LATE
WESTERNS

POSTWESTERN HORIZONS

LEE CLARK MITCHELL

LATE
WESTERNS

The Persistence of a Genre

University of Nebraska Press | Lincoln & London

Library of Congress
Cataloging-in-Publication Data
Names: Mitchell, Lee Clark, 1947–, author.
Title: Late Westerns: the persistence of a
genre / Lee Clark Mitchell.
Description: Lincoln: University of
Nebraska Press, 2018. | Series:
Postwestern horizons | Includes
bibliographical references and index.
Identifiers: LCCN 2017058304
ISBN 9781496201966 (cloth: alk. paper)
ISBN 9781496210692 (epub)
ISBN 9781496210708 (mobi)
ISBN 9781496210715 (pdf)
Subjects: LCSH: Western films—United
States—History and criticism. | West
(U.S.)—In motion pictures. | Motion
pictures—Social aspects—United
States—History—20th century. | Motion
pictures—Social aspects—United States—
History—21st century. | Social
change in motion pictures.
Classification: LCC PN1995.9.W4 M575 2018 |
DDC 791.43/65878—dc23 LC record available
at https://lccn.loc.gov/2017058304

Set in Scala OT by E. Cuddy.
Designed by L. Auten.

For Lucas

CONTENTS

ILLUSTRATIONS

ACKNOWLEDGMENTS

Two decades ago, I published a book on Westerns that approached the genre historically, explaining the popularity of the form within a social context. More particularly, I examined a handful of celebrated examples to understand how they addressed a shifting set of cultural anxieties when they first appeared, demonstrating how their very lack of narrative resolution— their ability to play mutually exclusive interpretations inventively against each other—contributed to a surprisingly broad appeal. Precisely by not triggering a single reading, allegorical or otherwise, they inveigled a far broader spectrum of readers and viewers into accepting their terms. Since that book, I have found myself drawn to less social and historical concerns in lieu of more formal considerations, if ironically at a moment when the genre has again shifted to a less obviously recognizable form. In place of cultural conflicts supposedly underwriting plot diversions, the shape and texture of aesthetic, distinctly generic moments have come to focus my attention even as I continue to wonder at the persistent attraction of the Western in a period so far removed from its ostensible historical venue. Perhaps that quizzical stance helps explain this book's dedication to a son neither familiar with Westerns nor drawn to them. The initial questions that grew into the discussions below first emerged in an imagined effort to explain what it is that might appeal to him in a genre that refuses to die. He still resists watching, but then again, his generation seems to watch fewer films than generations preceding.

Conditions were dramatically different for those of us coming of age in the 1950s, with movies losing viewers to television in what nonetheless seemed at the time like a golden age for film. And for Westerns. Though my argument below will tend to deny the notion of a classic Western, the sense that some films had indelibly marked the genre was clearly shared. Not until later, as television series stalled and violent films stretched the limits of what was deemed suitable for family viewing, did it become apparent how varied, malleable, even unrecognizable Westerns could be, seeming to defy generic prescriptions. John Wayne and Howard Hawks are on record in outraged contempt for the cinematic transitions they themselves contributed to, bending the genre in ways that have always excited and enraged. For that evolution laid bare what had been true all along, if never quite apparent: our expectations for genre resolutions are always being teased and transformed. That insight has led to a richer understanding of genre constructions themselves and how (as my abandoned working title for this book declared) they tend paradoxically to "read us."

If the list of those to whom I am indebted seems relatively small, it may be because my fascination with Westerns is less than widely shared in suburban New Jersey where the proffered mode tends toward the hip and urban, more *The Sopranos* than *Lonesome Dove*. The attraction of recognizable Western character types and plot encounters is simply not as strong in the East, or so I conjecture, and certainly not as it once was. Who knows what attracts us to different genres, though probably something midway between sheer escapism and self-projection. At least one explanation emerges from Leslie Fiedler's classic essay, "The Montana Face," written when he was an assistant professor in Missoula during the 1950s of his experience sitting on Saturday afternoons in a theater watching Gary Cooper Westerns, surrounded by cowboys gazing up at the screen slowly learning to become themselves. That process of cinematic self-formation has faded over the decades, at least so far as Westerns are concerned, while our viewings occur less often as joint experiences in theaters than with DVDs borrowed from libraries and films streamed on Netflix. Yet if that means that those with whom I have shared are few, they extend back for decades. Alan Mitchell was there first, my earliest companion to the Regent theater in Bay Shore, where as preteens we eagerly saw *Kiss Them for Me* (Stanley Donen, 1957) and *The Blob* (Irvin S. Yeaworth Jr., 1958) as well as *The Man Who Shot Liberty Valance* (John Ford, 1962). Fellow grad student Doug Gordon will recall our amusement watching Sergio Leone's spaghetti Westerns in a small theater in Brighton, England, where in 1969 conventions for cinema behavior were still prescribed, and indignation at viewers caught laughing at over-the-top Western performances still expressed. Decades later, Laurel Bollinger and Walter Hughes helped me teach Western courses at Princeton (where students occasionally showed up in high-heeled boots), and recently Maria DiBattista and Brian Gingrich have cotaught more sedate seminars on the same subject. As well, they have both kindly read chapters of this work in progress, as have Anne Sobel and Fareed Ben-youssef, casting critical eyes over flawed arguments to immeasurably good effect. Among others consulted, Carolyn Abbate and Dave Molk have ensured that my assertions about musical scores are at least not embarrassing. Those in the Western Literature Association who have listened attentively and shaped ideas presented in various papers over the years include Frank Bergon, Nancy Cook, Catherine Halverson, Bill Handley, Marek Paryz, Forrest Robinson, and Stephen Tatum.

The two University of Nebraska Press readers for this book, Matthew Carter and Andrew Patrick Nelson, offered astute assessments that saved me from silly excesses, helping to shape the whole into a more cogent performance (Andrew's contribution also included a recommendation for the book's present title). Bill Handley, the director of Nebraska's Postwestern Horizons series, has been exemplary in his encouragement, as has my editor, Alicia Christensen. Though it might seem unusual to thank a copyeditor, Brian King read the book with a care and intelligence that regularly compelled me to try to sharpen the argument. At Princeton, Daniel Claro, manager of the Digital Learning Lab, guided me through the perils of screen capturing, while Carolina Alvarado once again has created an excellent index. Lastly, I am indebted to publishers and journals who have allowed versions of essays to be reproduced in much-altered form:

the introduction, "'Who *are* those guys?': The Advent of the Beleaguered Western Hero," is reprinted with permission from *Once upon a Time . . . The Western: The Art of Western Film*, edited by Thomas Brent Smith and Mary-Dailey Desmarais (Montreal Museum of Fine Arts and the Denver Art Museum, 2017); chapter 3 is derived in part from an essay published in *Journal of Popular Film and Television* (March 2016), copyright © Taylor & Francis, available online at http://www.tandfonline.com/, doi: 10.1080 /01956051.2015.1074154; chapter 4 is derived in part from an essay published in *Quarterly Review of Film and Video* (June 2015), copyright © Taylor & Francis, available online at http://www.tandfonline.com/, doi: 10.1080 /10509208.2015.993911; chapter 5 is a much-expanded version of an essay published in *Papers on Language and Literature* (Spring 2018); chapter 6 is based on an essay that appeared in *Genre* (Fall 2014) and appears with the permission of Duke University Press; chapter 7 appeared in an earlier, much-shorter guise in *CineAction* (Spring 2016).

LATE
WESTERNS

INTRODUCTION

There's No Such Thing as Postwestern,
and It's a Good Thing Too

Consider a handful of scenarios recently set in the American West: a corpse repeatedly buried and disinterred on its journey south from Texas; two cowboys entangled in an explosive romance in northern Wyoming; an Anglo half brother and Hispanic American half sister in love (Texans again), no longer willing to ignore their incestuous desires; an Indiana businessman discovering, as if astonished, that his long-buried identity has erupted in the midst of small-town family life; a famous Western actor walking away from a film set to reassess his wastrel past in urban Montana; a wannabe cowboy in modern Los Angeles disrupting a broken family with his slightly demented six-gun aspirations. Each of these films was a critical as well as box-office success over the past two decades, and each (with perhaps the Indiana exception) was immediately labeled a Western. Still, despite recognizable venues, despite tall hats and high heels, despite even a shared fascination with masculine prerogatives and family roles, all of which has typified the genre from the beginning, these seem a far cry from films made famous by John Ford and Anthony Mann, Budd Boetticher and Sam Peckinpah. They are so different, in fact, that some scholars have argued not only that the genre has been altered decisively but that it has been transformed into something else entirely.

Of course, for more than a century the Western has perpetually tee-tered on the verge of exhaustion, only to revive in new forms. Almost as soon as it first appeared, viewers heralded its demise and ever since have applauded the passing of a genre that keeps rising from the dead.[1] The dramatic resuscitations supposedly performed by Ford's *Stagecoach* (1939), then later by Sergio Leone's *A Fistful of Dollars* (1964) and Peckinpah's *The Wild Bunch* (1969), then again by Clint Eastwood's *Unforgiven* (1992) and Jim Jarmusch's *Dead Man* (1995), followed by the unnamed films listed above: each offered heroic CPR to hackneyed materials, breathing life once again into an all-but-dead popular form. The question that keeps reemerging, then, is why this narrowly based vehicle—with among the most limited historical setting of any familiar genre—should continue to win over audiences more than a century after the lone cowboy had faded from view, appealing to ticket holders hooked by Hollywood's latest incarnation of America's foremost costume drama.

Why the regular turn again, even in modest new guises, back to quarter horses and small towns, to lone gunslingers and the curse of civic complacency? Why the resurrection of the Western as popular entertainment and, more compellingly, as a narrative means of addressing insistent social quandaries and cultural dilemmas? Why does the genre persist in winning our attention as successfully as action-adventure plots and spy films, space odysseys and zombie invasions, horror films and urban romances, murder mysteries and musicals? Jean-Luc Godard once pronounced the Western as "the most cinematic of cinematic genres," but that hardly forms a convincing claim even on its face, much less as an explanation for the genre's unusual staying power (O'Brien 1992, 38). For while the imperatives of the Western have altered over a century, they are still recognizably the same, or at least more or less similar in various configurations. Moreover (and this is a point worth conjuring), changes in the genre have been no more dramatic in the past two decades than they were in those preceding. When we pause to consider, it becomes clear that the question is larger than the Hollywood Western itself and encompasses why and how it is that genres persist, somehow hybridize, and otherwise evolve into new variations—but variations that are always recognizable.

In an earlier book, I addressed the appeal of certain Westerns at critical historical moments to explain how popular culture apparently helps resolve social crises. Chapters on films (as well as novels) spread over a century focused on what I argued were the deep if unspoken agendas driving these narratives: education and parenting, manhood and female liberation, among other topics. The present book offers a similar close reading of popular films from the past half century. But I no longer aspire to delve into contested political terrains or the cultural anxieties of first-time viewers, which draws them together even when plot resolutions seem indeterminate. Instead, I want to turn from divided social contexts to focus more intently on idiosyncratic aesthetic decisions and in the process address a fundamental question of genre itself: why do so many accomplished writers and directors (and importantly, Hollywood producers) choose to return to the Western if only to transfigure it and alter its trajectory? And how do their choices in plot, character development, cinematography, narrative sequence (among other features) reshape a genre that nonetheless remains recognizable *as a genre*. Of course, that inquiry could just as easily be extended to other popular forms (melodrama, say, or noir and war films, romances and fight movies), which have likewise been adapted cinematically, aesthetically, narratively over time without losing their generic identity.

For various reasons soon to become apparent, the Western best clarifies how fully genres change yet endure—indeed, how they *must* change *to* endure—and solicit our interest by confirming expectations while nonetheless diverging from them, inventively, entertainingly. That process, once understood, helps explain our routinely renewed interest in a supposedly identifiable genre regularly viewed as on its way out. The examples with which I opened differ little from countless others in the past in dramatically deviating from what is taken as a generic model even as they bear a "family resemblance" (in Wittgenstein's formulation) to their predecessors.[2] If these and other films are sometimes set on a long-ago frontier, just as often they abandon small, nineteenth-century towns for contemporary suburban, even urban locales; if they sometimes involve men on horseback, just as often characters speed by in cars or SUVs; if plots sometimes erupt out of violent confrontations, just as often they are driven by convoluted histories and tortured psychologies. The point is that whether or not familiar materials are immediately discernable, the genre persists, and does so in more or less recognizable forms. Even when major films deliberately defy these patterns, they still end up appealing on the basis of our cumulative understanding of prior Westerns, our appreciation for their variable materials and flexible structures. It is as if a fixed generic understanding were imprinted on our consciousnesses, with recent versions of the Western (like improvisations on jazz standards) compelling our admiration by their skill at revising underlying expectations, confirming how little we can escape a deep recognition of the genre that has always been there, fully itself.[3] Like Justice Potter Stewart's notorious threshold test for obscenity ("I know it when I see it"), we (critics and viewers alike) spot familiar generic constructions, which most simply begin in beginnings themselves with opening lines like "Once upon a time" or "In a galaxy far, far away" or "Theona, the hot-blooded lady-in-waiting at Elizabeth's court," or "The sky was the color of watered-down whiskey when Melba stumbled into my office." Whatever ensues may not be either fairy tale or sci-fi, historical romance or noir fiction, but setting, characters, diction, and narrative style all establish expectations for these modes, expectations that over time need to be stymied, encouraged, and playfully altered if they are to persevere.

The paradox of genres is that the longer they survive, the more they fool us into thinking they have always had a single "classic" form, which may explain why critics are sometimes inclined to affix a hyphenated "post-" to later examples.[4] That prefix signals something distinctly belated in subject matter or cinematic style, something that emerged after the genre's initial structure was supposedly settled and by which it would ever after be sanctioned. No one denies that genres are malleable, changing while remaining recognizable, yet the very attachment of "post-" to a genre confirms how unwilling critics are to treat them as fundamentally shape-shifting for each new generation, if only to stay current and sell tickets. Accompanying that unwillingness is a misconception about how genres first emerge, which is never immediate or self-contained and usually depends on a generous backward glance—thus imposing a retrospective coherence on examples based on factors selected well after the fact. Critics and viewers tend to impute similarities to these examples, granting a structural kinship to them that at the time may rarely have been acknowledged. Still, to agree that some examples are not obvious, or that genres regularly reshape themselves so long as they satisfy audiences, is not to deny that we nonetheless at any given historical moment refer to them *as if* more or less comparable, more or less fixed, distinguishable from competing genres with which they borrow and share. And the tautology underlying this interpretive confidence dictates that any genre's perceived structure remains contingent on the examples we choose to define it. After all, examples from any period in the past are as incompatible, sometimes even irreconcilable and chaotic, as more recent examples brought together to justify a presumed generic claim.[5] To repeat, no stable version of a genre transcends a particular moment, since genres are always being reshaped by each new potential member. But that hardly denies how fully expectations are aroused when people break into song or dance, or space ships loom on the horizon, or cowboy hats and chaps appear on full display.[6]

In short, the assumption informing this book is that the Western has been effectively "post-" all along, which is to say, from its very beginning. Consider that Owen Wister and Zane Gray were initially considered writers of "romance" when *The Virginian* (1902) and *Riders of the Purple Sage* (1915) appeared, both of which were first marketed as such. The Western novel still had to await its appearance *as* an identifiable genre, only gradually coming to be seen as sharing features with other instances of a category yet to be named. Genres are, that is, as much historical categorizations as theoretical constructs, posited retrospectively by critics, but also by filmmakers and filmgoers at the time of a film's production and consumption. Even if film noir and melodrama were labeled by critics well after the fact, viewers and producers didn't need a label to know what they wanted to see, which was simply "more of that!" And even genres that seem obvious to us, like musicals and Westerns, had to wait for expectations to settle into a pattern. As Andrew Patrick Nelson has observed:

> The films Fred Astaire and Ginger Rogers made at RKO in the mid-1930s were not marketed as "musicals," because audiences at the time understood that term to mean something rather different, namely the films being made at Warner Bros. and choreographed by Busby Berkeley. As with its literary counterparts, Western, as a "noun," was not widely used to describe a class of film until the 1920s, meaning that the viewer of *The Great Train Robbery* (1903) or *Hell's Hinges* (1916) did not know they were watching a Western. Even *Stagecoach* (1939) wasn't promoted as a Western, as the genre in the 1930s was associated with low-budget pictures. (pers. comm.)

That process, moreover, continues today in the blending, pilfering, and crossbreeding that happily keeps generic strains ever impure.

From a slightly different angle, one might add that the Western's own historical belatedness has been incorporated thematically, offering city dwellers a nostalgic vision imagined as having occurred in rural settings, and always for allegorized resolutions to urgent urban crises of labor and governance, of civil discord and economic conflict, of destabilized gender roles and contested precepts of parental obligation. But my argument for more recent, supposed "postwesterns"—which I prefer to think of instead as simply "late" in order to identify them chronologically without imputing anything like a generic break—is that their belatedness is apparent less in some distinguishable subject matter than in their inventive executions. As with other recent offerings in competing genres (musicals, noir, detective and horror films), they win our admiration not by repeating past performances but by altering and augmenting what has gone before, troping plots self-consciously (ever playfully) in ways that keep us riveted to the screen. Offering viewers innovative plot turns, offbeat character portrayals, and alternative landscape settings (or not), late Westerns often come upon us unexpectedly, triggering a consciousness of the genre only after the fact, helping integrate materials not obviously "Western" into a familiar format. Such films may well rely upon structural earmarks and cinematic allusions more than earlier generic additions did, along with other formal implications and citations meant to remind us of shifting generic tradition. Repeatedly, our interpretive capacities are tested by deliberate reminders of earlier Westerns, encouraging a generic interpretation of materials that might otherwise seem to invite something different.

The following chapters are not meant to be a sociological survey or historical accounting of anything like all late Westerns; they aim instead at offering a series of close readings of a handful of films to see in particular instances how our generic expectations are reshaped. They have been selected mostly from the past two decades to reveal how elastic (and healthy) the genre continues to be, as opposed to the somewhat prescriptive template imposed by a self-styled "postwestern" category. My argument extends from the premise that genres are always hybridized, consisting of a shifting array of thematic and formal constructions, never so distinct or finished as critics retrospectively make them out to be. In fact, my more aggressive claim is that recent "postwestern" critics are actually diminishing the power of the Western genre—and by extension, of all genres—not so much in limiting what recent versions have achieved but more in curtailing an appreciation of what earlier films themselves had already accomplished. After all, by flattening out the history of generic performance, as diverse and sometimes antigeneric as those earlier films also seemed on first viewing, these critics diminish the impact that genre outliers have had on genre itself, contributing to what it is and how our continuing enthusiasm is reinforced.[7]

When one pauses to consider, the casual definition offered by the American Film Institute already suggests how imprecise the category is: the Western is "a genre of films set in the American West that embodies the spirit, the struggle and demise of the new frontier" (American Film Institute, 10). And a partial list of "subgenres" offered by Wikipedia confirms a swirling array of crossed possibilities: acid, charro, and contemporary Westerns; electric, epic, euro-, and fantasy Westerns; horror, curry, and martial arts Westerns; meat-pie, sci-fi, space and spaghetti Westerns, along with simply "weird Westerns." Yet more sober discrimination leaves us equally aware of how mixed the genre is, when its unquestioned finest examples seem to defy an easy "family resemblance." Nonetheless, certain films *are* generally taken by viewers as definitive at certain historical moments, pivoting their understanding, and doing so precisely by revamping expectations in directions that then come to be seen as reconfiguring the genre. That rarely occurs in predictable ways or uniformly, as exemplified at any given era of successful movie making. Take 1952, and consider just three prominent films that year, all quite different in their innovations: Fred Zinnemann's *High Noon*, Howard Hawks's *The Big Sky*, and Nicholas Ray's *The Lusty Men*. Or jump to 1969 for an equally dramatic constellation of four even more disparate examples, as far apart thematically, in character portrayals, and cinematically as one might imagine: George Roy Hill's *Butch Cassidy and the Sundance Kid*, John Schlesinger's *Midnight Cowboy*, Sam Peckinpah's *The Wild Bunch*, and Henry Hathaway's *True Grit*. Whatever orientations the genre took following the release of these films, they were clearly diverse and uncoordinated. Or consider John Ford simply as the most celebrated Western director, whose films differ as much from each other as from other directors' Westerns and clearly poach from other generic fields. *My Darling Clementine* (1946) partakes at least as much of noirish, romantic, and melodramatic strains as it does of Western ones; and *The Searchers* (1956) could hardly be less similar in its narrative of obsession, adultery, racism, mixed in with comic relief. The genre's capaciousness seems at times almost antigeneric, though it confirms the influence of new outliers on its future. And at this point, it may be worth turning to well-considered theories of genre simply to see what is at stake in making claims about "post" or "late" versions. More generally, how are we to sort out the problems of bringing together such notably distinct films into a single category?

The most significant current theoretician of film genre may be Rick Altman, who has over some decades developed an understanding of genre as a tension between what he terms, following Fredric Jameson, its semantics and its syntax (or alternatively, its topic and its structure).[8] According to Altman, "We can as a whole distinguish between generic definitions that depend on a list of common traits, attitudes, characters, shots, locations, sets, and the like—thus stressing the semantic elements that make up the genre—and definitions that play up instead certain constitutive relationships between undesignated and variable placeholders—relationships that might be called the genre's fundamental syntax. The semantic approach thus stresses the genre's building blocks, while the syntactic view privileges the structures into which they are arranged" (Altman 1984, 10). Exemplifying the semantic model are definitions of the Western that rely on its supposed historical configuration, identified by Jean Mitry in 1963 as a film "consistent with the atmosphere, the values, and the conditions of existence in the Far West between 1840 and 1900" (cited by Altman 1984, 10). By contrast, later studies by such notable critics as John G. Cawelti, Philip French, and Jim Kitses would offer a syntactic model, emphasizing in Altman's words "not the vocabulary of the western but the relationships linking lexical elements. For Kitses the western grows out of a dialectic between the West as garden and as desert (between culture and nature, community and individual, future and past)" (Altman 1984, 10–11). Wisely enough, Altman settles somewhere between the two extremes of semantics and syntax, contending that only a combination of approaches can do justice to any genre.

Moreover—and this point is just as significant—Altman argues that holding fast to a concept of genre purity tends to privilege less innovative, more derivative films, ignoring instances that often prove commercially successful or critically interesting. Even so, prescriptive investigation remains the coin of the realm. "If genres are regularly treated like nation-states," Altman observes, "then dual citizenship has clearly been proscribed by current genre studies" (1999, 19).[9] And Celestino Deleyto agrees, if from precisely the opposite perspective, claiming that the "dominance" of supposedly classic examples actually "distorts the genre's history since these are 'exceptional' texts that do not reflect the way the genre works as accurately as more mediocre, less well-known films" ([2011] 2012, 219). Multiple pressures are always at work, altering expectations in any given decade for crossover influences from other genres, which in the case of Westerns includes most prominently noir, romantic comedy, crime films, and melodrama. Deleyto enjoins critics to treat genres less preemptively, indeed less generically, since they are constantly mutating, destabilizing our prescriptive assumptions, leading careful readers and viewers to "a chaotic view of genres [that] underlines their instability, the impossibility of establishing clear lines of demarcation, and the nonlinearity, unpredictability, and complexity of their evolution" ([2011] 2012, 222).[10]

Still, the misleading notion of doggedly categorical genres refuses to die, persisting despite ample evidence of so much spirited generic fluidity, with generic expectations ever ready to forge phantom structures of meaning that effect how we read individual films. That fascinating if paradoxical process happens to be what delights us, in failing to find perfect examples of unmistakable genres (at least those worth our ongoing interest) even as our inclination to believe in them nonetheless reinforces the expectations always at work. And in better films, those enlivened expectations tend to work us, exhilaratingly so. Such suggestibility, the implications of which inform the chapters below, begins with the very pattern by which genres are constructed. For difficult as it may be to list their essential, even generally characteristic components (their supposedly semantic elements), their narrative syntax tends to render them identifiable "as *processes*" by which interpretations can be aligned (Neale 1990, 56). [11] Syntax, not semantics, informs Altman's effective argument that genre definition is always retrospective, encouraging an idea of the category that did not (could not) exist when its first supposedly exemplary film was produced. In the early years of Hollywood, the absence of any such thing as a "Western" hardly prevented films from being made, but it did allow a series of variously intersecting subgenres to come together into what was at last perceived to be a coherent category (1999, 36–37). As Altman concludes of the unambiguous assumptions that have dominated Hollywood: "Our vision of the film industry as a self-confident machine producing clearly delimited generically defined products must be abandoned" (1999, 44).[12] Instead of a vehicle that fulfills a prescriptive set of features and structures, screenwriters and directors create films through idiosyncratic plot engagements, through cross-generic imaginings that at their best alert us into fleeting if evocative possibilities.

Altman's and Neale's wary skepticism about genre definition certainly informs my own interpretations, all of which indulge the play of generic disorientation. But while accepting their calm judgment that genres do not exist as such, I nonetheless am more interested in why we continue to entertain the possibility and what it means for the process of watching films that do not directly fulfill their presumed generic conditions. My interest in Westerns lies more particularly in why films that do not immediately strike us as such should be read *as* Westerns, assuming them to be what their obvious (usually semantic) materials lead us at first to believe they are not. The implications of that disorientation inform this book, especially in its focus on formal features rather than larger historical or cultural considerations, turning us back to aesthetic clues to a film's success and its determinate meanings. In concentrating on the viewer's ever-hesitant construction of meaning, the following chapters mean to provoke renewed attention on the regular slippage of generic labels, particularly as the appeal of genre itself causes viewers again and again to return to them, even in films that seem to avoid being read according to an identifiable category. As Altman claims in a provocative challenge: "Rather than assume that generic labels have—or should have—a stable existence, we must heed the examples of the woman's film and family melodrama, recognizing the permanent availability of all cultural products to serve as signifiers in the cultural bricolage that forms our lives" (1999, 82).

We rarely realize in the viewing experience how irrepressibly generic indicators (semantic, syntactic) shift our expectations. Or as Altman states, "In the popular mind genres are so tightly identified with certain readily recognizable semantic traits that they may easily be represented by no more than a suggestive element here or there. . . . Hollywood has throughout its history developed techniques that make genre mixing not only easy, but virtually obligatory" (1999, 132). It is that idea—that a "suggestive element" might transform our readings generically, and that "genre mixing" is therefore "virtually obligatory"—which seems to me most fruitful as a means of understanding the current production and broad appeal of late Westerns (as well, of course, as every other late genre). For there is finally no template that serves well for that presumed category or that otherwise confirms a singular identity. What seems obvious, certainly among films invoked in this book, is that recent Westerns may share a broad and conflicting array of available characteristics, but that any easily identifiable or coherent character is ever elusive and needs to be demonstrated.

To repeat, simple generic identification is not at all clear in many of the most successful recent films, given the ways in which cinematic framing alters understanding. The syntax of a film fundamentally changes the materials invoked so that even charged moments or conspicuous characters or familiar scenes that we presume are distinctively "Western" or "melodramatic" or "comic" depend on the sequence of which they are a part. Indeed, Altman argues that our interpretive gestures need to become ever more nuanced if only because of the various ways in which moments can be dramatized: a "device favouring filmic multivalency is what we might call *multiple framing*. By virtue of the context in which it is presented, any given event appears to be 'framed' by more than one narrative series, as if a single object were repeatedly photographed, but always against a different background, thus calling into question the sameness of the object across multiple photographs" (Altman 1999, 135). The result is that our understanding of scenes and their constitution is altered by the contextual expectations we are encouraged to hold, prompted both before and after such scenes appear. "What Western is not at some points a melodrama?" Altman asks rhetorically; "What musical can do totally without romance?" (Altman 1999, 141). Which is to say that genre mixing is and always has been the norm, apparent so often in films as to make claims for genre purity seem little more than a critic's fantasy. But the important point here, apart from innate impurity, is the way in which we as viewers delight in expectations aroused and diminished, with intersecting generic possibilities engaging us as much or more than any simple, straightforward narrative sequence. Carol Clover would seem to agree; in speaking of horror films, she has similarly concluded about the

> remarkable fit between horror and the western (or at least a certain kind of horror and a certain kind of western). . . . The case could be made that westerns are really horror "underneath," for the terms of violation and revenge in the western seem often to slide beyond an economic analysis into a psychosexual register. In fact, of course, if the two genres really do stand in the kind of reciprocal relationship that I have suggested, then it must be that both things are true—that each is the other's "underneath," that the terms of the one are inherent, if not manifest, in the terms of the other, and that each enables the other to be told. (1992, 165)[13]

The neat divisions by which we presume to interpret films generically keeps breaking down in all but the most simplistic examples, the rudimentary settings and uninteresting plots that have somehow come to be identified with a genre.

Why then do we nonetheless persist in the assumption, in parsing out separate templates to be presumptively associated with certain genres, then subgenres? Again, Altman anticipates the question, pointing to our desire to think this way as simply an inveterate inclination or a tired critical habit, and then attesting to the problems that result: "Built on a fundamental paradox, genre subsists because it seems to provide firm anchorage in a transnational, transhistorical substratum oblivious to the vagaries of time and place. Yet those who actually pronounce generic terms and invoke generic categories do so in such a fundamentally contradictory way as to preclude associating permanence or universality with the notion of genre" (1999, 193). We assume genres offer predictable narrative constructions for what often seems like a tumultuous, even chaotic turn of current events, and yet (as in the case of so-called "postwesterns") the very desire to adapt supposedly fixed generic interpretive structures to new films distinct from those preceding tends to destabilize the very conception with which we began. What we need to consider is not that genres *sometimes* shift but that they *always* do, and have so from the beginning, altered and shaped by creative considerations that are invariably belated, as critics new to the task impose a retrospective set of assumptions upon materials that are always fluid, hybrid, mixed.

The central question raised by Altman, Neale, and others, especially in terms of late entries to a supposed genre, is how to evaluate very different films that offer a revision of generic semantics as well as syntax—that is (to take the Western as example), in which both materials (rural setting, stalwart characters, western costuming) as well as narrative scope and structure (pursuits of revenge, or of justice, or simple self-defense) vary so much as to seem completely different cinematic experiences. Diane Borden and Eric Essman have positioned the argument historically in referring to a subset of Westerns and Western directors not usually considered "postwestern": "A series of key American films—which have been called 'post-Westerns'—have reinvented the genre: among them, John Huston's *The Misfits*, Sam Peckinpah's *The Wild Bunch*, Robert Altman's *McCabe and Mrs. Miller*, and John Sayles's *Lone Star* (1996). At the same time, filmmakers such as Sergio Leone, Werner Herzog, John Schlesinger, and Michelangelo Antonioni have re-viewed and reimagined the Western through European eyes and thus, in effect, have remapped the American moral landscape" (2000, 36). Each of these films and filmmakers seems to offer a variation in our thinking, a slippage from what we had presumed about the genre Western. And one might well add other canonical names, including Budd Boetticher, André de Tóth, Samuel Fuller, and Anthony Mann, whose work also signals the genre's success by getting us to respond nongenerically, excited by the prospect of materials pulled together in constraints we recognize as familiar, yet somehow developed in more imaginative and destabilizing ways. Once again, the historical arc of a genre can only be defined after the fact, though it depends on the suggestive generic elements introduced by the newest outliers, which will in turn alter the genre's shape.

"POSTWESTERN"?

Perhaps the very desire for stability in critical judgment draws us to the presumed clarity of genre divisions. Yet the indeterminacy of genres has always been true, giving the lie to any Platonic conception we share of genre itself. There is simply no "pure" strain of a genre, despite talk of a classic Western or an archetypal screwball comedy or a paradigmatic war film. However, distinctions made on historical grounds (between 1930s crime films, say, and those of the 1950s and '70s) tend to muddy the waters, hiding the ways in which a film supposedly of one genre may actually seem more akin to another contemporary instance of a purportedly different class. That is simply how enforced generic syntax works, often authoritatively as a policing mechanism, explaining why a term like "postwestern" seems at once misguided and misleading, hypostatizing a specific set of films as constructing a fixed genre, then locating a set of historical changes occurring *in* that genre as part of a "post-" development. Ironically, John Cawelti has noted an early use of the designation, but in a rather different sense from more recent practitioners: "One of the first critics to suggest that the traditional Western was in the process of being replaced by a Post-Western was Philip French who added a chapter on 'The Post-Western' to the 1977 edition of his excellent 1973 book on Westerns. However, French used the term mainly in the sense of 'modern' Westerns 'set in the present-day West where lawmen, rodeo riders, and Cadillac-driving ranchers are still in thrall to the frontier myth'" (1999,

102). In short, the term "postwestern" is as labile and slippery as the classic "Western" with which it purportedly contrasts.

Guided by Altman's identification of both semantics and syntax as generic constituents, we can understand French's "Post-Western" to have been conceived as more precisely a semantic shift, with any syntactical elements remaining more or less unchanged. Yet limiting the Western this way to a set of historical features or geographical earmarks seems somehow to miss much of what has always energized the ever-evolving, always-indistinct genre. Cawelti was aware of this myopia in wisely correcting French, then adding: "As the Western became increasingly tenuous as a coherent generic tradition in the 1980s and 1990s, the symbolism, the landscape and the central themes associated with this tradition found expression in a number of different forms" (1999, 102). In fact, though Cawelti shies from mentioning it, this claim happens to characterize every so-called genre, since films do not simply repeat each other either semantically *or* syntactically but regularly develop and evolve, mix and change. Carol Clover confirmed this truism in 1992 in response to the fear that "horror is declining" (1992, 234), leaving doubt as to what would replace it. On the contrary, she observed that other films were inventively adopting horror techniques without resorting to the notion that this constituted something like "post-horror." The Western, in other words, has become no more "impure" than any other genre, and certainly no more than it ever has been (all one needs to do is recall the various "subgenres" listed above).[14]

"Boundaries" of a popular genre are never secure or otherwise durable (nor meant to be), though they can occasionally appear so because they were (as always) established retrospectively, imposed by the present on the past. Late Westerns are no more distinctive as a group for their supposed thematic concerns than were earlier ones, or even other genres, despite the kinds of claims that theorists sometimes offer about supposedly characteristic "spectral landscapes," which revert to "scenes of absence and loss or to buried secrets" (Campbell 2013, 15). Those kinds of scenes have in fact been true of countless Westerns over the years, ranging from

Stagecoach or *My Darling Clementine* to Howard Hawks's *Red River* (1948) and Sergio Leone's spaghetti Westerns, extending in turn to nearly every other traditional genre film.[15] And one might well ask whether that is not also true of noir or spy films or zombie movies? Again, the claim that "post-Westerns are characterized by world-weary, disillusioned protagonists" (Campbell 2011, 369) seems to overlook a large swath of earlier Westerns, including *High Noon, The Searchers*, and nearly all of Boetticher's Western films—ignoring in the process countless examples from other genres (noir, most significantly).[16]

Conversely, some scholars have predictably taken the opposite tack, expressing skepticism about the effort to corral films generically. The dean of current Western critics, Edward Buscombe, unconditionally denies any "family resemblance" within the genre, even as he admits that certain semantic materials (setting, clothes, tools, horses) loosely hold distinct films together as a group. But in blanket tones, he rebuffs a "significant similarity between the plots of different westerns" ([1970] 2012, 14). Still, despite such dubiety about efforts to group films categorically, we *do* automatically recognize larger generic similarities even among the necessary variations that seem to preclude group identification. The point is that too much emphasis on the differences among films has the same effect as too great a concentration on what aligns them: it tends to close down more careful and nuanced discussions of individual films themselves. As Tag Gallagher observes, "rich lodes of ambivalence are overlooked" by genre critics who assume similarities become uninteresting or obvious just by being reflected in another film (1986, 212). Michael Kowalewski says it best in his dismissal of those more interested in pigeonholing popular films than in actually looking at them, and who effectively dismisses Richard Slotkin as a sociologist rather than a critic—as someone, that is, more likely to count images rather than to read them: "Slotkin's way of dealing with violence is as a represented fact, not a fact of representation. Or rather, he takes fictional instances of violence to be merely functional, bits of paraphrasable action that constitute part of an ideological 'index,' a plot or a narrative that we are to render intelligible by dint of interpretation" (1993, 18).[17] Of course, Kowalewski's appraisal applies as fully to cinematic critics as to literary ones. If the Western is not to be simply packaged and ear-marked as a collection of readily translated tropes—if, that is, the texture of so many recent films is to be appreciated precisely for their idiosyncratic achievement—then we need to turn away from prescriptive generic understandings to something more fine-grained and closely assessed. Even then, as Celestino Deleyto rightly cautions: "Asserting that a given film or group of films 'mixes' genres is not saying very much about the films: it is a premise of genre analysis, not a conclusion" ([2011] 2012, 228).

THEMATIC SHIFTS

First, however, as reminder, the Western has long focused on certain features that traditionalists count as essential and describe unhesitatingly: its celebration of what Philip French described as "the overwhelming landscape, the strange qualities of light" (1977, 104)[18]; its nostalgia for a simpler past and yet its progressive belief in the triumph of law and order; and most centrally, its display of manhood as the intersection of honor and self-reliance. In extolling these virtues sixty years ago, Robert Warshow famously argued: "Why does the Western movie especially have such a hold on our imagination? Chiefly, I think, because it offers a serious orientation to the problem of violence such as can be found almost nowhere else in our culture. One of the well-known peculiarities of modern civilized opinion is its refusal to acknowledge 'the value of violence.'" ([1954] 1962, 151).[19] Of course, the closer one looks at Westerns, the more these seemingly unequivocal features become ambiguous or contested, revealing a crack in the veneer of assurance about how fully sustained they actually are. And likewise, persistent strains exist among more recent Westerns that reveal less of a sharp divide from earlier films than an almost predictable, even calculated evolution of informing assumptions, attitudes, and styles (in short, narrative syntax) long associated with the genre.

Before developing the argument for this book in its attention to a handful of more or less recent films, I want to survey some of those thematic currents shared by others appearing over recent decades in which conflicts have reemerged as recognizable, if altered (once again) from a generation before. Westerns, after all, have long focused on a notable syntax of opposed registers (savage vs. civilized, farmer vs. rancher, justice vs. the constraints of the law), but the pitched social conflicts once decided by conventional plot resolutions are more or less insoluble in contemporary films: racial, gendered, and ethnic conflicts have multiplied exponentially; old mores are increasingly viewed not as redeemable but as irrelevant; and crucially, heroes seem newly hampered, less and less empowered to alter events or even to grasp local circumstances. Recent Westerns, it is safe to say, display the same mood of confusion evinced in earlier films over conflicts that initially seem unreconcilable, energizing the genre but no longer lending a sense of resolution.

Supposedly celebratory portrayals of manhood's stalwart stance, which had always been challenged in the more compelling films, have nonetheless diminished, raising questions about where the genre has left the cowboy hero. If renowned more often than not for calm restraint yet redoubtable martial skills, if tenacious on behalf of justice (even justice won through illegal means), the figure was nonetheless frequently conflicted. However unflinching the face of the typical Western hero—sometimes viewed as a knight in defense of American virtues of fair play, egalitarian acknowledgment, courtesy to the weak and quiet, good manners—that face has grown haggard in recent films as he self-consciously confronts a world that no longer esteems such virtues, or even recognizes them as such. Increasingly, Westerns now present their central figures in dismay, as if unsettled by either a ghostly past or a baffling present, or alternatively, perplexed by strangely altered social codes themselves. None of this is new, having energized Westerns from early on, even if the strains seem now more clearly emergent. In fact, recent Westerns might well be divided into three constellations of scenes that challenge the lone gunman's generic self-possession, ranging from haunting to bewilderment to self-denial. Coping with circumstances that no longer correspond to the world he has known, the hero embodies a larger culture's vexed anxieties over the pressures altering our traditional assumptions about social mores.

Exemplifying the first constellation of scenes is Clint Eastwood's *Unforgiven* as Will Munny (Eastwood) rides into Big Whiskey to avenge the death of his friend, Ned Logan (Morgan Freeman). A close-up of his face transfigured in anger when he learns how Ned has died shows him slowly deciding to take revenge, confirming how fully the past has come alive for him—a past he has repressed for a decade in sustained efforts to reform but a past he realizes cannot be escaped. Earlier, a solicitous Schofield Kid (Jaimz Wollvett) had been rebuffed by Munny: "I ain't like that anymore, Kid. . . . My wife, she cured me of that, cured me of drink and wickedness." Still, this very assurance attests ironically (given the genre's familiar resistance to change) that he will not in fact be cured; the obligatory scene of Munny's woefully inept shooting and riding as he trains to recover his earlier proficiency is set off against reminders that he is once again doing it for money, not principle. For all his protests, the film's trajectory traces the past's customary generic stranglehold on the present. Munny resists as long as he can, counseling the Schofield Kid that "It's a hell of a thing, killin' a man. You take away all he's got an' all he's ever gonna have." Yet against that conviction, Munny is transformed into the haunting figure of his own youth, becoming a killing machine in scenes that register the Western ethos as an appalling last chance, neither redemptive nor worth remembering. Fittingly, the film ends with rumors of him as an anonymous dry-goods clerk. Even the bold excesses of Sergio Leone and Sam Peckinpah had a transfiguring quality, registering "the value of violence" that Warshow identified as central to the Western. Here by contrast, violence represents nothing more than its own chaotic fury, in Eastwood's knee-jerk response to savagery that fails to resolve anything, much less to restore a redemptive social order.

That ghostly hounding of the present by the past has long characterized the Western, perhaps most dramatically staged in films by Ford, beginning with *Stagecoach*, driven by "The Kid" (John Wayne) vowing revenge against his brothers' killers. *The Searchers* (1956) revolves around Ethan Edwards (Wayne again) obsessed with finding his niece Debbie's abductor; and *The Man Who Shot Liberty Valance* self-consciously revives the past (Wayne now in a casket) in an effort finally to lay the dead to rest. Predictably less violent than more recent films, these and other genre examples also more tellingly register less regret at the force of the past's resurgence and its need to actually *be* resolved. If the cowboy hero had always been redeemed by his behavior, the swerve taken by contemporary Westerns lies in their evocation of an anguished response to the grip of the past, with the hero unable to escape either himself or his history, immured in circumstances where violence offers a mere fleeting respite from conditions that persist nonetheless. That transition becomes clearer in chapters below on *Lone Star*, Tommy Lee Jones's *The Three Burials of Melquiades Estrada* (2005), and James Mangold's adaptation of *3:10 to Yuma* (2005), in each of which the present is singularly haunted by past obligations, leaving a mystery that can only be fleetingly resolved in order to be forgotten and buried, confirming how little has altered with the dramatic discoveries unfolded in the course of each film. The past, contrary to the genre's persistent assumption, no longer seems to hold a reliable sway over the present, and even less so over the future.

The second constellation of scenes signaling something like a shared difference in recent Western heroes is epitomized in the Coen brothers' *No Country for Old Men* (2007) when Sheriff Ed Tom Bell (Tommy Lee Jones) expresses bafflement at a world no longer capable of being understood. His incomprehension matches the genre's larger reconfiguration of a Western hero now powerless to grasp motive, means, or opportunity. As Bell remarks at one amazed moment: "Signs and wonders. But I think once you stop hearin' sir and madam the rest is soon to follow." If the bewilderment here seems as old as the genre itself, the breach between civic understanding and social violence has expanded exponentially. It comes as no surprise that, in such a self-conscious genre film, the heightened contrast between expectation and ruthless reality should be defined in Western terms as something long familiar. Attempting reassurance, Bell's uncle Ellis acknowledges how fully violence has been the regular default position out West: "What you got ain't nothin new. This country is hard on people." But in fact, Bell rightly grasps how fully the burgeoning violence of cinema has become the incomprehensible violence of the West itself. The handheld cameras, the jittery eviscerating sequences, the need to remain imperturbable in ever more bizarre and imperiling settings, all define the confusing anarchy that reduces the hero to befuddled bystander. And that mood is extended in David Mackenzie's *Hell or High Water* (2016), in which the bewildered, elderly Texas Ranger Marcus Hamilton (Jeff Bridges) tries to fathom the rationale behind two brothers' reckless robbery of rural banks. He even interviews the surviving brother at the end and agrees to "finish the conversation" sometime in the future.

Robert Rodriguez parodies this evolution of the genre with *Once upon a Time in Mexico* (2003), offering a potent mix of carnage-filled ambushes, sudden abductions, and brutal mass assaults that share the violent vision elaborated by Quentin Tarantino. Plot logic is meant to confuse viewers, if only because El Mariachi (Antonio Banderas) himself is likewise bewildered by gratuitous brutality that exceeds our frenzied understanding, failing to resolve conflicts whose origins we cannot comprehend. Earlier Westerns invariably raised prospects for social resolution by the end. In *High Noon*, Will Kane (Gary Cooper) leaves Hadleyville confounded by the citizens' cravenness, but his very example suggests the town can be redeemed through its ignominy; in *Red River*, Matt Garth (Montgomery Clift) stands at odds with his step-father Tom Dunson (John Wayne) over the concept of legal contract, but the film ends with a clear promise of reconciliation. And in other instances, from *Stagecoach* and *My Darling Clementine* to Anthony Mann's *Man of the West* (1958) or Budd Boetticher's *The Tall T* (1957), transformation is always understood to be possible, whether imminent or not.

By contrast, recent films seem to explode onscreen, transforming the lone hero, now bewildered by the motiveless violence that erupts around him, into a stand-in for the viewer far more than earlier exemplars. In *Dead Man*, Jim Jarmusch's "psychedelic Western," the accountant William Blake (Johnny Depp) arrives in town after an exhausting train ride with a motley array of passengers that has already left him dumbfounded, only to stumble into ever more confusing encounters and mystifying violence. An Indian seer named Nobody (Gary Farmer) saves Blake after he is all but fatally shot, becoming a "walking dead" who then undergoes a delirious vision quest that precedes his actual demise at sea. Jarmusch focuses on imperturbable facial close-ups in this strange black-and-white film, confirming the puzzling nature of events in a genre that had once seemed almost too familiar. A similar strain runs through Paul Thomas Anderson's *There Will Be Blood* (2007), if from a one-hundred-eighty-degrees perspective: Daniel Plainview (Daniel Day-Lewis) registers a fierce stubbornness as central character in this peripatetic film, repeating his mining efforts ever westward and thereby exposing a remorselessness all but deathlike in the hero. Single-mindedness emerges time and again as a gesture of violence, leading at last to a brutal and senseless murder that defies any resolution to a history that was rarely what it seemed.

This strain of incomprehension in the genre, simply being unable to understand terms, is further manifest in Jon Favreau's *Cowboys and Aliens* (2011), whose title already reveals how fully the hero is thoroughly lost. Space aliens in 1873 New Mexico Territory come to represent everything that can no longer be explained in a West where amnesia and abduction dictate the plot. Together these films seem premised on a repeated refrain from *Butch Cassidy and the Sundance Kid*: "Who *are* those guys?" as one of the heroes bewilderingly asks. But where those fleeing partners at last discover an answer, current heroes engulfed in similarly baffling narratives remain mystified by antagonists who follow no recognizable rules.

If the hero has been both haunted and perplexed in recent Westerns, the third dislocating response that seems to characterize the genre is a profound disorientation about his own masculinity. Notoriously encapsulating that disorientation is Ang Lee's *Brokeback Mountain* (2005) in which men's mutual desire at last indulges the erotic gaze long lying at the heart of the Western. That powerfully repressed strain had always before been closeted, however acknowledged in the camera's adoring fixed stare, celebrating the fetishized costume, lingering over faces and bodies without quite entering into risky plot scandals of same-sex desire. Think of *Red River's* Montgomery Clift or *Shane's* Alan Ladd for only two prominent examples where masculine beauty is extolled through prolonged facial close-ups even as the yearning sustained by such shots remains off-screen. And then consider the host of other actors who have established male beauty in frequent close-up views as essential to the genre. Lee's film shifts desire from film viewer to actor even as it establishes how disoriented both central characters feel. No other film has been quite so explicit about same-sex desire in the genre (barely concealed in so many generic examples), though Andrew Dominik comes closer than most in his *The Assassination of Jesse James by the Coward Robert Ford* (2007). The plot hinges on the unacceptable fascination Ford (Casey Affleck) feels for James (Brad Pitt), with "hero worship shad[ing] into lust" as Roger Ebert observed: "Since sex between them is out of the question, their relationship turns into a curiously erotic dance of death" (Ebert 2007). It is as if inadmissible cupidity is converted into lust for extinction in a film that probes the unsettling psychological displacement so often structuring Western plots. The contours of masculinity are again reconfigured, exposing what lurks in the genre's recurrent celebration of the male body.[20]

Yet the disorientation of current Westerns extends to other than same-sex desire, as Sam Raimi reveals in *The Quick and the Dead* (1995), piling on violence, fake deaths, and quick-draw showdowns, but with the singular distinction of having the usual vengeance-seeking masculine hero replaced by "The Lady" (Sharon Stone). Or consider how Tommy Lee Jones offers a feminist reworking of the genre in *The Homesman* (2014), set in mid-1850s Nebraska Territory, with Mary Bee Cuddy (Hilary Swank) saving women maddened by pioneer life, escorting them back to Iowa. Having hired the drifter George Briggs (Jones) to accompany her east, she establishes at once her forcefulness in executing the trip and her psychological frailty as well, confirmed by her suicide near the trip's end. Quentin Tarantino shifts the Western in a different direction by setting *Django Unchained* (2012) in the antebellum South, where the black slave Django (Jaime Foxx) teams with Dr. King Schultz (Christoph Waltz), who promises him his freedom in exchange for help collecting bounties. Again, traditional roles are reshaped against a spaghetti-Western accumulation of blood and gore, as Django renews the modern hero's ruthless obsession in racially inflected terms.

Invariably, it comes as a surprise to realize how fully this century-old cinematic genre keeps reinventing itself, offering a triangulation of new directions in an era that might seem hostile to the self-assured classic hero. That very lack of assurance has made the Western figure alluring again, given his quizzical uncertainty conjoined with a stumbling awareness of the bonds of cultural repression. Underneath the familiar impassive face lies an expanded emotional register, revealing fault lines in standards that have come under review in larger discussions of American culture. If the question that recurs is why we keep returning to the Western to engage these issues, the answer may well lie in the genre's willingness to recast its central figure from a model of apparently confident restraint, of silence and skills, into someone more frequently haunted by the past, baffled by the present, and willing to question (if not quite challenge) social and sexual codes that had long seemed a minor part of his identity. His very emotional responsiveness seems a change impelled by changing times, allowing us to recognize how even those constrained by a gendered past (and by a genre's supposedly stalwart configuration) can recast their obligations and inclinations into something more sympathetic, even benign.

Of course, much of the resilience of the genre has to do with its focus on male bodies, which still express masculinity much as the genre always has. An older generation riveted our attention on the alluring visages of Gary Cooper, Clint Eastwood, William Holden, Alan Ladd, Jimmy Stewart, even John Wayne. The power of the newly revived Western emerges from the eagerness of a younger generation of actors to replay and redefine the role of Western hero: Russell Crowe, Chris Cooper, Johnny Depp, Heath Ledger, Matthew McConaughey, even an aging Clint Eastwood. The ideal remains much the same—of nonexpressive facial characteristics, of inarticulateness, of a stolid physical presence—amid far different cultural anxieties than existed a century ago. Part of the genre's enduring appeal lies in its inventive capacity to dramatize in straightforward, even seemingly simple terms the shifting (always contested) values associated with gender, civic behavior, law, even violence. Those narrative conflicts, presented earlier with confidence, lately with increasing bewilderment, have routinely made us understand how heroes only partially transcend the hauntings and misunderstandings of their age. It is hardly surprising, moreover, that this recent strain of perplexity and incomprehension is one that seeps into (and out of) other genres as well (including once again noir, thrillers, and sci-fi).

BORDERS

Much as a broad survey may disclose of common strains among late Westerns, I am more interested in what can be revealed through sustained analysis of far fewer films whose powerful styles have been uniquely influential—styles that coyly play on the borders of semantic and syntactic allusion. Focusing in this way may put me at risk of being accused of having too small a sample, but my argument for "genre expectations and border crossings" rests less on exhaustiveness than suggestiveness. Only a close reading of a few films rather than a sweeping review of many will reveal the distinctive characteristics that make late Westerns worthy of our attention. Having made that point, however, I should add that many of the films just referred to could also easily withstand closer scrutiny, as well as others, including: Kevin Costner's *Dances with Wolves* (1990), Clint Eastwood's *Unforgiven*, Robert Rodriguez's *El Mariachi* (1992), Mario van Peebles's *Posse* (1993), Jonathan Kaplan's *Bad Girls* (1994), John Hillcoat's

The Proposition (2005), Ed Harris's *Appaloosa* (2008), the Coen brother's *True Grit*, Quentin Tarantino's *The Hateful Eight* (2015), and Alejandro González Iñárritu's *The Revenant* (2016). Each of these, given more time and space, would offer further confirmation of inventive directions taken by late Westerns.

To repeat my initial argument: at a certain point in the history of any genre, semantic materials can become misleading, while narrative syntax (however altered and hybridized) can do its generic work alone without such visual cues. Early on, we learn to recognize generic patterns that emerge from a film (whether Western, noir, or comedy) via the balance between semantics and syntax, usually beginning with vivid visuals (boots and epic landscapes; gumshoes and mean streets; dancing shoes and fast-talking dames) as they become associated with certain narrative structures and relationships (the desire for revenge, or a dancer's grace, or a laugh). But as genres become well-worn, films often highlight their familiar status suggestively, not simply mixing in strains from other genres (which has always occurred, as discussed above) but self-consciously enticing audiences—sometimes teasing us with generic possibilities that do not pan out, at other times evoking patterns before we even become aware that generic expectations are being entertained. Late Westerns have been a surprisingly rich vehicle for such generic play, and their box-office success seems to confirm viewers' delight in the cinematic bait-and-switch operation (which can also seem like inventive double dipping). Occasionally, the process is so attenuated that films hardly seem Western at all, at least according to the supposedly "classic" genre ideal (fixed in the 1950s), until we realize how thoroughly a generic syntax informs the plot even without the usual visual markers. Conversely, other films are filled with semantic tags that seem immediately to confirm a Western identification, until we gradually realize how little they exhibit any interest in its generic syntax.[21]

Consider just such a case of two directors enthusiastic about the genre whose films investigate themes and traits long associated with the Western, but which still seem part of a more mixed, even uncertain generic identity.

Wim Wenders's *Don't Come Knocking* and David Jacobson's *Down in the Valley* both appeared in 2005 and together rely on clear genre features, oriented toward unstable family dynamics. Those links, however, hardly confirm their status as late Westerns and may be as confusing as they seem generically significant. After all, a film set in the West, starring figures in western garb, is not by virtue of those attributes alone a Western, and the question of why such films are mildly less interesting as late versions of the genre may be worth pausing to consider.

Wenders's film follows a cowboy star escaping his popular reputation, abandoning his current film commitment and literally heading back on the road. Having finally in late middle age become troubled by the life he has led, realizing at last the havoc he has strewn, the children spawned, the loves lost, he decides to confront his past directly. The plot weaves together his efforts to repair that life, nostalgic and misguided as he is. Yet little here reminds us of issues or cinematography characterizing the Western, certainly no more than family melodrama. Howard Spence (Sam Shepard) ruminates about his youthful dalliances, visiting towns in Nevada and Montana where he had spent time, but the film seems generically Western only insofar as he has become a generic Western film star. And Jacobson's movie seems a similar generic cross-mix, focusing on a twenty-something, would-be cowboy, Harlan Curruthers (Edward Norton), psychotically attracted to a cute teenager in Los Angeles. As he engages in escalating conflicts and shootouts, we are reminded less of Westerns than of crime dramas like Raoul Walsh's *White Heat* (1949) or Terence Malick's *Badlands* (1973). In both Wenders's and Jacobson's films, sets are meant to remind us of a worn-out genre only glancingly, without otherwise engaging conventions in recognizably generic fashion. The one theme they share is a testy concern with family dynamics, a persistent and central feature of the Western, perhaps more than any other. Attention to issues of parenting, of marital compatibility, and of children's obligations forms a recurrent strain in the genre, and in chapters below—including those about *3:10 to Yuma*, *Lone Star*, *Three Burials*, and perhaps especially

Fig. 1. Family melodrama of Howard Spence, revisiting his past and failing to communicate with his newly discovered son, in *Don't Come Knocking* (Sony Pictures Classics).

Fig. 2. "Am I gettin' through to you?" Psychotic Harlan Curruthers confronted by his girlfriend's father trying to protect his family, in *Down in the Valley* (Thinkfilm).

David Cronenberg's *A History of Violence* (2005)—it becomes clear that a dominant feature of late Westerns is still to remind us how important family remains. In that regard, both *Down in the Valley* and *Don't Come Knocking* do engage us, if not as compellingly as other candidates.

More generally, the films selected in the following chapters creatively turn their attention not only to the margins of family dynamics but to all sorts of other contested issues having to do with borders, whether geographic or economic; racial or gendered; cultural, legal, or social. Class conflicts are as unrelenting as racial strife, gender clashes as persistent as narcocorrido tensions, past historical grievances repeatedly hemming in the present, with violence always conceived as a necessary breach of borders that had otherwise seemed secure. These become means of reminding us of the genre's earlier semantic binaries (civilized vs. savage, privileged vs. powerless, East vs. West, and legal resolution vs. individual action), as well as of their translation from thematic questions into syntactical plot patterns, doing so formally in ways that inveigle viewers into accepting them *as* Westerns. In fact, the salient aspect of the more successful of these recent films has been their commitment to a form of aesthetic *border crossing* in their shots and cinematic angles, as well as their pivoting narrative sequences. Far more commanding than the habitual Mexican boundary that continues to center Western plots, or the riven family dynamics that likewise recur, are the cinematic "borders" that visually, sonically compel and shape our attention. While the films below are all Western in theme and setting, what distinguishes each is how its specific formal innovations transform a concern with borders aesthetically, making viewers aware of their own discernibly ocular borderline status. As much to the point, these films are not only generically mixed, but sometimes confusedly so, confirming how intriguingly impure the Western continues to be.

Admittedly, film noir is the generic thread that keeps reappearing in the weave, less as interloper than an essential aspect of directions taken by late Westerns. And that is ironic since no species of film defies the constituent features of the Western (or its "serious orientation") so dramatically as noir, which in contrast to colorful Panavision landscapes characteristically focuses on cramped urban quarters shadowed by claustrophobic fears.[22] Far from the nostalgia associated with the Western, a strain of dread pervades film noir for a past that continues to haunt the present, leaving sparse faith in anything like benign future prospects.[23] The Western tends to be civic minded, or at least regularly addresses such issues, while noir seems bent on purely individual and selfish ends. And even more conspicuously defining noir is its apparent immutability of character, of inscrutable femmes fatales who dictate seemingly fated plots even as they cow the pliant men they engage to carry out their wills. As if in sheer revolt against the tested restraint of Western heroes, noir luxuriates in mayhem and bloodshed for its own sake, void of redeeming virtue, as the mere culmination to action, ending plot itself.[24] Yet noir's influence is among the more persistent subjects in the following chapters—including those on John Sturges's *Bad Day at Black Rock* (1955), Delmer Daves's *3:10 to Yuma* (1957), and *Lone Star*—and registers one significant reason for the Western's continuing appeal.[25] Different as the genres have always fundamentally been, cross-fertilization has led to strikingly innovative cinema in the past, most prominently Raoul Walsh's *Pursued* (1947), *High Noon*, and Anthony Mann's *The Naked Spur* (1953). Still, each of these films tends to meld noir techniques to a Western vision celebrated by Warshow, reinforcing both "the value of violence" and masculine self-restraint. While that melding continues in the late Western, any sustaining belief in violence as a continuing "value" has all but entirely disappeared.

The following chapters concentrate on aspects of late Westerns that make them creative extensions of a genre that continues to reinvent itself, sometimes through idiosyncratic scenes, or odd characterizations, or unusual formal dimensions. Granted, nothing about this is unique to the Western, nor could it be, given how mixed the genre has been. Indeed, thematic as well as formal features tend to bind competing genres more closely to each other in any clear-cut historical period than to their generic precursors, based on the way audiences consume films and the way in which the industry obliges in satisfying their desire. Graphic violence, "self-conscious" camerawork, fragmented narratives, and the influence of film noir prevail with late Westerns and will focus the discussions below, but these features also characterize thrillers and melodrama, horror and space and war films. Still, one vivid change *is* peculiar to late Westerns, in the often deliberate turn from the supposedly premier feature that lent its name to the genre—its celebrated, wide-open landscape. The efflorescence of the Western in the 1950s corresponded with the introduction of CinemaScope and later the Panavision widescreen processes that actively competed with television, offering an aspect angle (2.39:1) that allowed stunning, sweeping panoramas of western scenes. Yet recent films that continue to rely on similar wide-aspect ratios are counterintuitively often swung away from distant vistas, pointedly refusing to focus on landscapes at all. Instead, cameras are turned to interiors and closed spaces with lenses focused on faces rather than far horizons, deliberately angling away from the suasions of earlier films in what sometimes seems like a tacit effort to induce in the viewer a longing for such scenes. That effort was anticipated as early as the 1950s, certainly with *Bad Day at Black Rock* and Daves's *3:10 to Yuma*, but also with Jacques Tourneur's *Stars in My Crown* (1950), Fritz Lang's *Rancho Notorious* (1952), *High Noon*, and *The Lusty Men*. Moreover, many of these films were shot self-consciously (even defiantly) in black-and-white in an era of enthusiastic color photography, with Daves's cinematographer Charles Lawton Jr. using red filters to emphasize the parched landscape brought on by the drought that pressures the narrative. Again, the very absence of a conventionally luxuriant landscape, here as in other films, paradoxically signals a defiance of familiar Western cinematic norms.

The second formal aspect that characterizes films addressed below is how frequently so many of them resort to odd, even disruptive camera angles, drawing attention self-consciously to their cinematography. Again, this hardly distinguishes Westerns from other genres and, in any case, is hardly new. But something mildly more furtive occurs in the look of recent films as figures (usually masculine) are held up to examination from unsuspected perspectives, making us look at them afresh if only to pause and realize that we never fully knew them nor could succeed in gaining greater understanding. Cinematographers explore odd angles on central figures—including Roger Deakins in *No Country for Old Men*, Dariusz Wolski in Ridley Scott's *The Counselor* (2013), and Stuart Dryburgh in *Lone Star*—that have the effect of disarming the viewer, inducing a sense of dissociation, often as a means of aligning us with the hero's confusion and befuddlement. Accompanying the unexpected use of close-ups and singular framing techniques is the frequent fragmentation of narrative itself, with the customary chronology of events that proceeds in a more or less straightforward fashion undone by flashbacks and prolepses, inserted sequences that remind us as much of noir as of Westerns. Again, that is the fruitful legacy of genre mixing; effects that transcend any supposedly single genre are immersed in something like a tidal pool that stimulates adulteration and hybridization.

And again as well, hybridization had been anticipated most notably in *The Man Who Shot Liberty Valance*, even earlier in *The Searchers*, both of which reveal John Ford's deep indebtedness to noir in his effort to enact how fully legend and facts create one another. But now the perceived problem of history has taken a more dominant role with almost all the films below obsessed with the grip of the past on the present, unsettling as that coercive process continues to be. Consider the basic plots of *3:10 to Yuma* and *Lone Star*, of *No Country for Old Men* and *The Counselor*, in each of which some previous event or decision handcuffs possibility, asserting an all but inflexible hold that leaves characters (and viewers) unable to move on. *A History of Violence* is perhaps the most prominent example of this stifling backward pressure, if from another angle, and the same may be said of *Brokeback Mountain*, appearing the same year.

That helps explain why these films so often focus on figures struggling with an array of personal obsessions, which borders on the psychological distress displayed in other genres (crime films, for an obvious instance, but also noir and horror, spy films, even thrillers). Perhaps the most obvious candidate among earlier Westerns is Ethan Edwards in *The Searchers*, though Will Kane in *High Noon*, Jeb Rand (Robert Mitchum) in *Pursued*, and almost all of Jimmy Stewart's characters for Anthony Mann's 1950s films appear similarly afflicted. In each case, the obsessions pinpoint ways of acting as a man that have long obsessed the Western, involving worries about obligation and honor, ignominy and martial skills. Among more recent films discussed below, Pete Perkins (Tommy Lee Jones) in *The Three Burials of Melquiades Estrada* and Sam Deeds (Chris Cooper) of *Lone Star* are obvious figures plagued by events long since passed, whose efforts to right that past or otherwise understand it define the sometimes repetitive narrative motion of their films. But that dynamic had been anticipated by the stubbornly persistent John Macreedy (Spencer Tracy) in *Bad Day at Black Rock* as well as Dan Evans (Van Heflin) in Daves's *3:10 to Yuma*.

Lastly, an overriding theme links these late Westerns in ways hardly obvious at first glance: their persistent misgivings about supposedly settled questions of identity. To state the issue this way risks a certain unnecessary vagueness, especially since the theme recurs in so many forms of contemporary cinema, hardly making it a distinctive feature of Westerns. Consider the film adaptations of Robert Ludlum's series beginning with *The Bourne Identity* (1980), perhaps the most dramatic version of doubt being cast on what the central character is and was. Bourne, because of his amnesia, is unaware of his combat expertise and survivalist skills. The films below inquire even more deeply into that seemingly contemporary issue, perhaps because the Western itself has unquestionably assumed the identity of the hero, his masculine virtues and gender identification. Now however (as suggested in the review above of recent thematic preoccupations) that assumption has all but evaporated. *The Counselor* offers Cormac McCarthy's self-conscious investigation of selfhood, having characters themselves discuss the relation between actions and character, desires and personality. From a different perspective, *A History of Violence* similarly investigates our common understanding, transforming the central character's dual identities into the film's central drama. To a lesser degree, so do *Three Burials* and *Brokeback Mountain*, if in both cases from different underlying perspectives. It is worth adding that the sequence of chapters below moves from 1950s films that anticipated how Westerns were already becoming self-conscious about identity, turning genre conventions against themselves, to more recent examples that have built on that premise, questioning the processes of obsession and selfhood, and doing so via formal techniques that themselves become ever more provocative and self-aware.

Like all late versions of successful genres, Westerns have begun to direct their attention to categories earlier taken for granted, which may explain the breakdown of specific ideals as well as notions of coherent identity. Certainly, films have become more self-conscious, aware of their own preoccupations, with some examples discussed below clearly meta-Westerns intrigued by their own generic structure. One might almost claim that late Westerns are by definition "meta," resisting being immediately identified in semantic terms but revealing through their inventive syntactical borrowings a view all the more self-conscious of a tradition, a legacy, a genre. Then again, what makes a genre recognizable is a willingness to acknowledge certain conventions even in bending or defying them, making all members of the class to some degree self-conscious (hence, "meta" all the way back). One need not recall the comic self-consciousness of two of the most successful Westerns—Elliott Silverstein's *Cat Ballou* (1965) and Mel Brooks's *Blazing Saddles* (1974)—to realize how fully the genre has always been aware of its own construction and how broadly that self-consciousness is part of the pleasure of Westerns, which by the time they are identified are always comfortably late.

CONCLUSION: ANTICIPATIONS

The following chapters offer, as promised, intense close readings of individual films, beginning with *Bad Day at Black Rock*, itself already an unlikely Western. After all, an aged, one-armed man arrives at a barren Southwestern town in 1945 to present a dead son's medal for bravery to his Japanese father, only to discover the father is also dead under untoward circumstances. Nothing redeems the town as the site of a conventional Western: its drab setting; its almost exclusively male community; its lack of any visible economy; its mix of craven citizens and maniacal bullies. The whole seems nearly a parody of Western conventions arranged in a modern setting, with a central figure posed stubbornly against a community that refuses to grant him any leverage. Moreover, the film's formal features—from its paradoxically sparing use of CinemaScope to its oddly angled shots—challenge the very assumption of a wide-open West that would seem the burden of the setting's appeal. Yet despite negating the materials it borrows, the film nonetheless endorses the viewer's identification of it *as* a Western. And this is the point: that Sturges deconstructs the genre element by element but leaves the viewer with a sense that the Western has remained somehow intact, as ghostly and persistent as the figures that people it. In short, we are encouraged by a film that seems hardly supported by the narrative itself, which anticipates late Westerns to follow, interrogating the very terms it invokes to establish our expectations.

The second chapter makes a leap from the 1950s to the '90s, crossing over decades that have been well-discussed (Todd Berliner, Andrew Patrick Nelson), following the debacle of Michael Cimino's *Heaven's Gate* (1980) and the revival precipitated by *Dances with Wolves*. More importantly, the discussion turns to a different problem of many Westerns (indeed, of many genre vehicles) in their adaptation of fictional narratives, then adaptation of earlier films—a problem pursued in various subsequent chapters. James Mangold's *3:10 to Yuma* offers an intriguing instance of the late Western since it reconfigures Delmer Daves's earlier version, itself an adaptation of Elmore Leonard's 1953 story. The chapter thus traces a plot adapted for the allegedly "classic" period of the film Western, then transformed into a late Western, half a century later. Clearly, the genre remains recognizably the same, supporting my argument that no break occurs into the "postwestern." But it *is* true that Daves and Mangold use generic materials idiosyncratically in films that may appear at first similar but nonetheless turn out to impress us as fundamentally unallied because of the very different historical periods from which they emerged. In their substantially different levels of violence, in altered cinematic techniques (close-ups, camera angles), and in dramatically varied characterizations: in each aspect, these directors create versions of a story that reveal more about contemporary standards of cinematic pleasure than the supposed coherence of the Western genre itself. Indeed, Daves's allegiance to genre assumptions contrasts with Mangold's turn to certain thriller expectations, explaining why the latter's film veers into mild if entertaining incoherence. The fragmentation that predominates in the late Western has the effect of overtipping the balance of plot, and in the end mangling the genre—though nonetheless to the pleasure of viewers, suggesting something about a more recent desire for fragmented plots and gratuitous violence.

John Sayles's *Lone Star* offers in turn a substantially different version of the late Western, taking the occasion of Hispanic and Anglo cultural differences to concentrate on an array of epistemological borders: between history and myth, parent and child, male and female genders, as well as racial and cultural matrixes. These are all central aspects of the generic Western, though Sayles self-consciously places them under scrutiny, making this even more than earlier examples a late Western about Westerns themselves. And the cinematic structure of the film compounds these efforts through a fragmented presentation that engages viewers in the problematic seamlessness of any narrative sequence. In every way, *Lone Star* ponders the question of unified identity, shared and nearly shared, simply by dramatizing the contrasts that allow for coherence itself to be achieved.

The following chapter on *The Three Burials of Melquiades Estrada* continues to investigate this strain of self-consciousness, asking why the film begins in a deeply fragmented narrative fashion, presenting a series of gestures, scenes, and themes that remind us of the Western genre yet fail to contribute to a recognizable sequence that might generate a coherent story. Even the meaning of the central event—the shooting of Melquiades (Julio Cedillo) that prompts retribution from his closest friend—is left indeterminate since his killer may actually be as "innocent" as he claims to be, saying that Melquiades first shot at him. Only as the rancher Pete Perkins defiantly seizes control of these disparate scenes, abducting the border patrolman Mike Norton (Barry Pepper) and compelling him to return the corpse to Mexico for proper burial, does the narrative begin to cohere. Only then do the disconnected, even senseless materials of the film's first half come together as a resurrection of the Western itself. The film resuscitates exhausted materials, affirming how fully the myth itself creates the facts that seem to support it, exemplifying in the process the central argument of this book.

In 2005 two films vividly challenged assumptions about the ongoing success of the Western: Ang Lee's *Brokeback Mountain*, which scandalized expectations, and David Cronenberg's *A History of Violence*, which barely seemed to fulfill them. This chapter begins with a focus on the classic Western's concern with family dynamics and then turns to the genre conventions surrounding that theme, which shape our experience of each film so differently. In one case, we are led to read scenes as Western because of their clear semantic valance, but the overall syntax seems quite distinctly drawn from the school of melodrama, which alters that response. In the other, what appears forthrightly as a crime thriller gradually becomes clear (again syntactically and this time in defiance of semantic materials) as a narrative to be viewed through expectations dictated by Western conventions. The premise pursued through previous chapters here comes to a vivid contrast in making us realize again how fully our cinematic experience of a late genre depends upon films that have long been assumed to constitute that genre.

The sixth chapter focuses on the Coen brothers' *No Country for Old Men*, returning us to the question of adaptation (of Cormac McCarthy's 2005 novel) and in this case to a film that initially solicits us as a Western yet through its cinematography persistently denies that that is what it is doing. Beginning in nostalgic voice-over and a series of frontier landscape scenes, the film almost immediately shifts from a familiar Western mode to noir techniques, involving odd camera angles (close-ups, overhead views), shadowed lighting, claustrophobic settings, and abrupt editing transitions. Indeed, the film soon seems more noir or thriller than Western, though the contradictions and tensions among generic markers clearly reflect a self-consciousness about genre expectations. Translating the novel's verbal spaces into cinematic juxtapositions, the Coens make us realize how persistently the late Western turns self-conscious about its own generic dictates.

The final chapter seizes on Ridley Scott's *The Counselor*, extending the pattern of other late Westerns in crossing among generic expectations, mixing and matching materials, offering a hybrid that is once again little different from the hybrids of earlier "classic" Westerns except in being so self-conscious. Yet in this case, the argument I advance is that the film's fleetingly apparent invocation of genre conventions (Western, noir, thriller) teases us with a seemingly "late Western" syntax but finally refuses to submit. *The Counselor* hardly touches on issues of family or masculinity that have been the focus of other Westerns early and late, even if it pursues questions of borders that have been central to them. Indeed, the frontier borders that other films have conceived as political, ethnic, or cultural have become in McCarthy's script and in Scott's cinematography deeper epistemological and moral divisions, separating us from the coherent figures we take ourselves to be. *The Counselor* finally undermines twin notions of morality and character long associated with the Western and held dear by viewers: that we can actively choose the kind of life we want to live and that we can choose the kind of person we would like to be. The fragmented, dissociative aspect of events in the film, which at first seems familiar, finally undoes any more integrated or progressive plot we might hope to imagine for it. Granted, the film is self-conscious about this pattern by having characters repeatedly ruminate on the problem of coherent identity: on the disjunction between doing and being, between expectation and consequence, and more generally between the view of oneself one takes internally, prospectively, and the perspective one is forced to take (as others have) after the fact. Granted as well, the noir and thriller elements so central to the film are contrasted with generic Western expectations about loyalty and masculinity. But in seizing on syntactic generic elements that refuse to link together or otherwise add up, the film makes clear how little it is a late Western, which may well help explain its lack of critical acclaim or box office success.

This array of films is not meant to reveal a single strand to the late Western or anything like a concentrated "postwestern" mentality. On the contrary, the continuing strength of the genre rests in its openness to other mediations, other influences, other genres. And that has been true since early years. The fact that a particular semantic strain seems to identify a "family resemblance" hardly answers for the extraordinary staying power of the genre, which depends as much or more on its syntactic resonances, on patterns that evoke our continuing concerns about family, gender, civic responsibility, even violence itself and its suitable expression. The late Western is an effort to keep these concerns alive and well in popular entertainment and, even more, in our cultural dialogue. How else might that occur? In what other genre (romantic comedy, mystery, sci-fi, horror) are those important considerations ever given such sustained and self-conscious, if altogether fictional, expression?

1

GHOSTLY EVOCATIONS IN
BAD DAY AT BLACK ROCK

Normally, a precredit sequence sets the tone for a film, generating the overall mood for nearly everything that follows. But *Bad Day at Black Rock* defies that familiar axiom in opening with a high helicopter view of a Southern Pacific train bisecting an arid landscape at top speed, urged on by a sustained acoustic clamor. The sequence registers an all but unstoppable force accompanied by a loudly percussive score, generating an immediate emotional turmoil that far exceeds the mystery that follows. Soon, the predictable transition from frenzy to exhaustion occurs as the passenger Streamliner slowly pulls into the ominous setting of Black Rock, Arizona, its whistle now reduced to uncanny blares, alerting us (through cinematic pacing, sound track, and lackluster setting combined) to how fully this community looms as little more than abandoned ghost town. The irony is that this sequence is dramatically, all but self-consciously counterpoised against the rest of the film, as if the largely static plot that follows were meant as strident contrast to the world here approaching. Another way to understand so dislocating an introduction is that its very intensity alerts us to other discrepancies in a noir Western, a film that consists as much of interior scenes held in medium frame (counterintuitively opposed to the genre's characteristic mode) as of epic CinemaScope landscapes. And even those views of barren terrain are regularly drab and washed out, evoked in thin sepia tints. Characters (all men, with one exception) rarely move around freely or unconstrained in loose configurations but instead are militantly lined up, found sitting or standing in place against walls and windows, as the camera persistently angles down on the hero, John J. Macreedy (Spencer Tracy), placing him in turn in a routinely subservient position. Moreover, Macreedy's strangely enigmatic undertaking, unexplained until late in the film, seems eerily like a mirror image of the town's behavior in safeguarding its own secretive, history-burdened dilemma.

In fact, the film's opening introduces the first of various paradoxes, heralding the vibrant, electrifying arrival of an outside world (the first time the train has stopped in over four years), only to let off an aged, apparitional figure who seems little different from the ghosts he will soon encounter. A specter enters a community of kindred phantoms, who become suddenly animated by his presence even as he embodies a mystery they are increasingly desperate to suppress. As we learn much later, Macreedy has arrived simply to honor his dead army comrade, to deliver the Medal of Honor Joe Komoko earned in saving Macreedy's life to Komoko's father, as a belated gesture of respect. He has no reason to suspect anything untoward has happened until the town's blustering intransigence arouses his suspicions about stories of the elder Komoko's death. None of that is apparent at first, except in the sheer draining away of the opening's profusion—its dynamic orchestral range, its hyped-up visual transitions—as if the wide-open landscape made so familiar by the Western genre were being undone by a noir plot of a shamefully buried past, one that adamantly refuses to stay buried. And curiously, when that past is finally laid bare, we discover the Japanese subplot has nothing to do with the whole and does not explain the plot transpositions. For all its lingering power, the Asian backstory (unusual as a theme in 1955) emerges as merely a Hitchcockian MacGuffin, a past trauma that signals the present's racism and small-mindedness but otherwise contributes little to the film's dynamic strains.

The paradox of *Bad Day at Black Rock* resonates more profoundly in the assortment of strangely dissociated plot materials brought together into a more or less familiar configuration. Characters who first appear little more than zombies, devoted to endless, undead behavior, rearrange themselves

Fig. 3. Southern Pacific Streamliner as unstoppable force bisecting the landscape at the opening of *Bad Day at Black Rock* (MGM).

into patterns that eerily remind us this is a Western. Long before the genre had exhausted familiar possibilities, the film seems prescient in anticipating ways that later Westerns would surprise us into deconstructively imposing remembered paradigms on scenes in order to grasp a narrative trajectory. The formally spectral look of *Bad Day* confirms this legacy by quietly invoking the genre's more usual visual appeal, if only by contrast with what is here absent or etiolated, the desolate landscapes and washed-out settings. Sturges brilliantly reveals how even his tired mise-en-scène cannot avoid the Western's continuing structural power to persuade. And characters function likewise, as perverse deformations silently enforcing a genre from which they so obviously diverge: the lone (if elderly and disabled) figure unswervingly committed to righting injustice; the craven (if perversely powerful) community riven by dissension, challenged by external threats; the open (if desolate) frontier, transforming individuals for the better; and above all, the prospect of starting over again, escaping the past (if a past no one acknowledges, so never in fact to be successfully escaped from). Each of these gestures seems antigeneric, unsettling us as viewers, since the film's very defiance of familiar patterns makes it slowly recognizable *as* a Western that focuses on the dynamics of Westerns themselves.

Vague quotations from the tradition alert us to that heritage, beginning with the telegraph office placed near the railway station that replicates the recurrent scene in *High Noon*, with tracks converging toward the horizon—though here as symbol of constraint rather than ready access of violence. Hector David (Lee Marvin) tilted back in his porch chair gestures recognizably to Wyatt Earp (Henry Fonda) in *My Darling Clementine*—though with no sense of civilized ease in the posture. And Macreedy's stalwart patience in the face of local, browbeating thugs reminds us of countless other Western heroes who have dominated the big screen. More generally, the film arouses expectations for a genre otherwise familiar through costumes, gestures, and attitudes in a distinctive locale rather than for its recognizable plot (after all, the initiating event in this case is hidden, arbitrary, finally a lie). The menace of Black Rock the town, its bullying and taunts, expresses a generic motif that seems at once excessive and unearned. No reason exists for this threatening dynamic at the very beginning, at least that we can discern, intimating how fully local spirits embody the very historical self-consciousness that will destroy them. The crime that has occurred in the past, that has clearly silenced the present, and that requires a revenant outsider to set a town free: this is the mysterious narrative premise that promises to bring Black Rock alive once again, as it simultaneously signals the dead will at last be allowed to rest in peace.

More importantly, the film parades distinctive (if mixed) generic materials for their own sake: a past revealed by the very energy of making it secret (noir? melodrama?); landscape surveyed not for celebration but simply to register its drabness (Western? Italian neo-realism?); the promise of working economies exposed as empty, perhaps senseless (crime or gangster films? road films?); and masculinity tested as a series of otherwise shallow gestures (action-adventure? historical epic?).[1] In that uncertain parade, *Bad Day* at once adopts signature features and yet moves relentlessly forward as an exposé of the redemptive aspects to which the Western genre has long laid claim. Granted, this deconstructive reading of a genre film has become a familiar practice in recent decades, though earlier directors had themselves created films with this in mind, most pointedly John Ford in *The Man Who Shot Liberty Valance*, which has long been cited as having initiated the practice. It comes as something of a surprise, however, to realize that screenwriter Millard Kaufman and director John Sturges should already in 1955, in the midst of the Western's efflorescence (a year before *The Searchers*), have exposed the genre's continuing power to persuade by focusing so intently on its limits.

AN ALIEN WORLD

Should one have wanted to waken the dead, the frenzy of *Bad Day*'s opening sequence would offer a suitably appropriate tone, registering sonically and visually the rousing of another world. The combination of strident, overwrought music with a landscape that holds vague appeal, all filmed via a camera that zooms, hovers, and glides: how else might the past be brought alive? Strangely, this scene was unplanned, with Sturges initially having chosen to introduce Tracy descending from the train with no sound other than prairie wind. The producer Dore Schary had "decided not to have any music. Only sounds. First the quiet of the speck of a station in the heart of desolation. A wind blowing, a yowl of a coyote, the far-off horn of a diesel engine, then the roar of the train" (1979, 279). Previews, however, revealed viewers were "puzzled" by this ambiguous entry, and the present scene was added as an afterthought: a Streamliner seen hurtling across the landscape from different points of view, arousing intrigue at this maniacal machine in an incongruous garden.[2] As well, contrary to the initial decision to use only ambient sounds throughout (wind, clocks, slamming doors, automobile horns), a young André Previn was hired to compose an orchestral sound track following the success of *High Noon*, which had suffered a similar failure in previews before Dimitri Tiomkin's score was added. Previn's music is far more dissonant than Tiomkin's, relying on a series of string repetitions over the blasts of a syncopated, off-kilter brass, all in sixteenth notes. Immediately, the viewer is unsettled by sonic discontinuity, with the music imitating the noise of a train in its clipped ostinatos punctuated by "stingers" (loud discordant punctuations), each of which comes when a credit interrupts the scene. The woodwind trills and continuing brass syncopations never settle into a clear counter-rhythm but keep fragmenting in a sequence that remains at once recognizable and somehow new. Gradually, actual sounds (clacking wheels, shrieking steam whistle) start to cross over the musical sound track as the train pulls into the station.[3] The completed sequence—which began with the camera seeming to fly *into* the front of the train, then over alongside it, accompanied by the brass and percussive score that corresponded to Schary's desire for "something loud, throbbing, and martial in undertone" (1979, 280)—suggests a mildly sinister, emotionally fraught advent to the town of Black Rock, as a solitary, apparently elderly, clearly burdened man disembarks. The opening is done, closed off, underlining its flagrant contrast with the cinematography of the rest of the film. Hereafter, we have a more or less silent, cinematically benign view, slow-paced and understated. And the figure who finally descends as a phantom ready to confront the town—a town we will learn that desperately wants to remain inert—is himself an ironic gesture against the plot to come: a figure unutterably weary, conspicuously aged, acutely handicapped.

Critics have disparaged this opening scene as "overstated," an otherwise irrelevant addition to the film, but its very theatricality arouses self-consciousness about what ensues.[4] For the film contrasts this melodramatic opening with its closing view of the same train slowly departing from a depleted town, with narrative returning us to the status quo before everything was disrupted by the stigma left on this community. The contrast of loud, initial agitation with quiet, closing enervation reinforces the aftermath of murder fully disclosed, incapable of being suppressed, no longer urgent. That sudden transition from turmoil to calm seems to encapsulate the film's own disclosure of murder settled to memory, long since resolved, and now simply there to be suppressed. Part of the logic of this opening sequence is to pressure viewers into resisting the slip into inertia, to maintain an energy that corresponds to what we later learn of Macreedy's obsession. After all, he is the paradoxical figure of absence, the ghost witness of a historical past that refuses to die, and yet the immediate presence of ongoing accusation as well, keeping the energized citizens now fully alive. The town itself is presented as the antithesis of any such energy, statically self-alienated and thoroughly impotent to effect any change. And while the sound track periodically reasserts an ambient emotional energy, that mood is rarely sustained in productive ways. Strangely, one of the few insistent sequences of dramatic emotion occurs in Coley Trimble's (Ernest Borgnine) brutal car chase of Macreedy, where the non-diegetic score is remarkably absent as all we hear is the violence of his honking car.

Just as dramatically and deliberately, however, visual details match the film's unnervingly muted acoustic realm, its mise-en-scène extending a singular dreariness from landscape scenery to personal wardrobe to interior furnishings. The Western celebrated by John Ford and Anthony Mann, André de Toth and Budd Boetticher, appears here as bleached out and comfortless, a dingy palette lacking much that might catch the eye.[5] All is ghostlike, revealed as if through deadened eyes. The only deep-hued color is Reno Smith's (Robert Ryan) red baseball cap, worn as emblem of revived emotional rage but also offered as a singular (and dramatic) contrast to all the other washed-out tints of clothes, furniture, interior decor, weathered buildings, thread-bare desert hues. He is, as the singular demonic figure through the film, identified by this ironic blotch of blood-red color, drawing everyone else in the town under his aegis. The script itself expands Howard Breslin's brief story description to corroborate more elaborately this sense of insignificant void: "The town is minute, dismal and forgotten, crouching in isolation where the single line of railroad track intersects a secondary dirt road. The twin strips of steel glisten in the fierce sunlight, fencing the dreary plain from the false fronts of the town. In b.g. is the bluff of a black stony mountain. Against this ancient mass the houses of Black Rock's single street are scanty in number and insignificant in architecture, a conglomerate paint-peeled modern trussed together with rusty nails and battered tin strips torn from signs." And then, confirming this physical dilapidation, it stresses "the quality of inertia and immutability—nothing moves, not even an insect; nothing breathes, not even the wind. Town and terrain seem to be trapped, caught and held forever in the sullen, abrasive earth." When Macreedy arrives, he is described as smiling "a sad, distasteful greeting to the town, its wretched dust, its mean, modest buildings" (McGuire and Kaufman 2015, n.p.). And with Spencer Tracy's tight-lipped grimace, the agitated music almost immediately subsides into a static rhythm, though the reason for his pause is left mysteriously unanswered. Curiously, the craggy, sallow features of Tracy's face (drooping, deeply creased, immobile) form a living embodiment of the arid landscape itself, exposing him as an autochthonous figure, giving expression to the land's memorial demands.

Again, the long panoramic shots intercut with credits, spurred on acoustically by off-balance music, inject an energy into the landscape that it cannot produce on its own: "The composition of each shot has that hard, sun-beaten texture of American primitive painting—pressurized in its simplicity—best exemplified, perhaps, by the work of Grant Wood." In a genre that nearly everywhere celebrates landscape, Sturges evokes a region reduced to the most provocative extremes of "dismal," "dreary," "barren," and "empty"—or as the script once more needlessly adds: "The morning sun lays over this wasteland of the American Southwest, a gigantic yellow bruise from which heat waves like bloodshot arteries spread themselves over the poisoned sky."[6] Perhaps, given this joyless if surreal terrain, it is unsurprising that so few outdoor scenes should be shown, rather than simply alluded to through windows.[7] Macreedy's central (mystery-resolving) jeep ride out to Adobe Flats is itself shot in relative close-up, with Sturges resisting the suasive advantages of a CinemaScope technique that was the very reason for adopting it (the first MGM film to be shot with this lens). The oddness of these scenic choices and notable omissions has been best (if elliptically) captured by the director Wim Wenders in a telling comment:

"You could say of this John Sturges film that it doesn't show a succession of images, but of sentences. A whole dozen of these sentences are written up in the display cases of the theatres showing *Bad Day at Black Rock*" (2001, 48). That is, the dreariness of setting demanded by the script seems better detailed as a verbal conceit *in the script* than visually in the film itself, which we translate into expressions of exhaustion. Another way of putting it, as Wenders bluntly adds, is, "In this film all details were really details!" (2001, 49). Deftly, the film expresses the script's assertions of a drab venue, with nothing warranting either further effort or greater attention.[8]

The physical town of Black Rock itself is deliberately filmed to appear enervated, drained all but completely of life, with its telegraph and gas stations, its dusty street and storage sheds, its hotel lobby and spare rooms, all self-consciously invoking the morphology of a ghost town, little more than a worn-out movie set. Whether peering in or looking out, that slightly fabricated impression of scene prevails, as Wenders further claims, in observing that our sense of "backdrops of the landscape that constantly show through windows or doors have more in common with paintings by Magritte than with the real landscape shown in the outdoor scenes. But even these look much more like a mile-wide, sky-high stage-set built in a gigantic studio. This endless artificiality confused me a lot at the beginning of the film, because I could only trace it back to the colours" (2001, 49). Still, that inauthentic palette unsettles us only initially until we realize a stock cinematic response is generated throughout that extends to characters' interactions. In fact, Black Rock consists of only seven buildings, clearly defined as isolated, part of a civic collective dying off.[9] No effort is made to persuade us of a reasonable economy here, certainly not one based on agricultural production; the murdered Japanese Komoko supposedly chose the place in order to farm, but what crop might he possibly have cultivated? And no other prospects seem apparent. Reno Smith does admit to running the Triple-Bar Ranch, a ranch neither seen nor referred to, with nobody else expressing an interest in cattle or cowboys. Sheriff Tim Horn (Dean Jagger) does initially ask about Macreedy's purpose in town—whether he is "selling cows or seed corn"—as if those were part of an otherwise invisible economy; but like the physical town itself, the gesture seems spurious. The local mortician-veterinarian, Doc Velie (Walter Brennan), emerges as the most expansive citizen on the subject, telling of eager argonauts who discover only pyrite: "They rip off the top soil of ten winding hills. They sprint in here, fog-heaved with excitement, lugging nuggets, big and bright and shiny. . . . Is it gold? (he bangs the rock down next to the scales) It is not! Do they quit? They do not!" As he adds, confirming the economic suspicions we have had all along: "Then they decide to farm. Farm! In country so dry you have to prime a man before he can spit, and before you can say 'Fat Sam' they're stalled, stranded and starving. They get weevil-brained and buttsprung." The very premise of so many Westerns, so often devoted to the plight of beleaguered farmers against railroading interests or overbearing ranchers, is undermined on-screen, suggesting how little this aspires to match generic codes.

As well, in defiance of the familiar saloon girls, school marms, and society matrons, Black Rock confirms part of the reason for its barren ghostliness in being nearly all one gender, flouting generativity itself. In a genre that has often shoved women to the margins, making them more or less inessential, this film further presses limits by excluding them nearly altogether. Yet men themselves are scarce. The shooting script called for "loafers" and incidental onlookers, but in fact only two such scenes were included, as Sturges later observed: "There's almost nobody there except the principals. Few extras. It's the most unrealistic staging ever. It's like a Greek tragedy: theatrically true but realistically false. I sometimes wonder how I pulled that off" (Lovell 2008, 100).[10] The whole constitutes a dismally enervated masculine realm coupled with a "sense of isolation and desolation" that contributes, as Neil Campbell argues, to "a community of the living dead, full of silence, absence, and bereavement" (2013, 83). True as this comment seems at first, that slide from silence through absence to bereavement itself appears not quite right if only because grief becomes among the last emotions evoked by the film. Even less do we assume that Black Rock represents an entire viewing audience's emotional slant, where "everything is trapped, contained, and deathly, symbolizing the postwar world of containment and suspicion, a McCarthyite culture of repressed anger and paranoia played out as western exceptionalism, traditional values, and masculine power" (2013, 85). In fact, 1950s America was no more a "world of containment and suspicion"—at least, distinctively or predominately so—than our own NSA-driven era of surveillance. And while Joseph McCarthy himself may have exhibited the "anger and paranoia" alluded to here, the entire culture can hardly be summed up so sweepingly or monochromatically.

Still, at a minimum, the lack of any productive or otherwise noticeable activity in town confirms its ghostliness and does so distinctly athwart generic expectations, bringing us back as viewers to our own quizzical confusion about Macreedy's resolve. Nothing seems to happen in this static space, though it gradually becomes clear that the town's inertia results from the weight of history bearing down on it ("four years ago something terrible happened here"), with the death of Komoko representing the end not merely of Japanese American aspirations, but of any fruitful possibilities, since his death corresponds with the last train to stop at Black Rock. The film has frequently been cited as the earliest to address the acrid legacy of internment policies during World War II and the persistence of anti-Asian attitudes in the postwar period. Reno Smith gives full animadversion to this xenophobic provincialism in his references to "a lousy Jap farmer" and rejection of "loyal Japanese-Americans, that's a laugh. They're mad dogs." But the absence of Komoko, even in flashback, makes such attitudes seem somehow drearily conventional (if otherwise predictable) in a film so clearly pitched against them.[11] Moreover, larger racial perspectives are inadvertently invoked in the treatment of Macreedy, whom a newly appointed sheriff Hector treats contemptuously as a (black) "boy . . . boy . . . boy." In the repetition, we are reminded of all forms of prejudicial exclusion, of cultural and psychological oppression enacted via slurs that reduce an antagonist to immaturity and childishness. In short, a town that otherwise seems alien and unrecognizable in physical as well as verbal treatments reveals the kinds of ethnic, gendered, and cultural divides that have always beset Western plots.

A CRAVEN TOWN

Ironically, the Western has frequently celebrated the kind of staunch independence that Frederick Jackson Turner notoriously claimed was characteristic of frontier communities. Yet in doing so, the genre invariably pitches a stalwart individual against the passive, sheeplike tendencies of those he both protects and defies. *Bad Day* turns this convention on its head by defining Black Rock as a community of hard-bitten souls bound together by guilt, resistant to outsiders who do not share their secret. Still, that condition itself tacitly invokes the genre's obsession with borders that has been apparent from the beginning, of men without women, of locals cut off from an outside world, of Anglos guarding their history of racial violence. Like any ghost story, however, the past resolutely refuses to die, aligning the living dead against the figure who threatens to expose them to light. The paradox of this genre film is that it reveals cravenness as itself a kind of perverse strength, binding together those too weak to stand on their own and thereby ironically fulfilling the claim of stalwart independence so often attributed to the West.

The pervasive attitude of the town, apparent in Macreedy's initial encounter with the telegraph operator Hastings (Russell Collins), is aggression toward those who do not share its past. Yet as Hastings's surreptitious loyalty to Smith makes clear, that aggression is only the obverse side of a pervasive timidity. All Hastings can later do, in offering Macreedy lemonade, is to mechanically repeat the mantra, "I'm just a good neighbor." And that sentiment confirms for even the better citizens a resistance to becoming involved, as Doc Velie dubiously acknowledges: "I feel for you, but I'm consumed with apathy. Why should I mix in?" Civic obligation, a sense of moral propriety, any residual duty towards one's neighbor: all are swept aside in the general sense that collective action on behalf of positive values is insufficient as rationale. Macreedy himself seems to have been party to this logic in conceding that "I was washed up when I got off that train." As he admits, conceding he is like everyone else: "I don't know. I was looking for a place to get lost, I guess."

That unwillingness to break free from the past, to abide however dispiritedly by its imprisoning bonds, and to become a mere spectral presence, is confirmed spatially by a visual turning inward, sequestering characters paradoxically once again behind an invisible border. Cinematographer William C. Mellor focused on closed interiors rather than panning open spaces, effectively shutting down the prospect of physical freedom or visible choice. Macreedy all but steps from the train into the hotel lobby and, later after a bath, returns to his room to lie on his bed where Hector bullies him (a scene that cites a similar hotel-room sequence in *High Noon* and anticipates many more in *3:10 to Yuma*). Thereafter, the camera remains constrained by small rooms through long, fixed shots that all enforce interior confinement. Whether Macreedy rouses sheriff Tim in his jail, or meets Doc in his vet's office, or confronts Smith's confederates in the town bar, the West is represented as quarantine rather than absolution. Even the occasional outdoor scenes present distant mountains as mere backdrop to strained discussions or tense encounters, highlighted by Macreedy driving a jeep to Komoko's burned-out homestead at Adobe Flats. And that extended view consists primarily of close-ups, as he picks flowers or gazes at the windmill creaking in the wind or listens in the stillness for the splash that finally follows his rock dropped down the well. The ghostly scene nicely evokes Komoko's distant presence when suddenly, a contrast occurs not visually but sonically as Coley Trimble runs Macreedy off the road, honking repeatedly, guffawing maniacally, ramming the jeep with his Packard, all in close and medium shots—reminding us via head-on views of the film's opening, though this time shorn of musical accompaniment. The sequence is structured as an interlocked arrangement of silence, investigation, sudden realization, then threat, but within a noir focus on the psychology of faces rather than a Western turn to landscape and space.

Given how fully civic cravenness is reinforced by Mellor's cinematography in the film's claustrophobic concentration on closed rooms and close-ups themselves, still the overall sense of inadequacy is compounded more generally by the plot backstory, which seems oddly flawed. For while covering up a murder always silences those in the know, in this case too many unanswered questions still loom. Why would an Asian American settle in so eminently Anglo a community, with no one else accompanying him, to live in isolated circumstances as a farmer where no other farms exist?[12] And why is it that no one besides Reno Smith, the casual killer, expresses antipathy towards the Japanese? The death of Komoko is clearly what today would be termed a "hate crime," but he exists solely as someone about whom we know nothing at all, an absent cause supposedly responsible for all that follows, though it is unclear whether the town's cravenness follows or precedes his death. That is, since he is merely an emblem of race consciousness (little more), his death is linked to nothing particularly Japanese. And it seems that the town's unwillingness to resist Smith was as much the impetus for Komoko's death as the result of it. The thin community of Anglo men (and one woman) is bound together by nothing so much as the oppressive sense of being exposed to the light. Everyone is terrified in a world where telephones fail to work as they should (because one is always overheard), where cars are easily disabled (because someone might flee), where secrets are passed and therefore motives left invariably suspect.

Again, Mellor's cinematography perfectly captures this abiding sense of trepidation that tips over into fear of one another and especially of outsiders. That cumulative uneasiness is registered most powerfully when Smith holds court in the hotel lobby before his crew glances through the window to watch Macreedy, while we in turn watch them superimposed on his mirrored reflection.[13] That very appearance of their own bodily images overlaying scenes they view intimates the psychological constraints that enforce their imprisonment *by* the past, with the cinematic frame revealing inner recesses exposed over faces and figures still haunted

Fig. 4. Reno Smith holding court with fellow citizens in Black Rock's hotel lobby, watching John J. Macreedy through the mirroring window in *Bad Day at Black Rock* (MGM).

by what has occurred. Repeatedly, characters peering through windows seem split off from themselves, hampered psychologically by the guilt that accompanies what they see and what they do not (since only we as viewers can see both). Earlier, Doc Velie had surreptitiously observed Macreedy with what is shown to us in a similar double image, making the very apparitions of deeds once done appear in the cinematography itself, spectral presences reflected both off the glass and seen through it. In this sense, not only does the past seem eerily immanent, but present figures are revealed as ghosts, liminal presences not fully alive but consumed by a zombielike need to preserve a past *as* past. They have become animate corpses revivified simply because some external energy has momentarily imbued them with a sense of vitality. And their secret is revealed in accidentally mirrored reflections, exposing the entire community of Black Rock as a collection of undead figures, explaining why they have no other purpose (no vocation, no economy, no other lives) than to defy death itself.

Kaufman constructed his screenplay self-consciously to elaborate this spectral theme, strangely enough, building out from the central opposition between a mysteriously intrusive protagonist and the resident forces opposing him. The logic of borders once again is enforced by fear. As he claimed: "Any work is only as strong as its heavy (or heavies), and that's an axiom. If your bad guy isn't strong, your good guy, who goes up against him, is diminished; he doesn't present much of a challenge, and without a challenge you have no conflict of any deep consequence" (2008, 80). One could say that the entire plot has been conceived as a schematic of good (or bafflement) versus evil—less to uncover a mystery that finally seems to make little sense than to expose the forms of behavior that go into making a plot. More specifically, Kaufman drew on supposedly classical notions of plot dynamics in which evil is construed in a series of distinctive formulaic figures who separately harass the protagonist, described by him as the Brain Heavy, the Dog Heavy, and the Cad Heavy (2008, 79). That triumvirate corresponds to the oppressive figures confronting Macreedy: Reno Smith ("the intelligence behind the gang. . . . A figure of respect and authority" [2008, 79]); Coley Trimble and Hector David ("the sociopathic killer, the enforcer" [2008, 79]); and Pete Wirth (John Ericson) ("what in a pre-Freudian era was called 'weak,' a follower, a bed-wetter" [2008, 79]). The film, in short, was intended to portray a species of menacing threat arrayed against the innocent outsider, all in a plot structured according to classical determinants representing psychological forces that emerge out of the past.

While Sturges used the newly invented CinemaScope lens sparingly on landscape, to little effect, it turned out strangely effective in transforming close-ups and interior spaces. An inherent weakness of the anamorphic lens had dictated a conventionally awkward blocking of actors as well as what seemed like unnecessarily sharp filming angles. As Kaufman observed: "CinemaScope, which worked so well with wide-angle shots of the desert and the wild blue yonder, had its problems focusing laterally on people. In any set-up more complex than a two-scene, the characters were lined up

Fig. 5. Watchful citizens lined up in a row on the town café's front porch in *Bad Day at Black Rock* (MGM).

and frozen in place like figures on a horizontal monument" (2008, 81). That helps explain the apparitional rows of men sitting on the hotel's front porch or the frequent closed-in scenes of figures awkwardly confronting each other. At first it seems characters were meant to be presented in a Kabuki-like drama, following established forms, even generic expectations for the ways in which dynamics are worked out through personality, leading to a dramatic revelation. But in fact the cinematic choices were more obviously intended to be oppressive, as Kaufman observed of Sturges's decision to frame "all the heavies individually and collectively in key scenes on a physical plane *above* Macreedy, i.e., they look down on him, they dominate whatever space he occupies" (2008, 76–77).[14] As he continues, "They are on the deck of the shabby hotel, arrogant and imperious, as he walks below them on the dusty road; or when Tracy sits uncomfortably on a bench in front of the garage as Reno Smith (Ryan) towers over him at a gas pump. . . . I made no reference to the interrelated altitude of characters in any given frame. The contribution was entirely John's" (2008, 76–77). The film's unusual camera angles reinforce a pervasive sense of not simply antagonism but of dominance, with Macreedy's appearance repeatedly, obsessively cast as beleaguered by a citizenry committed to denying their past.

That presentation of Macreedy is complemented by Tracy's characteristic comportment: patient, long-suffering, soft-spoken, at times passively agreeable in the face of menace. His advent into Black Rock, moreover, replicates Komoko's as an outsider, an anomaly who clearly fails to share local values. Curiously, Macreedy's own bearing conforms to traditional Japanese forms of behavior in avoiding conflict and resisting boorish challenges. By midway through we realize he is the phantom embodiment of Komoko haunting the town, refusing to let it rest in peace. His arrival has formed an understated plot repetition, acting in ways we imagine Komoko must have, met with the same rejection Komoko presumably received—the aspersions, rebuffs, and active provocation of a tight-knit, close-minded (defiantly racist) community. Not only is it impossible for the past to stay repressed, but its energies seem to be a close repetition in the present of something we can only imagine historically, with Black Rock residents snooping once again in response to a stranger's inquisitiveness.

Thus, as we now finally realize long after, the frenzied opening of the film resonates (if only in retrospect) as announcing the return of the repressed, as strident harbinger of a past that refuses to stay past. And in that, the entire film registers a tension between the tight, inward-turning community and the figure who emerges as that past's heraldic ghost. Smith gives perfect expression to this sentiment in his outburst to Macreedy: "I don't know. Somebody's always looking for something in this part of the West. To the historians, it's the 'Old West.' To the book writers, it's the 'Wild West.' To the businessman, it's the 'Undeveloped West.' They say we're all poor and backward and I guess we are. We don't even have enough water. But to us, this place is our West. I just wish they'd leave us alone." For Smith, as for so many others in a genre that regularly extends Turner's simplified myth of frontier escape, the American West is a place not simply to protect oneself but to close off the past from the present. Of course, his defense of their characteristic response—of being "suspicious of strangers. . . . Hangover from the old days. The old West"—is met by Macreedy's equally accurate retort: "I thought the tradition of the old West was hospitality." This standoff between wary distrust and generous accommodation defines not simply the range of civic responses in the West but the internal range of responses exhibited by each man separately, one closing down mutual exchange, the other eager to open up possibilities.

Where silence fails, however, deceit might have succeeded in preserving that silence, and the intriguing aspect of the plot backstory is that Smith deliberately lies about the past, claiming Komoko "was shipped to one of those relocation centers" after Pearl Harbor, unaware that Macreedy has checked sources and found no mention of Komoko. The film's plot itself seems to succumb to this inconsistency since Joe Komoko's presence on the Italian front was itself unlikely, as historians have shown. After all, historical protocols dictated he would have been immediately dismissed from military service after Pearl Harbor.[15] The confusion about the elder Komoko's presence in Black Rock, like his son's in Italy, seems of a piece with the seemingly motiveless violence in the past as well as the present. The town has not so much reverted to violence as continued to perpetuate it, which is proclaimed analogously in Smith's first appearance with a dead buck tied to the hood of his station wagon. As Macreedy observes, "There aren't many towns like this in America. . . . The rule of law has left and the gorillas have taken over." Confirming that straightforward judgment, Smith later easily suggests that Macreedy could be "just disappeared." And his explanation of the "spreading" infection that has been brought to Black Rock curiously identifies the disease as his own, confirmed in the musical score that once again signals fear, anxiety, and common sympathy with Smith's view.

Yet just when Macreedy has sent a telegram to the state police for needed assistance, when the possibility of his death has already been announced ("They're gonna kill you with no hard feelings," Doc Velie asserts), the ghostliness of his role is transformed redemptively in an encounter that both reveals the past and offers something like a present reenactment. At Sam's Bar and Grill, Macreedy is once again confronted by Coley Trimble, who picks a fight in a scene set carefully against the greasy spoon's windows. This time, however, in contrast to other mirroring scenes of split image and self-division, the windows are grimy (and revealingly unreflective), the view is occluded, and characters no longer seem quite like specters of the past. Or rather, Macreedy finally acts in a way that establishes the past, his own and others', as clearly delineated. He resists Coley by offering a model of conduct that, far from defying Western ideals for masculinity, is simply a more dramatic reinforcement of a role reiterated in countless earlier genre instances. Macreedy's regular accommodation of others carries to an extreme the kind of silent self-possession characteristic of Alan Ladd or Gary Cooper faced with similar gestures of aggression. And in this, paradoxically, he does not simply remind us of Komoko's own presumably deferential demeanor but returns as the ghost of Komoko himself, an Anglicized version of Akira Kurosawa's contemporary meditations on medieval samurai style (meditations themselves inspired, ironically enough, by American Westerns). Various specters emerge in this scene of martial arts in Arizona, as if to demonstrate how irrepressible genre conventions are in the depiction of traditional masculine self-possession, even with behavior that appears somehow non-Western.[16]

CONCLUSION: FALSE RESOLUTIONS

Bad Day at Black Rock oddly defies the genre it brings to mind, with the ghostly conduct of its characters corresponding to its own mildly spectral status as a Western. Critics have frequently noted its incorporation of major anxieties of the 1950s (McCarthyism, civic complacency, racism, abraded community bonds), but few have observed that its plot and cinematography register a defiant generic self-consciousness, with Welles and Sturges deliberately stripping the Western of its all-too-familiar features and inverting, even derailing, its customary formal appeal. And these efforts still fail to dissuade us as viewers. After all, the genre is obsessed with the hold of the past on the present if only in its focus on what a future promised by Frederick Jackson Turner might hold. Like noir films, Westerns often seem haunted by memory of actions and occasions that trigger a need to repair what has occurred. Macreedy becomes the representative figure for this ghost of the past, both as character and as narrative engine that brings the genre alive once again. In that, he reminds us of other classic films driven by events that precede or begin them: of the Plummer boys' false testimony that sent the Ringo Kid to jail before *Stagecoach* commences; of the initiating bond in *Red River* of contract (or is it compact?); of the fitting arrest of Frank Miller some years before *High Noon*; of Ethan Edwards's repressed love of his sister-in-law that drives *The Searchers*. In each of these and other Westerns, the past is a continuing burden, living on in consequences that need to be exorcised before characters can move on.

Macreedy thus comes to stand not only for Komoko but more generally for every other Western ghost of the past, making clear in the process that that is how the genre regularly functions. Having stripped plot down to a simple inquiring visit by a stranger, Kaufman and Sturges then reduce events to no more than a contest over that inquiry, developing the tension between silent power and a need to know, between transgression and retribution, between a buried crime and its exposure, into the structural basis on which Westerns (and many other genres) depend. For all its ostensible realism, the whole is (in Rob Nixon's words) "actually highly stylized, and extremely pared down in the spare, economical and underpopulated manner of a Road Runner cartoon, with the same sudden violence exploding in a barren landscape" (Nixon, n.d.). Not only is behavior reduced to a series of theatrical gestures, but the plot becomes a self-conscious consideration of the way in which the past is inescapably plotted, always containing a mystery that may make little sense but dictates the present nonetheless. Moreover, in so deliberately excluding narrative elements that traditionally constitute the Western—frontier economics, gendered relations, even the actual dynamics of racial conflict—the film more thoroughly concentrates attention on the past's hold over the present in a fashion familiar generically as much from noir as from Westerns. The pressure of historical consciousness and the burden of ongoing guilt serve as threaded themes in *Bad Day*, consuming both powerful and weak together.

Moreover, the whole occurs in an all but exclusively male realm, reducing behavior to a least common denominator, not only tightening the focus on a central mystery but doing so in the absence of any other relevant issues. This stripped-down version of plot still fails to resolve itself acceptably, leaving questions no longer hanging but also offering no solution for the problem introduced by the film. Macreedy is already self-conscious about this dilemma midway through in realizing that everyone else in the town wants the problem of the past to disappear, or as he phrases the impasse to a recalcitrant Pete Wirth: "I know your problem. You'd like me to die quickly, without wasting too much of your time . . . or silently, without making you feel too uncomfortable . . . or thankfully, without making your memories of the occasion too unpleasant." The speech converts Pete into an ally but little is otherwise served here, and by the conclusion the town has failed to pull itself together in ways the narrative would like to suggest.

In its generic self-consciousness, *Bad Day* casts doubt not only on the capacity of this Western but of all Westerns to ever effect a neat laying to rest of the past. Sheriff Tim may round up the guilty, who are bundled off by Sand City police, and Doc Velie can intimate hopefully that what has happened will transform Black Rock. But little reassures us that any genuine recovery is about to occur in a community hardly recognizable *as* a community, making the contention nothing more than a false promise.[17] Macreedy does finally give Komoko's Medal of Honor to Doc in grudging response to his plea for a gesture that might redeem the town, but the very rhythm of the scene seems to deny that prospective hope. The Southern Pacific pulls in slowly, cautiously, contrasting vividly with the film's opening that announced a new beginning; but otherwise everything remains in place, unchanged, unable to transcend the past or otherwise forge ahead. The rhythm of these closing moments is halting and unrelieved, again in contrast to other, more celebratory Western endings, offering a reminder that past transgressions cannot be so easily remedied. And in thus failing to offer a resolution—in leaving the town of Black Rock immutable, drab, and static—Sturges exposes generic aspirations as having been built upon nothing other than our willingness to believe in them. Instead of having freed itself marginally from its historical mistakes, the town represents the very onus of history, of a past that has become inescapable, burdensome, inevitable, finally doomed.

Cinematography again confirms this paralysis in the focus on still moments, on closed spaces, on interminable conversations that continue until they abruptly end, without anything being settled. Viewers are implicitly encouraged to create a narrative (whether of race, or revenge, or masculinity) that is not actually made explicit in the film itself; we impose generic forms of the Western on elements that remain misleading or tantalizingly apparent only in parts. We weave a progressive interpretation out of materials finally unforthcoming and indeterminate. As the film concludes, it drains away the animation, the anxiety and freneticism that opened it, but there is little sense of closure in whatever satisfaction we feel—satisfaction mostly at how fully Sturges has turned the tables on us. Macreedy's physical turn from Doc at the end is a turn away from the film proper, though that gesture dismissive of the Western's traditional promise has become a well-worn Western gesture itself. Miscreants may have been successfully rounded up and arrested but nothing seems to have changed.[18] All that is left are those who themselves are no longer actually there, the ghosts like Reno Smith for whom "this place is our West."

2

CATCHING THE *3:10 TO YUMA*

The question intriguingly posed by *Bad Day at Black Rock* was whether a film that notably lacked (even flouted) the Western's semantics could come together syntactically in a convincing generic pattern. The question initiated by Daves's *3:10 to Yuma* is analogous if not quite the same: how does adaptation of a text shift our understanding of generic constraints? And in the salient transformations Daves made to the Elmore Leonard story on which his film was based, the shifting pressures reshaping our view of the Western come into a more distinct profile. Add a half century, and James Mangold's adaptation of an adaptation, *3:10 to Yuma*, offers an additional test of how the genre continues to stay alive and, in tandem with Daves's film, allows us to speculate why certain shared plot materials and generic ingredients can be distorted yet remain recognizable, as resilient as a flattened capsule toy or a twisted straw hat that regains its shape. For all their differences, the adaptation of Leonard's story into Daves's film, then Mangold's, remind us how flexible the Western's syntax can be, and always has been. That realization may seem inconsistent with issues raised in the last chapter, though again we are made aware of the power of generic assumptions to dictate narrative interpretation and of the way in which those seemingly stable assumptions shift over time. As well, the contrast of adaptations turns us to the question of aesthetic choices made, as well as to the influence of social and cultural pressures. Especially given how little film genres remain pure, always transecting and energizing each other, the choices made by directors need to be measured and weighed. Multiple adaptations of a single narrative, then, invite value judgments (often invidious), even as we realize that supposed fidelity to an original text is at once an impossible criterion and one that nonetheless perpetually hovers over most discussions. That makes it worth pausing here at the beginning (and in the transition from 1950s films to those a half century later) to review some of the problems inherent in adaptation, especially since those problems have prompted a considerable wealth of critical discussion.[1]

Recent studies divide those faithful to an ur-text from others adamant about the unearned advantage accruing to simply being first. Colin Mac-Cabe cherishes the former position in a book that "considers the question of 'truth to the spirit' to capture something important but . . . also implicitly raises questions of value that are routinely dismissed by adaptation studies" (2011, 8). Thomas Leitch has persistently advocated the latter, proclaiming that "fidelity as a touchstone of adaptations will always give their source texts, which are always faithful to themselves, an advantage so enormous and unfair that it renders the comparison meaningless" (2007, 16). The two camps have long appeared deadlocked along this theoretical border, though a closer look reveals both engaged in similarly formal appraisals. MacCabe relies on André Bazin's 1948 call for a mutual evaluation in "reading novel and film as illuminating each other" (MacCabe 2011, 21), while Leitch demands we focus on "essentially aesthetic" considerations for originals as well as their adaptations (2007, 5).[2] In fact, the camps sometimes seem less divided than appearances first suggest in a critical realm where too many others (as Kamilla Elliott remarked more than a decade ago) are fleeing formalism altogether for cultural studies and poststructuralism (2003, 5). Consider how uncannily similar the fidelity proponent David Kranz sounds to Leitch: "The heart of fidelity criticism is the *comparative textual method*, which allows critics to put a source and a film adapted from it side-by-side in order to see what the similarities and differences are, what patterns emerge from the variety of these contrasts, and what these patterns might say about the consciously or unconsciously intended meanings in both source and adaptation" (2008, 203). The imperative for attending closely to an original as well as its adaptation owes to the fact that neither one preempts the other or has a necessarily superior claim, but that both offer a perspective on what the other singularly achieves.[3]

What then does one make of an adaptation of a previous adaptation, especially in terms of a basic narrative structure construed as somehow distinctively Western? What do adaptations reveal about generic considerations and, more specifically, about the pressures subsequent adaptors feel as plot is constrained by a genre template that keeps shifting over time? Moreover, how does a further turn of the screw alter an understanding of patterns and meanings? In fact, questions raised by reworkings challenge both adaptation *and* fidelity studies, especially in the response to Leonard's original story, in the substantial changes each film makes to his bare-bones structure. Daves can be considered "true to the spirit" only by a considerable stretch, transforming the original narrative in ways having little to do with its "spirit," though in the process achieving something perhaps more compelling as a cinematic experience. By contrast, Mangold took his adaptation further afield, adapting Daves's film in ways far less obviously linked to Leonard's story yet offering nonetheless an "updating" of the genre that corresponds more fully to expectations for action-adventure films in the twenty-first century. That raises the question of what Daves gains by complicating Leonard's spare plot, and what Mangold gains in turn as he reshapes generic expectations more dramatically. The very impurity of the Western becomes apparent in the sequence of avatars, allowing us to see how generic assumptions are both always in place and yet always being challenged.

Leonard's short story covers nine hours in a western hotel as a deputy waits to put a convicted felon on a train to prison, guarding him against the prisoner's roaming gang. Daves's film offers an "expansion" (Leitch 2007, 99) of the story that lasts ninety minutes, filling in the relationship of farmer Dan Evans (Van Heflin) with his son, adding scenes that seem mildly digressive with his wife, introducing an alcoholic assistant who is gratuitously tortured and killed, and ending with the sudden nobility of the prisoner, Ben Wade (Glenn Ford), as he helps Dan escape. A half century later, Mangold's film adds twenty-five minutes, introducing far more (and more melodramatic) details, of marauding Apaches and Chinese laborers, of Pinkerton agents and Civil War history, creating in Wade (Russell Crowe) a figure more darkly vicious than his earlier incarnations and yet more sentimentally inclined, someone who actively betrays his own men who in turn end up killing Evans (Christian Bale).

The sequence from initial bare story through increasingly lengthy films offers an intriguing trajectory, from minimalist clarity to a denser unfolding of psychologies and motives, and finally to a violent if somewhat muddled drama that shares the title of Leonard's original but resembles it only tenuously. No reason exists for Mangold to have subscribed to some Platonic ideal of the original narrative, but it is worth teasing out the increasing expansion of these adaptations into a Dionysiac frenzy if only to understand the continuing significance of both films as well as the tenor of their hold on initial audiences. The fact that both did well in box-office sales is testament to an ability to capitalize on contemporary expectations for enthralling themes and familiar treatments. And though Mangold's film becomes increasingly incoherent, that need not constitute (as Todd Berliner has persuasively argued) an aesthetic or critical flaw.[4] The comparative analysis Kranz recommends should reveal not only the patterns defining the source story and its adapted films, but help to explain how such different vehicles with the same title nonetheless achieved both critical success and commercial appeal.

Notably, Leonard's spare style, his dynamic (if skeletal) characters and intriguing plots established him very quickly for Hollywood producers as an appealing author whose fiction invariably resulted in notable films.[5] Yet from the beginning, he "saw how easily Hollywood could screw up a simple story" (Leonard 2003, xiii), anticipating the tin ears and stale market ideals of industry moguls charged over a half century with adapting his narratives for the big screen (first Westerns, then crime thrillers, and latterly romantic heist films). The transformations of his early story,

"3:10 to Yuma," begin with changes to character, fixed and constant in his vision but progressively more mercurial, indeed unpredictable, in its film adaptations. As well, the movies elicit conflicting responses to their formal features themselves in the transition from Daves's languid use of a long lens and sustained interior shots to Mangold's intensely brief close-ups and frenetic handheld sequences, reflecting the shift from Leonard's construction into ever more deeply subjective geographies. What starts as a simple story with a clear trajectory of economic motive and moral integrity shifts gradually into a less systematic if more exotic psychological terrain with the breakdown in emotional coherence linked formally to a more slippery, disjointed camera effect in the framing, sequencing, and duration of shots.

A large part of the triumph of adaptations lies in their unveiling of hidden meanings, sometimes nascent, otherwise unseen, transposed by a new medium or fresh configurations to reveal what now has become compelling. Of course, the augmenting of scenes, the shading of characters, the manipulation of emotional registers needs to be measured against a final synthesis that defines the work—a synthesis that may be unlike the initial structure of possibilities, fulfilling what had only been latent or undeveloped. Such changes, moreover, expose something of the film's historical context (often, the pressure of contemporary cultural concerns), suggesting aesthetic and narrative possibilities otherwise unapparent (often, a consequence of altered audience expectations). Leonard's "3:10 to Yuma" forms a paradigmatic case in the very economy of its plot and character, and Daves's film nicely develops its incipient concern with masculine identity into a range of issues related to the so-called Silent Generation, including uncertainties about civic responsibility and parental authority. Mangold adapts Daves in turn for parents of Generation Z, troubled by children who simply dismiss their assumptions, spouses who talk past each other, and economic structures that seem more unyielding and forbidding than in the past. Of course, reading larger significance into these plot trans-formations risks ignoring the effects of overdetermination and leads too readily to reductive sociological claims, as if reflection theory allowed us direct access through idiosyncratic narrative patterns to underlying social anxieties.[6] But what is fascinating in the rehandling of Leonard's spare verbal structure is the transpositions that occur, the visual reshaping that directors offer to fashion their own allusive narratives.

Granted, Mangold's most dramatic reworking involves the filial tension introduced by the teenager William Evans's (Logan Lerman) defiance of his father. And this can supposedly be taken to register a change in paternal relations from the 1950s as portrayed by Dan Evans's loyally supportive son Matthew (Barry Curtis) in Daves's version. But the more revealing aspect of successful adaptation consists not in thematic but formal changes that disclose via aesthetic choices those pivot points around which cultural anxieties cluster. Controversies resolved via plot are finally less telling than camera movement, which often defines cinematically those convoluted pressures that led to conflict in the first place and thereby signal a refusal to succumb to straightforward judgment. The following discussion is an effort to understand how two versions of a story can differ so dramatically—not simply in terms of straightforward plot but more importantly in terms of less direct but still compelling cinematic presentation—and how those formal differences point to larger ideological considerations. What also intrigues in this instance is why, half a century after Daves's film, when the Western had already been conceded to be in severe decline, James Mangold chose to return to materials that might have been considered distinctively mid-twentieth century and then to alter them as significantly as he did.

MINIMALIST STYLE

Weighing in at little more than fourteen pages, Leonard's story condenses events to a handful, which may have been what made it attractive as a vehicle for something more. Paul Scallen, earning $150 a month as deputy, is assigned to accompany Jim Kidd to the railroad that will transport him to prison in Yuma. Notably, among judgments merely hinted at, the story leaves uncertain whether Kidd was unjustly convicted of murder. As Scallen asserts, "A jury said he didn't do it" (Leonard 2003, 189), leaving purposely vague who in fact murdered the stage driver. Yet Leonard interestingly allows an equivocal history to drive the narrative, suggesting how little importance attaches to background episodes. Kidd may even be innocent, so far as we know, with neither man holding the other responsible and everything reduced to the immediate personal conflict between them. Extraneous concerns are simply dismissed as Kidd indefatigably tests Scallen's devotion to his assignment. Despite taking the job for no more than the pay, Scallen refuses to renege on his agreement while baited by the offer of an additional increment, leaving Kidd to realize in "startled" recognition that Scallen cannot be bought: "Maybe you come higher than I thought" (Leonard 2003, 185). Leonard's story focuses on nothing other than the ethical tension dividing the two, depicting a shift in balance between basic twin desires: to fulfill a bound duty despite emerging threats and strains, and to escape from possibly unjust restraint.

For his part, the outlaw Kidd seems assured throughout: "Confidence. It was all over him. And even with the manacles on, you would believe that it was Jim Kidd who was holding the shotgun" (Leonard 2003, 187). Moreover, the presence of his lieutenant Charlie Prince reinforces a promise of imminent freedom. His adversary's emotional toll consists, on the contrary, of escalating unease, barely held in check: "Scallen knew fear at that moment as fear had never gripped him before" (Leonard 2003, 192). Prior to the story's conclusion, only one violent outburst occurs when the murdered driver's brother breaks into the room to be quickly disarmed by Scallen. That moment crystalizes the dilemma resting at Leonard's narrative center, as Kidd reveals at its concluding moments: "I don't understand you. You risk your neck to save my life, now you'll risk it again to send me to prison" (Leonard 2003, 190). Moreover, Scallen's mixture of emotional stasis and irrepressible fear is augmented through Leonard's spare scenic description, his understated account of what at first seem like irrelevant details: the signs of stores "lining the rutted main street to make it seem narrower. And beneath the signs, in the shadows, nothing moved. There was a whisper of wind along the ramadas. It whipped sand specks from the street and rattled them against clapboard, and the sound was hollow and lifeless. Somewhere a screen door banged, far away" (Leonard 2003, 191). In a narrative tight-lipped about Scallen's reflections, the scant depiction of various kinds of silence coupled with desultory details offers something like an objective correlative of his psychology. And the taut tension between the men culminates in an expected moment of emotional violence erupting into emphatic sound, a flurry of action, with Scallen out-shooting Charlie Prince and his confederates. All Kidd can offer, having failed to escape, is grudging admiration.

If this characterization sounds slightly odd for a Western story, it may be worth keeping in mind Geoffrey O'Brien's insight a quarter century ago, when he claimed, counterintuitively: "The classic Western is customarily less epic than it is a study in claustrophobia and repetition, offering not wide open spaces but dead ends, the canyons and defiles of ambush, the mesa beyond which there's nowhere else to hide, the alleys and stables where men on the run are cornered. 'They've got this whole town boxed up.' Open space being lyrical rather than dramatic, the Western's formal problem becomes one of making space ever tighter and narrower" (1992, 40). By that token, Leonard's is a Western *par excellence*, succeeding marvelously in manifesting the deep claustrophobic strain that regularly inhabits the genre, of incarcerating characters into Poe-like spaces where walls constrain, space is locked down, borders loom everywhere (taking diverse forms), and psychologies are unduly curbed by forces unavailing.

Partly Leonard achieves this effect by forging a narrative itself as laconic as his characters, perhaps more so. After all, the story occurs all but entirely in dialogue, with speech only rarely interrupted by exposition or brief description. Access to personality, other than what might be gathered from spoken exchange, seems deliberately withheld. Straightforward, even stripped-down psychological realism tilts a Kidd persistent in striving to escape against a Scallen refusing to sell out, with sparing exposition that barely distinguishes this from a play (or screenplay). The oddly placed "silent early morning mist" of the opening sentence intimates a strain between the men (with the word "silence" repeated soon after, confirming their tension), just as the train's noise in conclusion registers Scallen's mental agitation: "the iron rhythm of the train wheels and his breathing were loud in his temples" (Leonard 2003, 193). Consider as well the somewhat tedious mundane progression of the day as it begins: "The sun came into the room after a while. Weakly at first, cold and hazy. Then it warmed and brightened and cast an oblong patch of light between the bed and the table. The morning wore on slowly because there was nothing to do and each man sat restlessly thinking about somewhere else, though it was a restlessness within and it showed on neither of them. The deputy rolled cigarettes for the outlaw and himself and most of the time they smoked in silence" (Leonard 2003, 185). The scene's very stillness parallels the strain between the two men, confirmed during the shoot-out itself: "There was a fraction of a moment of dead silence that seemed longer" (Leonard 2003, 192). Moving directly, concisely, always straightforwardly, the event apparently lasts little more than the amount of time taken to read it, and in thus ranging among a circumscribed set of emotions effectively narrows the reader's response.

CONFLICT AND IMPLICATION

Testifying to the story's resonances are the efforts of Halsted Welles, the scriptwriter for Daves's film, in fleshing out a bare-bones plot, stitching together elements left nascent, conferring new dimensions to the whole, introducing formal innovations that adroitly reinforce a thematic vision left otherwise tacit. Leonard's Scallen, for instance, happens to note "indifferently, 'I think it's going to rain'" (Leonard 2003, 182), a single brief observation altered by Welles into a transforming condition, creating a long drought that first induces Evans to take the job of escort. The film concludes with a rain storm that serves (a bit magically) as an almost allegorical summation. More generally, the addition of vignettes of civic malaise, alcoholism, sexual desire, and explosive violence, all enhance a central focus on masculine fear (and cowardly behavior) that prompted the initial narrative. Welles's backstory of what had presumably led to the arrival in Leonard's account at a Contention, Arizona, hotel foregrounds not just masculinity but paternal relations, opening with Dan Evans (the renamed Paul Scallen figure) and his sons watching the stagecoach robbery that is the ostensible cause for the arrest of Ben Wade (the renamed Jim Kidd figure). That opening then expands to include Evans's relationship with his wife Alice (Leora Dana), incorporating the supposed heart of 1950s family life, which is otherwise referred to only fleetingly in Leonard's story when Scallen recollects his "wife, then, and the three youngsters. . . . He didn't know why they had come to him all of a sudden" (Leonard 2003, 186). And to strengthen the story's domestic theme, Welles adds Wade's dalliance with a barmaid that leads to his capture not just to confirm Wade's lack of self-discipline, casually putting himself and his gang at risk, but also to mark a contrast with Evans's character as devoted husband and father. Alice's family dinner with Wade then reveals a further difference in values, with Welles reinforcing Leonard's two-man drama by elaborating various other forms of masculine behavior, including the addition of Alex Potter (Henry Jones) as Dan's assistant, the aging alcoholic who offers a suitable generic contrast to the hero's earnest sobriety.

But Alex also registers brutality's effects in a film that considerably escalates the story's minimal play of violence. Nearly our first view of Wade depicts him callously killing his own gang associate held hostage before shooting Bill Moons, the driver and hostage taker. In short, Welles transforms the otherwise benign Jim Kidd of Leonard's original into a heartless murderer, a melodramatic propensity compounded by Wade's lieutenant, Charlie Prince (Richard Jaeckel). Emulating his boss's values, and more ruthless in expressing them, Pierce seizes Alex, casually shoots him in the back, then orchestrates his hanging in the hotel, leaving a hauntingly shadowed scene of a body swinging in an empty lobby. The dramatic noir cinematics of Alex's swaying corpse are meant to arouse our abhorrence of the violence added by Welles himself to the narrative. For if the tenuousness of Kidd's supposed innocence ignited our curiosity about his potential for violence, that potential has been creatively transformed by Welles into the stark, compellingly unambiguous figure of Ben Wade.[7] Moreover, Glenn Ford's chilling display of thin-lipped charm—shifting from easy amiability to psychopathic dispassion—offers the perfect expression of our own uncertainty about what he actually feels, or is otherwise capable of doing.[8] Welles nicely exploits this aspect of Leonard's equivocal prose in complicating our notion of character as a series of intersecting possibilities, of figures we think we know but whom we find, under emotional pressure or due to changing circumstances, to act quite the contrary. And the cinematography and editing of the film contribute to this seemingly malleable construction of character, as Michael Walker observes of scenes following Wade's counsel to Dan to take care of his wife:

> The sequence of shots that then occurs is very suggestive: a deep focus shot of Dan sitting tensely at the window in the foreground, with Wade lying on the bed in the background; dissolve to a pan across the dusty road into town, empty of life; cut back to a medium shot of Dan; cut to the road from a different angle, with the gang members in the distance, riding in. It's as if they have been conjured up by the tensions between the two men, both as a censor—echoing Prince's return to the Bisbee saloon twenty-four hours earlier, when he arrived to break up the love scene between Wade and Emmy—and as a way of redirecting Dan's urge towards violence. (1996, 144)

Throughout, the film underscores a convoluted notion of character at odds with itself, of psychology denser and more conflicted than Leonard initially conceived.

That thicker sense of personality is further exposed in a feature absent from the original story: the timidity of Bisbee, Arizona, where Wade and his gang arrive after the robbery. Only an initially reluctant Evans and the town drunk can be convinced, despite principled anger and general dismay, to escort Wade to the railhead. Collectively fearful of what the gang is capable of, everyone else declines, and as Evans and Alex discover when they arrive with their prisoner, Contention is no different. Faced with the threat of the gathering gang, deserted by men the stage owner has hired (indeed, finally abandoned by the owner himself), the two discover the same civic response enacted in other contemporary films—*High Noon*, *Bad Day at Black Rock*, Nicholas Ray's *Rebel without a Cause* (1955), Don Siegel's *Invasion of the Body Snatchers* (1956), Nunnally Johnson's *The Man in the Gray Flannel Suit* (1956)—revealing something of the era's anxiety about timid collective behavior. Welles constructs his scenes to accentuate this conflicted masculinity, transforming Leonard's elliptical evocation of Scallen's mild anxiety into Evans's more apprehensive, if nonetheless gradually stalwart assertion of character. Duty offers a clear hand-hold, dictating behavior when feeling protests, with Welles narrowly drawing the lines: "I've got to, that's all. . . . Honest to God, if I didn't have to do so I wouldn't. . . . The town drunk gave his life because he believed that people should be able to live in decency and peace together. You think I can do less?" It is as if the film adaptation introduced stark figurative borders (civic obligation, fatherhood, honor, reputation) hemming in masculinity but also redeeming valued principles.

The casting of Van Heflin lends to this performance a suitably troubled and urgent tone that makes Evans more accessible in his self-division. His gnawing insecurity, his stolid, often morose aspect, contrast effectively with Glenn Ford's smoothly polished self-possession and all but duplicitously graceful ease.[9] Yet Welles complicates things by introducing another side to Dan's personality that is strangely, ironically akin to Wade's guilefulness, suggesting he is neither so upright nor candid as he appears. His wiliness in getting Wade to surrender in the bar, demanding first restitution for himself, then his boys, then his cattle—all as a delaying tactic allowing allies to sneak up on Wade—testifies to a certain unanticipated deviousness. And later, a further depth of character is revealed in the perceptible interest he takes in Wade's offered bribes; he may refuse, but we nonetheless detect the growing effect of temptation.

This slightly malleable, nicely indeterminate quality to masculine psychology emerges more fully in Welles's elaboration of contexts missing in Leonard's abbreviated account. But even in scenes nearly the same, the film surprises. Consider the guarded walk to the station, which Leonard offers as a predictable tussle between adversaries but that suddenly becomes in Welles's version an unexpected reversal of intention. Following nearly an hour of screen time in which Wade has pressed his case for freedom, he and Evans carefully make their way through Convention's back streets, with the camera revealing their growing alignment in an assortment of two-shots that suggest a conjoint anxiety, then their mutual alliance framed side by side, capped by Wade's sudden refusal to give Charlie Prince a clear shot at Evans. Wade in fact enables Dan to escape from the gang in what seems at first a mystifying betrayal of friends as he jumps onto the train. Critics have found his explanation unconvincing, that he helped because Dan shielded him in the encounter with a murderous Bob Moons.[10] But the final gesture of placing his gang in peril might also be construed as offering a more complicated view of Wade, with Welles extending the process of character construction he had applied to Dan Evans, confirming how fully identity is not simply fixed and settled but always slightly capricious and incalculable, certainly changeable, sometimes contradictory. Wade's expressed envy of Dan's marriage and children, and the respect that seems to develop between the two, attest to something like a modern Stockholm syndrome of paradoxical bonding. Even if not, the film transforms Leonard's stable constructions into figures whose expressions as well as the framing of faces, the frequency of close-ups, suggest psychologies more interestingly conflicted. Dan appears at once fearful and steady, tractable yet wily; Wade is ruthless and charming, yet potentially reliable; Alice emerges as both steadfast yet uncertain.

Welles intensifies Leonard's account, however, not simply in transforming characters into conflicted figures but in widening the pressures they feel, stirring a mix of popular anxieties about gender, class, and social obligation into a mildly strange brew. Dan Evans, for instance, is no longer a man in need of cash but someone overcome by economic constraints, family pressures, and inner conflicts, who only at last redeems himself from intractable dilemmas. Consider how little we learn from Leonard of why Scallen would risk his life for $150 a month (with Leonard himself "disappointed that it did not remain so in the film version" [K. Jones 2013, n.p.]).[11] The story concentrates simply on isolated moments, not motivations or psychological patterns, which is of course the basis of any story's appeal. If Geoffrey O'Brien is correct, that abbreviated fictional style itself contributes to the sense of claustrophobia Leonard achieves, of psychologies dictated by narrowing forces. The film, however, contemplates character differently (though achieving a similar sense of claustrophobia) by revealing pressure points against which behavior can be measured, beginning with Dan's resignation before hardships that must be borne: "You have to watch a lot of terrible things. People get killed every day. Lightning can kill yuh. Three years of drought killin' my cattle, that's terrible too. What can I do, I can't make it rain. You expect me to cool off the sun?" And the fact that stage owner Butterfield (Robert Emhardt) offers exactly the price needed to pay for water rights explains Dan's willingness to accept the job despite his civic indifference. The film, however, traces an emergent sense of rectitude aroused, then enforced by the very commitment he has reluctantly made, with Dan's behavior itself initially shaping his belief, followed by a growing sense of civic obligation that has arisen from the act of obligating himself contractually. Again, Van Heflin's demeanor expresses fittingly the haunting inner divisions, with his very casting meant to contrast with Ford's slick performance, his serene countenance and easy smile.

That increased sense of psychological complexity that nonetheless effects a similarly claustrophobic ambience is compounded by Dan's domestic life, which Welles unfolds as a series of marital tensions extending the narrow self-sufficiency of Leonard's Scallen. Kent Jones goes so far as to claim that "the core of *3:10 to Yuma* is a marriage . . . with its wearinesses and projections of fear, its longings and its renewals" (2013, 7). That description indicates how fully Welles has reconfigured Leonard's story, even if Jones overstates the misalignment between Dan and Alice, who rarely seem in doubt about the other and whose minimal scenes together reaffirm the centrality of family life. As she says of his commitment, "The boys are so proud. . . . And I'm proud too." Even in failing to dissuade him, she still abides by his decision in a film whose leisurely pacing encourages a viewer to want to know why characters act as they do. What begins with Leonard's simple physical maneuvering of Scallen—the kind of narrative motion that film seems best able to configure—shifts to a more nuanced psychological view of why a father and husband acts as he does, and the pressures he feels in following conscience.

Charles Lawton Jr.'s cinematography reinforces this reconfiguration of Leonard's story by concentrating on individual bodies at odds with themselves.[12] The black-and-white production itself confirms this impression, borrowing from a noir preference for shadows and angular shots that stress a psychological dislocation. And the film's high-contrast aspect (often relying on red filters) heightens the focus on isolated bodies: "The result is a western that looks like no other," Jones again observes; "the texture of its images alternately stark and lustrous, enhancing the loneliness of houses, animals, and human figures against the endlessly flat earth and wide-open skies" (K. Jones 2013, 9). True as this is, it misleads us into recalling Daves's panoramas as constituting the bulk of the film when the contrary tends to be true: an arid landscape appears occasionally, as in the opening when the stage crosses the terrain or Wade's gang rides to his rescue through high cacti, or high-angle shots offer a circumscribed view of desolate towns and gathered groups. Yet Lawton's camera focuses more frequently on facial expressions: Alice yearning, smiling, hopeful in her early scenes alone with Dan; or Wade seducing the barmaid Emmy as their tender expressions evoke emergent desire, then sympathy; or the back and forth one-shots of Dan and Wade in the Contention hotel room as they test each other's mettle. Occasionally, Lawton alternates angles on figures to shift our perspective, as in shots of Charlie Prince, glimpsed first through reflections in store windows, then through high-angle perspectives. Alice

Fig. 6. High-angle panorama of Alice Evans and sons watching husband Dan ride into town, hoping to survive economically when "all this will be green," in Delmer Daves's *3:10 to Yuma* (Columbia Pictures).

is first presented, as Simon Petch observes, "so that the camera begins by looking down at her and ends by looking up at her. The least introverted of the film's major characters, Alice here is characteristically looking beyond herself" (2007/2008, 53).

If Lawton moves the camera around to capture multiple subjective states, he relies as well on elevated angles that register something like the opposite: an objective view of bodies simply configured in the land-scape, apparently cut off from each other and from a collective sense of community identity.[13] The stage entering Bisbee empties its passengers impersonally, seen from an aerial perspective, and we return in the next scene to a similar perspective on that same stage with Wade as passenger crossing wide-open country, watched by his gang. Daves was known for his devotion to the high-angle boom rising above the action in deliberate and often dramatic contrast with close-ups, revealing via visual detach-

Fig. 7. Close-up of family tensions over the dinner table, sparked by contrasts between father and charming killer, in Delmer Daves's *3:10 to Yuma* (Columbia Pictures).

ment the claims he makes about characters' emotional lives. And that characteristic perspective is later confirmed under cover of darkness, as the scene pitches downward in a high shot of Dan, Alex, and Wade riding off from the Evans ranch. The next day, Charlie Pierce dramatically walks the main street of Contention, watching a funeral cortege return to town, the whole filmed once again from a boom. Compounding these wrenched angles and pitches is a noir emphasis on shadows and light, reflecting the way in which setting itself is divided, cross-hatched, otherwise patterned and blistered to suggest a less than unequivocal realm. "Stylistically, the film gestures habitually to the play of shadow and reflection," Simon Petch has claimed, "directing us to speculate on what is happening beneath the external action. As sunlight slants through doors, windows, or across the street, shadows fall across faces, and bodies cast shadows, suggesting that individual lives may both shape and be shaped by dramas of which the participants are unconscious" (2007/2008, 49). The camera seems independently to adumbrate aspects of subjectivity not otherwise conveyed by the film, with shadows creating "a drama in which human figures mean more than they know, in which surfaces hint at hidden depths, even the fusion of psychic and material" (2007/2008, 51). The claim is a strong one, suggesting how Daves transforms Leonard's minimalist materials into a more fully realized psychological drama.

Yet a lingering question concerns the film's relation to the story that inspired it, especially given that proponents of fidelity studies often adhere to a more traditional test of "truth to the spirit." Apart from the basic structure of a bare-bones plot, it is hard to see much of a connection between the "spirit" of Leonard's story and of Daves's film. One is an exemplary odyssey that pits adversaries against one another and, in its terse homage to Hemingway, offers little purchase for larger interpretation. The other elaborates an unhurried rumination on issues familiar to the genre Western (as well as other significant films) at least in the mid 1950s, including masculine obligation, domestic negotiations, parental insecurities, filial interactions, and inducements to civic accountability, all as part of the persistent cultural conversation of the era. In short, the central premise to Leonard's creation of Scanlen, accepting the charge of getting Jim Kidd to the train, gave Welles a scaffolding on which to lay out narratively a series of confrontations central to gendered, ethical, even political questions of the day. Both texts succeed on their own, though Leonard's mastery is directed to a more circumscribed vehicle.

The triumph of Welles's adaptation, matched by Lawton's cinematography, lies in transcending Leonard's materials to create a meditative film that confronts its era's concerns, yet seems to reach beyond them. The film, in fact, achieves something like an understated calm best expressed by Wim Wenders in admiring its apparent tranquility: "In Delmer Daves's black-and-white Western *3:10 to Yuma* there takes place the gentlest and most peaceful story that you have ever seen happening in a saloon. You watch eternity go by" (2001, 10). For Wenders, whose own films concentrate largely on places and explore their ramifications at the expense of plots of cause and effect, this comes as high praise. And in a film whose very title indicates its preoccupation with time (keeping it, if nonetheless imprisoned *by* it), and where the sound track confirms both urgency and abeyance, the idea that scenes might give a sense of time suspended is at once a paradoxical yet strangely satisfying effect.[14] That effect, moreover, is achieved not simply in the saloon, as Wenders suggests, but throughout in the mentally ticking clock that accompanies the mere wait for something to happen.

MANGLING PLOT

A half century later, that cinematic allure prompted a remake of the film, though the contrast between the two versions could hardly be more exaggerated. The first question to ask is why the choice was made, and the presumptive answer is that the initial claustrophobic conceit stirred cultural anxieties that continue to resonate. Indeed, the taut economy of Leonard's original story, in its spare structure and minimalist mode, allowed for disparate interpretations with different notions of character expressed through distinctive cinematic styles. And without a doubt, Mangold's version succeeds—as Daves's did—in vivifying issues troubling its audience through a plot and performances that seem to correspond to changed social assumptions as well as altered cinematic conventions (with the psychosexual attraction that Charlie Prince [Ben Foster] feels for Ben Wade now fully on display).[15] Yet the very demands dictated by twenty-first-century Hollywood cinema—for colorful action, gratuitous and splashy violence, nonsequential narrative, among others—contributed to the film's commercial success even as it tested formal coherence. Pete Falconer, in fact, argues that Mangold deliberately cast his net wider than Welles, in transforming a source familiar to few viewers today (in Mangold's words, "probably one percent of one percent of America is even aware of the title" [Mangold 2007, n.p.]) into something like a meta-Western for the twenty-first century: "the newer *3:10* is as much an adaptation of the

Western genre as it is of any specific predecessor. Many aspects of the 2007 movie can be attributed to its having to address the peculiar status of Hollywood Westerns in the early twenty-first century" (Falconer 2009, 62). Yet in his own words, Mangold admitted that the genre could only be revived by a more or less free-wheeling treatment that indulged its "fever[ed] . . . dreamscape" possibilities: "Westerns are about our great mythical landscape, our Mt. Olympus, in which all of the great American themes are played out in this kind of fever dream. That's what I tried to keep in focus: not being so fastidious about tradition or history that we trampled on the dreamscape of the Western" (Barker 2007, A15).

Ironically, though Mangold himself had long (and publicly) revered Daves's restrained film as a classic, calling it "great" (Mangold 2007), he felt the need to dilate the narrative dramatically by adding characters and fragmenting issues that Welles had earlier woven together in a meditation on masculine psychology. For some viewers, that dilation tested the power of a generic syntax to integrate its Western materials.[16] The breakdown in shared cultural assumptions, often at what might seem a superficial level, makes this adaptation symptomatic of tensions it could not resolve, which may paradoxically explain its commercial success. For the film perfectly embodies its moment, diverging in the process from Leonard's initial text and Daves's adaptation, exemplifying the way in which a genre slides askew. Part of this larger transition has to do with the shift from Leonard's focus on uncomplicated action to Daves's more internalized view of Evans as the subject of contested masculine ideals. Finally, Mangold's dominant tension—the taut antagonism between Dan and his son William, a conflict that seems irresolvable—marks a transition from simplicity to something like formal incoherence. As Todd Berliner has shown, however, sometimes incoherence can signal both aesthetic and commercial success, since it so often structures the films that most engage us.[17]

Perhaps the sharpest difference between the films occurs in their look, in cinematic choices that render the two barely recognizable under the same title. Ratcheting up Lawton's visual style considerably, cinematographer Phedon Papamichael focuses repeatedly on extreme close-ups of faces offered in fleeting succession that has the effect of accentuating a similar randomness of emotion, regularly trumping a settled vision of solid conviction or quiet character. Psychologies so various, seen so intensely, seem flattened without being explained, once again seizing on Leonard's endorsement of a claustrophobic perspective but enacting it through a camera that focuses on Ben Foster's maniacal gleam, on Russell Crowe's easy charm, on Christian Bale's anguished, melodramatic regret, none of which can finally be understood independently. And the very heightening of tension by inflating individual responses leads to a disjointedness that makes us lose track of plot progression—or rather, makes us appreciate a strangely contemporary psychology that depends upon intensely local, thoroughly limited gestures that suggest a Twitter-like attention span. Narrative sequence is broken along various psychological borders that do not quite cohere, with the discontinuity confirmed by Papamichael's moving the camera not only near to faces but near to everything else as well. Scenes of blowing up a safe are shown as close focused as the glowering eyes of Wade's gang drinking in a saloon or Dan pleading with a neighbor, then Wade.

At the same time, none of Lawton's lingering long shots survive, much less the soaring crane overheads that had lent a sense of sweeping comprehension underwriting our overall command of the narrative.[18] The effect of this protracted close-up vision is intentionally contrary to the earlier film, unsettling our perspective, fragmenting the narrative, and undercutting a sense of stability, which itself becomes exciting cinematically. As Mangold admitted: "By the end of the movie I'm hoping you're in a complete quandary. Not an unpleasant one but actually a joyous fruit salad of confusion in terms of whom to root for. That's where movies get interesting" (Esther 2007, 29). This happens to characterize contemporary action films more generally, which often appeal by their jittery, self-consciously handheld attention, immersing the audience in viewed events and thereby contributing to some perceptual "confusion." Cinematic style

Fig. 8. Dan Evans in anguished close-up, his self-possession and masculinity challenged, in James Mangold's *3:10 to Yuma* (Lionsgate).

thus tends to undo the effect of landscape panoramas in refusing to allow a break from the more focused, local, and interior psychological spaces revealed in the film. In that sense, Carol MacCurdy misreads Mangold, claiming he "adds an extended midsection covering the posse's long trip so the audience would feel more acutely 'the claustrophobia in the hotel room' from having traveled with the characters" (2009, 287). That would only be true if, like Lawton, Papamichael had offered panning and long shots rather than a series of close-ups on the trip to Contention. There is, in fact, no real distinction in the framing through Mangold's film, so no particular contrast in our response is elicited. And by the end, we have a memory only of a certain helter-skelter sequencing that has made it difficult to follow the plot (however provocative) in vivid contrast to Leonard's story.

Thematically as well, Mangold shifts the narrative focus by opening not with either Evans or Wade but with teenager William reading a dime novel in bed, setting the film in a context of popular cultural expectations that regularly defy actual facts (and this, pitched to an audience disposed to allow how fully "fake facts" shape the history we live). The whole ends with a similarly skewed perspective, as Evans and Wade arrive at the station to find the train delayed in a curiously ironic conclusion to a film titled with timely precision. Between those terminal points, the narrative is packed chockablock full of violent distractions and red herrings, slicing and dicing the Western genre to include random parts, pulling together rapacious ranchers, murderous Apaches, and craven citizens along with disgruntled Chinese railroad workers, bounty hunters, and the butchered evidence of Civil War legacies, all simmering together in a stew of iridescent filial tension. The film's allure and its considerable box-office success depended on this mixture of scenes and styles, leaving more traditional, formal cineastes to wonder what holds the hodgepodge together.[19]

Notably, the question of appropriate masculine behavior central to Welles's script (and more traditional Westerns) has become somewhat muddled, partly as a matter of casting. But it also might be construed as a gesture against the very notions of masculinity that had so long dictated generic concerns, representing a more complex, more complicated vision of supposedly "manly" behavior than the Western had taken as its own. From this perspective, Christian Bale ironically, uncannily resembles his adversary Russell Crowe rather than offering a contrast, with both actors being conventionally handsome, self-confidently assured, even dashing. But as well, crises seem pitched more as physical tests than as trials of conscience. Bale's Dan Evans is hampered not by inner character as such (which had been revealed earlier in the unease of Van Heflin's face) but corporeally through the loss of his leg in the Civil War, requiring a prosthesis that from the beginning defines his moral standing. More generally, crises are inflated melodramatically, presented as exorbitant moments of conflict in every aspect of characters' lives. The community's inability to help one another in Daves's film, when a neighbor declines Evans's request for a loan because he too is strapped for cash, becomes transformed into full-blown civic corruption a half-century later. Evans is cruelly oppressed by money lenders who burn his barn, scare off his cattle, and meet a further request for a loan with contempt for the "cripple." Furthermore, they admit to having damned Evans's creek to force him out: "Sometimes, a man has to be big enough to see how small he is. The railroad's coming. Your land is worth more with you off it."

Everyone now is venal, with Charlie Prince promising two hundred dollars per man and those who decline his offer still agreeing they will not risk defending Wade. Dan himself is swayed by cupidity, converted by example, as he explains in taking the job: "You're gonna promise more than that, if I put the scourge of the Southern Line on that train. I want a guarantee that Hollander and his boys never set foot on my land again. And that my water's gonna flow. And I expect you to hand my wife one thousand cash dollars when you see her." Unlike Van Heflin, whose progress in the film occurs as a gradual accession to the civic premise embedded in his initial agreement, Christian Bale reveals very little of his emotions, never wavering or seeming uncertain, persistently standing toe to toe with the adversity he confronts.[20]

This melodramatic revision (which forms another version of borders intensified and hardened) extends to other plot relations, including the Evanses' marriage, reconceived by Michael Brandt as a fraught union. Adapting Welles's screenplay, he portrays them as visibly tense from the beginning, with Alice (Gretchen Mol) outraged at having been kept in the dark by her husband's secret financial dealings: "You lied to me, Dan. . . . You told me we made payments to Hollander. . . . We're supposed to make decisions together." But this forms only part of her anger, given his treatment of her and their sons, explaining her opposition to his taking the job of guarding Ben Wade. And he returns the feeling: "I'm tired of watching the boys go hungry. I'm tired of the way they look at me. I'm tired of the way you don't. I've been standing on one leg for three damned years, waiting for God to do me a favor, Alice. He isn't listening. It's up to me." Oddly, in contrast to Daves's film, Alice drops out midway through, suggesting that issues dividing them were not only *not* resolved but only further exacerbated by events. Matrimonial contentiousness seems finally not to matter, or to matter simply as fodder for melodramatic conflict.

That conflict is compounded in the standoff between generations, as the tension between Evans and his hostile adolescent son becomes ever more pronounced. Dismissively claiming "You don't take care of nothing"; later loudly retorting "I'm never walking in your shoes"; William repeatedly disobeys until the outlaw Wade arrives. Suddenly starstruck, he is unable to avert his gaze, gathering up the gang leader's spent pistol shells as if secret treasure. Staring at him agog over supper, William registers the hero worship a fourteen-year-old might feel for a man more dashing than his all too familiar, sedentary father. In fact, much of the first part of the film dramatizes the broken relationship between father and son, as conflicting concepts of masculine behavior are revealed and dismissed. What Leonard had assumed as the way in which a man might act, uncommented upon, simply accepted, has become in Brandt's version a tortured affiliation. And to the extent that films embody popular premises, the version of paternal control celebrated in the 1950s has broken down over the half century into a fractious relationship between self-empowered offspring and impotent father, with wife and mother pushed abruptly aside. Suddenly, surprisingly, the relationship is patched when William witnesses Wade's killing of Tucker and McElroy and instantly sees the wisdom of self-control, realizing where his alignments ought to be. He thereafter requires little encouragement to assist his father in getting Wade to Contention, adopting a suitably supportive filial role in watching out for pursuers.

That reversal of allegiance—as abrupt as it is unexpected and as little questioned—not only forms the central emotional transition of the film but reveals its melodramatic conception of character. Where Welles and Daves conceived of inner conflicts tested by circumstance, leading to resolution in action, Brandt and Mangold instead depict characters as either melodramatic extremes or as constellations of incompatible impulses with little apparent concern for their inner resources or hidden psychology. They exist more or less simply as entertainment, a diversion from dilemmas that otherwise remain irreconcilable. Mangold himself has admitted how much he delights in genre-bending, cross-gendered, border-crossing performances, stepping outside the box.[21] And significantly, Brandt shifts attention from Evans to Wade as the film's central focus, aligning with William's own sudden fascination. It may be that Wade's melodramatic self-division seems more compelling for contemporary viewers than Evans's stalwart undertaking. He first appears drawing a hawk on a sketch pad, attesting to the outlaw's artistic sensibility, an imputation given further weight by Russell Crowe's hair style and mellow self-presentation. In Bisbee, after seducing the barmaid, Wade further validates his artistic talents by sketching her undressed in a flamboyant echo of Leonardo DiCaprio's performance in James Cameron's *Titanic* (1997). Crowe follows Glenn Ford in his thoughtful alertness—taking Evans's horses but tying them up, offering to pay for Evans's lost time—and does so with a similar mercurial charm, though adding an irrelevant scholarly pose, confirmed in his ability to quote scripture, again an apparent affectation. He is at once more solicitous of Alice and more curious about Dan's military past than in Daves's version. Part of this change in Michael Brandt's Wade is attributed to his self-serving ego, enjoying the effect of his quicksilver charm as he relies on it to slide through life: "You know why I'm so hard to lock away, Dan? People *like* me. Farmers give me shelter. Cattlemen give me food. Judges let me off. Jailers let me out. Law-abiding citizens out there feel strangled by their shitty little lives. And me . . . well, I'm like the bird that should never be caged." But underneath the easy affability is the suggestion of blank nullity, of someone unable to value the moment or feel heartfelt sympathy.

And Brandt compounds Wade's chaotic character by adding scenes of gratuitous violence that thoroughly contradict his benign view of himself. He viciously stabs Tucker (Kevin Durand) with a fork simply because he was taunted, and later for a similar reason pushes McElroy (Peter Fonda) over a cliff. He even points his commandeered rifle at Evans before William disarms him, then briefly becomes reconciled to his prisoner status. Brandt's screenplay seems unable to resolve the issue of Wade's mercurial character, piling on scenes with little predictive sequence or psychological continuity. Wade beats Dan and then escapes, challenges Chinese workers to free him from handcuffs, then is recaptured and tortured by a railroad magnate before using dynamite to escape once again. In fact, by the concluding march to the station, Wade's inconsistencies have compounded beyond all coherence, as he first warns Dan of the rescue attempt, then shoots his loyal lieutenant Charlie Prince along with others in the gang striving to save him. Whatever sense of fidelity he feels has been supplanted by a new commitment to Dan, even as that commitment is left thoroughly unexplained and inexplicable.

Brandt shifts the focus to Wade for his engagingly unstable, self-divided (all but psychotic) personality, which offers the film a theatrical flair on which to capitalize. But as already intimated, Evans has also been altered by Brandt into an exaggerated version of Welles's reluctant rancher. Van Heflin's performance suggested muted anxiety, but always in the context of assurance about his own judgment, whether in his role as father, husband, or citizen. By contrast, Bale's version seems somehow hollowed out, haunted by an inability to corral his feelings into socially tractable forms and by a larger sense of inadequacy figured physically in his absent leg. The 1950s version of "father knows best," endorsed implicitly by Daves's film, is held up for due examination and rejected in Mangold's more dubious version of character. When Dan Evans is overpowered by Wade, he guiltily admits the loss of his limb resulted not from military daring but cowardly flight: "All I know is I lost it running, scared and blind and in retreat. You try telling that story to your little boy, Wade. And you watch his eyes." Later, he adds out of a misplaced confessional impulse that he has not been particularly stubborn in standing up to other ranchers but has persisted simply because his younger son is tubercular. In this, he appears to viewers almost as mercurial as Wade, suggesting that both figures have been constructed from melodramatic features, shifting emotionally among a range of possibilities. Brandt's script suspends the configurations of personal identity that had seemed firm in Welles's screenplay, loosening up personalities into a medley of disparate impulses, creating disjointed figures out of discordant parts. And that very lack of cohesion seems to lie at the heart of the film's appeal, in proffering characters who accord with popular conceptions less unified and consistent than Daves's mid-century audience would have presumed.

At the same time, Brandt meets contemporary viewing standards head-on by introducing substantially greater violence into the action, often gratuitously. The subdued stage robbery opening the film, added by Welles to confirm Wade's guilt, is now a crazed gang attack initiated by a Gatling gun. And Mangold heightens the violence substantially by having multiple robbers killed, ending with Wade driving Evans's cattle into the stage, toppling it. Cinematically, the scene appears more frenetic than the original, with the camera energetically engaged in close-ups, action sequences, and abrupt cuts that collectively lend a visceral excitement to the scene. Later, Charlie Prince brutally encourages others to kill the Pinkertons and then gut shoots Byron McElroy (Peter Fonda) in a gratuitously callous act. All the murder and mayhem is a surprising addition of violence to the earlier film's opening, which consists of Wade simply if ruthlessly killing Moons. And the violence thereafter expands exponentially: Prince sets fire to the prison wagon with Crawley inside, then shows his loyalty to Wade by defying others in their gang. We learn as well of inordinate bloodshed everywhere else in the past, particularly in Wade's revelation of McElroy's habitual ruthlessness: "Ask Byron here. He's killed dozens of people. Men, women and children. Miners. Apache. . . . When it comes to killing, Byron McElroy doesn't think in terms of man or woman or even child."

Compounding the film's excesses (of a piece with contemporary action films), Brandt introduces Apaches to the mix, the evidence of their presence provided by scalped miners sprawled on the side of the road. The embodiment of this boundless violence is Charlie Prince, Wade's alter ego, in his maniacal slashing through bodies as he reiterates "I hate posses," or "I hate Pinkertons," until he ends in a savage burst of gunfire shooting Evans multiple times, watched by his son and Wade in a dramatic rewriting of Daves's final scene. The ensuing execution of the gang only confirms the film's incoherence, further attested to by Wade's calm acceptance of being re-arrested, with William left to mourn all that has passed. Adding nearly an hour to Daves's ninety minutes, Mangold's adaptation delights in scenes of rabid violence that are part of a long tradition in popular painting and film, but that in this case neither resolve nor integrate issues of masculinity and civic responsibility pivotal in the ur-text, the reason for the adaptation.

CONCLUSION: CLAUSTROPHOBIAS

Unfair as it may seem to compare Daves's adaptation with Mangold's, their separate successes raise intriguing questions. After all, adaptations always reveal something about the periods in which they were made: the choices of what to expand or delete, the strategies by which scenes are recast, the ways that textual and cinematic gaps are either summarily resolved or continue to resonate long after. Leonard's short story imagines the relatively straightforward experience of a man compelled, for reasons unexplained, to accompany an outlaw to a train despite the threat of his escape. Daves dramatically augments this economical premise by engaging issues of masculine self-control, of economic adversity, of domestic conflict over the choices a family needs to make. And he does so in an adaptation that, while far from faithful to all but Leonard's bare structure, succeeds in integrating its diverse issues into a powerful study of a man under pressure coming to terms with what manhood more generally might mean in the mid 1950s. In his revision of Daves, not Leonard, Mangold tilts into an apparent chaos of scenes, pulling out stops with maniacal glee, toying with stock materials of the Western in an all but parodic fashion. Partly, the incoherence of the whole is signaled by characters inexplicably dropped (like Alice Evans, midway through); partly in the magical transition that others make (like William, also midway through); but mostly, in the quick introduction and dismissal of a whole array of figures, each irrelevant to the next sequence, all as segregated and bordered off from one another as are the scenes of the film itself. That experience of visual incoherence, however (again, as Todd Berliner has shown), is part of the very texture of new versions of established generic films, and speaks to a completely different set of cinematic standards (understandably, perhaps predictably so) from those reconfirmed by Daves's 1950s film. The marvel of Mangold's adaptation is the way in which it reveals in a stripped-down narrative structure the possibilities of engaging issues that a half century later still seem urgent.

Keep in mind that the three versions rely on very different stylistic ploys, none particularly privileged, though each devoted to the same narrative journey. Leonard's writing aspires to a Hemingwayesque transparency, with sentences constructed to avoid either elaborate qualifications or diversions, propelling a story meant to be just as straightforward. Perhaps few ways exist in which that verbal style can be replicated on film (as adaptation studies proponents are quick to remind), but in any case Welles and Daves alter Leonard's style considerably not only in being more forthcoming where Leonard prizes concision but in expanding the narrative generally to seize on issues pressing contemporaries in the 1950s. As well, the camera itself is given a prominent role, used self-consciously to make us aware of a story being told in a way that Leonard regularly avoids with his clipped prose. Brandt and Mangold extend this impulse, both in an unraveling plot that unspools frenetically and in the framed sequences involving handheld cameras, fragmented fields, and extreme close-ups. We lose sight of the fact that the original plot was essentially static and tightly focused: a man needing to guard another in a landscape more psychological than physically real, facing external threats and understandable anxieties, nothing more. Still, it seems apparent that the plot's very economy attracted interested directors and scriptwriters if only because the central tension seemed to beg so many questions: Why did Scanlen agree? What was Wade guilty of? What kind of men were they? Could they be altered by their experience? Welles, like Daves, realized that the simple armature of plot allowed for a fascinating assortment of character revelations, of alternative interpretations of gendered behavior and family dynamics, even of notions of human psychology, all pitched towards contemporary concerns. And the modest increase in violence revealed a failure to contain certain energies within civic processes, anticipating (however unintentionally) what the sixties would bring both to America's streets and its screens.

The urgency of questions broached in the first film had faded entirely by the appearance of the second, which understandably was created for a generation sharing neither its grandparents' ideological concerns nor their cinematic habits. If the suppressed intensity of the initial story unfolded aptly in Daves's answerable style, Mangold's adaptation endorsed something like an emotional chaos that seems irrepressible, speaking to itself alone, though admittedly in an era in which negotiated calm no longer finds itself readily championed. Contemporary standards for violence have risen dramatically, of course, in part due to Western practitioners themselves who followed Daves in the decades thereafter (Sam Peckinpah, Sergio Leone, Clint Eastwood) as well as so many other action-adventure film directors. Perhaps now, it is possible to see why Mangold chose Daves's film to adapt and did so successfully. For in the transition from Leonard's straightforward narrative, to Welles's refiguring of masculinity into a more ambivalent, untoward conception, the possibilities emerged of wringing further a glistening version of claustrophobia that could once again redefine the Western genre.

The heart of the Western has been a more or less traditional conception of masculinity that has increasingly seemed irrelevant to conventional urban life, perhaps especially so in films beginning in the 1990s, following the success of *Dances with Wolves, Unforgiven, Posse,* and George P. Cosmatos's *Tombstone* (1993). In these and others, narrative linearity breaks down as a cumulative plot progression, which corresponds to divisions characters experience within the films themselves. Mangold's effort is just as extreme, as an adaptation that transforms admittedly disconnected moments from its original, adding more scenes that refuse to pull together in a film that nonetheless succeeds on its own terms. Moreover, though radically different both narratively and stylistically from its precursors, Mangold's film clearly evokes similar questions about identity, obligation, and masculinity that Leonard first addressed, if for a new generation. The sequence from story to film, then to film again, has been one in which the fullest revelation has been about generic resilience. For in proving how powerfully an ur-text can command popular attention, even in a series of radical transformations over a half-century, Leonard's story is exemplary. As well, we realize once again not only the inventive divergences taken by late Westerns but as well the significant continuity, semantically and syntactically, between them and earlier genre examples.

3

BORDER-CROSSING
IN *LONE STAR*

The Mexican American border has long been a prized venue for Westerns, well before the closing moments of *Stagecoach* when the Ringo Kid (John Wayne) assures Dallas (Claire Trevor) that she will soon "get to my place across the border." As they ride off, another character approves: "Well, they're saved from the blessings of civilization!" In the genre's recent resurgence, that border looms larger than ever, exemplified prominently in *El Mariachi* and *Once upon a Time in Mexico*, Billy Bob Thornton's *All the Pretty Horses* (2000), John Lee Hancock's *The Alamo* (2004), *The Three Burials of Melquiades Estrada*, *No Country for Old Men*, and *The Counselor*.[1] Each of these prominent instances seizes on some aspect of Hispanic contrast to explore cultural divergence, political disparities, or the repercussions of a drug trade that binds both sides ineluctably together. Yet perhaps no film has dissected the notion of borders so ambitiously as Sayles's *Lone Star*, which is set on the Rio Grande in fictitious (self-consciously named) Frontera, Texas.[2] He himself characterized the work as "a story about borders," taking the occasion of cultural difference to focus on an array of other borders so as to render the category all-embracing and thereby potentially all but meaningless: borders between history and myth, present and past, parent and child, genders, and of course racial and cultural matrixes (Anglo, African American, Hispanic, Native American).[3] Moreover, the film's cinematic structure compounds these thematic strains through a splintered presentation that reminds viewers (ambitiously, once again) that no narrative sequence can be seamless. In almost too many ways, the film ponders the question of unified identity, shared and nearly shared, by dramatizing contrasts that allow coherence itself to be achieved.

Like a number of other "late" Westerns that are the subject of this book, Sayles's film is clearly a meta-Western, addressing syntactic patterns crucial to the genre and doing so well before we as viewers are altogether aware. The Western has always relied on a series of assumed borders (occupational, civic, regional, gendered, generational), and as often as it has questioned those borders in local configurations, it rarely expresses skepticism about the drawing of border lines themselves. By contrast, *Lone Star* deliberately invokes that reluctance to deconstruct the genre, to reveal and finally question the premises on which understanding of the West has been shaped by popular fictionalizations. Borders that have been simply assumed and accepted as part of the Western's syntax are here confused, interrogated, misaligned, and disputed. In this, the film offers a tacit extension of the skepticism registered in *Bad Day at Black Rock* and *3:10 to Yuma* about the contours of the genre it represents, taking its lead from no one as much as John Ford in questioning a past it mythologizes, revealing how history at a distance may appear to glow but up close becomes deformed and disquieting. Faith has too often simply displaced fact. Moreover, the film—for all its semantic identification as a Western, defined in terms of casting, setting, and costuming—depends on a syntactic crossbreeding that relies heavily on generic patterns associated more with noir and mystery, revealing again how impure this Western (like all notable Westerns) actually is. Clearly Sayles is fascinated by the hold a genre has on our interpretive impulses, and in variously complex ways draws attention to the narrative pleasures we so un-self-consciously indulge. His film's fissures and discontinuities, moreover, require increasing awareness at the effort taken to make sense of the plot, and more generally to understand a genre invariably built on confident assumptions about the binaries that structure our interpretive world.

Lone Star, in short, succeeds by probing discriminations we otherwise assume obvious, revealing slipperiness among accepted categories, and in the process confirming how identity is always constructed, not found. Or as Sheriff Sam Deeds (Chris Cooper) learns from the entrepreneur Chucho Montoya (Tony Amendola), after Montoya has gouged a line in the Mexican soil with his heel: "Step across this line. . . . You're not the sheriff of nothing anymore." The gesture is a resonant one, not only in silently bridging present and mythological past (reminding us of Col. William B. Travis's apocryphal appeal to those doomed at the Alamo) but in signaling how borders marked in dirt are the very basis for civilized discourse. They represent symbolic judgments that, however tweaked or altered, define values hammered out of the past, shaping the present. As the film variously argues, moreover, trying to escape or simply erase such history is always futile. *Lone Star*'s triumph lies in showing how borders at once reinforce and erode each other. Sometimes they work in concert, at others they are at odds, so tensions among ideological tenets (of race, gender, history, civic ideals) offer not a mutually enabling structure but an evolving set of assumptions about how one ought to behave.[4] In short, the film's ambition is to draw borders together, marked by formal intersections that repeatedly alert us to this central tension. Before understanding that aesthetic effect, however, we need to sort out thematic conflicts that emerge along the Rio Grande.

TEMPORAL AND GENERATIONAL

Immediately, right at the opening, borders are established as the film's principal conceptual category, though in ways neither natural nor obvious. And though the concept happens to be central to the Western, the genre is put into question before we realize it is in play. A buried hand with a Masonic ring is unearthed, as Cliff Potts (Stephen Mendillo) lectures his fellow Army sergeant Mikey Hogan (Stephen J. Lang), who is operating a metal detector, about distinctions among cacti and beers. The land itself is desolate, scree barely covered with succulents, as Cliff reads aloud the taxonomies provided by his pamphlet, describing the difference between nopals and yuccas, then between lead and gold mines, contrasting them to the "hundred-fifty varieties of beer" prized by Mikey Hogan. In turn, Mikey examines the ring and wryly queries, "Was Coronado in the Masons?" just as opening credits splash garishly across the screen accompanied by a loud mariachi tune. Everything from the outset proclaims a series of singular contrasts of brash boundaries and isolating conditions. Even the film's Panavision Super 35 cinematography deliberately stresses this condition, as Sayles admits in his focusing on "the horizontal look of the border. It's not mountainous, it is a very long, absolutely flat horizon line, and we wanted, at least in the beginning of the picture, to isolate people in that flat, wide land. . . . Widescreen gave us that feeling of just a few people fighting over that little thin strip of river where the good land is and which is surrounded by scrubby desert" (Carson 1999, 218). The entire sequence introduces a theme of appropriate categories, even in so seemingly insignificant a realm as succulents and hops. And Mikey's telling question about Masons is later matched in his studio when Cliff asks quizzically: "What's a pistol slug doing on a rifle range?" The queries engage the problem of reliable borders that introduces the murder mystery on which the film is based. For as Sam Deeds concludes, registering the tone of all that follows: "This country's seen a good number of disagreements over the years."

The next scene compounds this border crossing, shifting it from physical to historical, making us realize subliminally that classifications are being challenged. In her classroom, Pilar Cruz (Elizabeth Peña) describes to the mother of a new African American student her diverse group of black, white, and Hispanic students (as well as "a couple Kickapoo kids"): "a pretty lively mix." Then suddenly, she signals another conflicted border, the terrain between parents and children, when she learns her own son has skipped school: "He's going to wish he was dead." Before we can absorb the diverse issues introduced, it is clear that everything hinges on tensions between conflicting entities, as if tension itself were the binding link among disparate scenes. That uneasiness is even manifest in the posters of celebrated Anglos and Hispanics hanging on Pilar's classroom walls, to which she adds the somber face of Geronimo. In the absence of any sequence among these conflicts and distinctions, we are left unable to grasp a narrative thread as thematic resonances overlap. Each scene self-consciously engages problems among borders ill sequestered or otherwise muddied and contested. And as the scenes ensue, they alter our readings of each preceding, unsettling strict discriminations that characters initially bring to issues.

By the time Sam encounters his manic-depressive ex-wife Bunny (Frances McDormand)—so "tightly wound" over the college football draft that she seems in another zone as well—we have come to appreciate how much less plot matters than thematic parallels. The only explanation for this odd encounter in the midst of a border film seems the unusual strains between two such disparate personalities, confirming the absence of any borderless union at all.[5] In fact, Sayles sharpens the conflicts by stressing other overlapping perspectives: "I wanted people to get that idea that the answers Sam is given are always going to be influenced by the person who's giving them. . . . Sometimes they're lying. Or lying to themselves. But always keeping to that idea that this is not what happened—this is how I remember what happened" (G. Smith 1998, 229). Memory itself forms a demarcation from the experience as it really occurred. Already, the divide between past fact and present remembrance is signaled as a split that reminds us of the ongoing tension in so many Westerns, where revenge or restitution are conceived as goals toward which the plot aspires.

Still, for all the ways *Lone Star* addresses conflicts among singular viewpoints, its central mystery concerns the border between present and past, as Sam Deeds unravels the reasons that former Sheriff Charley Wade (Kris Kristoffersen) was murdered and by whom. The importance of that temporal boundary is signaled by the first genuinely intriguing transition between scenes, when Mayor Hollis Pogue (Clifton James) begins to tell the story of Sam's father, Buddy (Matthew McConaughey), as the camera closes in on Sam's face, then down to a basket of tortillas that morphs into

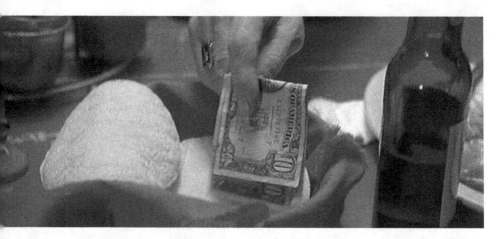

Fig. 9. Morphing pan shot from the present to 1957 as an account of corrupt Sheriff Charley Wade snagging a payoff is narrated in *Lone Star* (Columbia Pictures).

a similar basket in 1957, before pulling back to reveal Wade blithely snagging a payoff of three ten-dollar bills tucked in the pile. Cinematographer Stuart Dryburgh establishes visually the ongoing life of the past, in the still-vibrant tension between "your old-fashioned bribe-or-bullets kind of sheriff" and his long-dead deputy Buddy, who seems guilty of Wade's murder. As importantly, their tense standoff ends in the transitional pan back to Sam's animated face in the present, of which David Shumway observes:

> The shot embodies the idea that the past remains alive, and that people past and present are inextricably bound to one another. . . . This seamless temporal shift is accomplished not only by the long take, but also by lighting. When we first entered the café, it was broad daylight. But when the camera pans up to show Charlie [*sic*], it has become night. The café itself, which looks clean and well kept in the present, looks dark and dingy in the past. But it is significant that the story Hollis is telling took place where he is telling it. History in *Lone Star* is there, present in the form of people and things that were part of it. (2012, 93)

This notable morphing pan has the effect of eliding time, reasserting the hold of the past on the present, self-consciously making a temporal link that works more effectively than a simple cut or dissolve or fade.[6]

In this, the sequence self-consciously declares itself a cross mix of Western and noir by confirming how fully history persists in shackling and shaping the present, as the present defiantly continues to assume it remains unfettered, even free. Memory seems bound to actual history in this unusual cut, though memory is only one version, sometimes mystifying us in the very ease of transition or leaving us clueless at the behest of characters who otherwise deny the past, deliberately muddying the waters. Hollis in the present repeats his account of Buddy standing up to Wade, though he refuses to confess his own actual guilt for what ensues. And likewise, Otis Payne (Ron Canada) deliberately misleads Sam, claiming he never saw Buddy after this encounter. The two sole witnesses to Wade's violent death effectively segregate that past, keeping it hidden, in a pattern of deliberate obfuscation that is replicated throughout.

Past and present are at once linked and divided, with Sayles more generally complicating temporal frames by breaking them up. He offers a sequence that we must in turn reconstruct to ascertain after the fact an overall chronology, one that begins with Mercedes Cruz (Míriam Colón) crossing the Rio Grande as a young girl in 1945 and ends with Mercedes's daughter Pilar and Sam at the ramshackle drive-in half a century later. As importantly, Mercedes's flashback is one of the latest to come in the narrative sequence. The film thoroughly entangles history, looping it erratically back on itself, with accounts by all the major characters (Otis Payne, Sam Deeds, Hollis Pogue, Pilar Cruz) presented in a similarly fractured fashion. As Neil Campbell observes, "Sayles's characters exist within this liminality, perpetually engaged with the consequences of living during centuries of 'intercultural crossing and mixing' through which particular stories and memories become 'official' while others become marginalized or deliberately repressed" (2011, 208). Even so, the film also registers a need to untangle history as a contested terrain, one that has always been up for grabs—something that Westerns rarely do, or presume they need to, confirming again its self-consciously meta-generic status. That concern with history makes reference to similar moments in earlier Westerns. Pilar leads a history class on "Mexican independence" that deliberately echoes a scene in *The Man Who Shot Liberty Valance* when Ransom Stoddard (Jimmy Stewart) teaches English to a heterogeneous schoolroom (Hispanic, Anglo, African American), and shifts to a lecture on the origin of America's civic ideals.[7]

Yet where Stoddard imposes his political vision on a docile class of subordinates, Pilar (in a subsequent scene) barely controls a contentious argument about textbook accounts that allegedly misrepresent Texas's past. Anglo parents argue against Hispanic Americans about their shared history, testing who has the right to author (and thus authorize) a normative story, all but coming to blows. When Chet Payne (Eddie Robinson) finds himself fascinated by photo blowups of native Americans on his grandfather's wall, the lesson seems well learned, as Otis details the history of Indians and African Americans intermarrying a century before. This series of oddly irrelevant exercises (at least in terms of plot advancement) is crucial for demonstrating why public history matters, speaking to the borderland identities central to the film. In response to Chet's question whether he himself is "part-Indian," Otis responds: "By blood you are. But blood only means what you let it." The paramount claim for contested identity, pressed by the film in multiple forms, at last requires being stated straightforwardly in the conflict between inheritance and choice and in the discriminations that need to be drawn in any individual case. Again, *Lone Star* refuses simply to agree with presumed historical claims, to accept the past as necessarily determinative, which has invariably formed a shaping premise of the Western.

That difficult renegotiation of what political and social history actually mean day to day, reflected in the textbook argument, echoes other unresolved tensions in the film that are more personal: perhaps most pointedly, the strains between generations. Sam Deeds tries unremittingly to fathom the career of his mythical father so as to lay bare Buddy's guilt for murdering Charley Wade. Chet deals with his overbearing military father Del Payne (Joe Morton), whose hard-nosed demeanor is borne out of resentment against his own father's abandonment of him. Pilar copes as a second-generation Mexican American with her mother's vehement if antiquated beliefs about assimilation, as she simultaneously worries about the discontent of her own son Amado, who scorns her middle-class notions of suitable behavior. In each case, a younger generation feels somehow inadequate—or as Minnie Bledsoe (Beatrice Winde), the former co-owner of Big O's roadhouse bar, responds derisively to Sam when he identifies himself as sheriff of Frontera: "You just Sheriff Junior." Fenton (Tony Frank) had already expressed an older generation's disdain in referring to Buddy's son Sam as "all hat and no cattle." Yet part of the film's revelations lies in the converse, in a younger generation coming to realize the considerable burdens imposed on their elders, accepting in the process a legacy that bridges past and present. Once more, Sayles holds up for examination a central theme of the Western, but instead of simply presenting filial resentment at misplaced parental discipline, he repeatedly has characters reassess their own initial reactions.

Hardly apparent at first, the film's narrative thread begins with Sam's bewilderment at reports of Charley Wade's death and his father's presumed involvement: the two bound together in a pattern characteristic of the mystery genre. Yet the primary mystery has to do with Sam's reasons for wanting to know, which are never more than hinted at: Is it envy at his father's civic reputation? Or a response to having been thwarted by Buddy as a parent? Does he more generally need to modify, perhaps transform the past? The psychology underlying his search is never clarified, and Chris Cooper's performance remains credibly opaque, rarely suggesting through expression or response his feelings about what he discovers or why he persists. Still, from the beginning he does openly wonder whether Buddy is "on the short list" of suspects and soon after quizzes Hollis about the well-honed story of his celebrated father in an effort to achieve greater civic transparency: "People have worked this whole big thing up around my father. If it's built on a crime, they deserve to know." A certain idealism spurs him on as he delves into the past, staying up all night to review facts, then accidentally learning from a jail trusty that a witness of Eladio Cruz's murder still exists. Yet a full two hours into the film, Sam still remains ignorant of the past that has shaped him, falsely supposing Buddy killed Wade, with only Otis's disclosure at last revealing his father took the fall for Hollis. The blending throughout, moreover, of mystery and noir generic patterns reinforces how fully Sayles is continuing to probe the Western's own reach.

Of course, the genre has long dealt with violence itself as a necessary aftereffect of violence—with earlier malfeasance (often legal) or oppression (often racial) or trespass (often occupational) having led to the need for extralegal revenge and restitution. As Janet Walker observes: "In countless westerns, events of disturbing proportions, events that are markedly anterior to the fictive present, propel the actions and the retaliatory violence of the narrative" (2001, 220). But rarely are those events represented as secrets or as protracted, shadowy forces rather than clearly legible outrages that continue to haunt recollection. And that difference once again reveals Sayles's intriguing willingness to investigate what Westerns so often tend to take for granted. Even after the flashback of the shooting of corrupt Sheriff Charley Wade, the misleading construction of events persists in playing out scenically as the camera aligns with Sam's blinkered assumption that Buddy fired the gun. The film tenaciously delays a mystery that looms as large for us as for Sam, who only at last comes to terms with his father's behavior by realizing his own unsuitability for the job of sheriff ("Hell, I'm just a jailer. Run a sixty-room hotel with bars on the windows"). The long-delayed adumbration of Buddy's actual "innocence" has finally freed him to define himself, no longer the son of a supposed legend but someone able to stand on his own, independently. His view of his father, moreover, is comparable to Pilar's relationship with her mother, who likewise holds a "mythological" stature as self-made entrepreneur. Weaving through the film is Mercedes's past as an undocumented immigrant, though that too is revealed partially, fragmentarily, as she tries to comport herself in the guise of an assimilated, unhyphenated American.

Each of these filial relationships reveals a growing sympathy for parental self-justification in contrast to a pattern animating most Westerns that side with children *against* the past (*Red River* and *The Searchers* are prominent examples, but consider also Ford's *Fort Apache* [1948], Henry Hathaway's *True Grit* [1969], and *Down in the Valley*). With Sam, the realization that Buddy did what was needed despite breaking the law cultivates a more tolerant judgment of flawed moral behavior (and notably, this view marks an unusual acceptance of what Robert Warshow termed "the value of violence" [(1954) 1962, 151], if after civic moderation has replaced the need for it). Mercedes comes grudgingly to accept her own past through the example of others encountering similar perils in a scene that merges her earlier crossing of the Rio Grande (with Enrique [Richard Coca] helping his girlfriend do the same in the present). And prior to this, Del Payne acknowledges that his son need not follow him into the army in a gesture that confirms his acceptance of not only his son Chet but his own father Otis as well, realizing he has been as demanding as Otis had been of him. Sam, Mercedes, and Del each accept a more balanced view based on their renewed understanding of parental and filial bonds. Yet divisions between generations do not simply disappear in this series of insights, any more than do the borders that exacerbate gender relationships: of Sam and his wired ex-wife Bunny; of Del squabbling with Celie about their son; of Otis with Caroline, the latest of various wives and girlfriends, expressing a bemused view of each other. The difficulties of fathoming the "opposite sex" seem little different from grasping the entanglements and complexity of any border group.[8]

Throughout, Sayles focuses on foundational conflicts of the Western, creating a film that pitches generic expectations against ever more uncertain conclusions. Emotional conflicts between parent and child, husband and wife, past and present, all emerge in *Lone Star* as divisions that resist being bridged, at least at first. That process resembles most the generative experience of narrative itself, always unfolding in the present as we try to decipher the past. And the fragmentation of separate narratives that are woven together arbitrarily—so much so that the film compounds the strategy by jumbling sequences laid out more straightforwardly in the screenplay—suggests how important parallels are between them, aligning similarly, at times reinforcing each other. Perhaps the most remarkable part of Sayles's treatment is his lightness of touch, shifting from straight-forward narrative evolution in any single set of characters as a means of reinforcing the process of reconciliation, whether as part of parental control or filial obligation.

LEGAL AND CULTURAL

Reinforcing this obsession with temporal and generational borders are other similar tensions, so many that they risk confusing viewers about what is at stake. But certain salient divisions loom, including the troubled line between civic duty and institutional violence, represented less in the mystery of Charley Wade's death than in his sadistic fashion of sheriffing. That tension between shady police enforcement and the rule of law is played out in flashbacks confirming Wade's behavior: his tormenting of Otis; his bullying of Buddy; his ruthless shooting of Eladio Cruz in the back; his brazenly extracting bribes. Yet while Buddy offers a humane contrast of civic service, Sam discovers his father also played along, in one case prominently diverting ten thousand dollars for "widows's benefits" to Mercedes since "Charley killed her man." As well, Sam learns from the prison trusty, Pete Zayas (Sam Vlahos), that his father employed him on county time to build his patio gratis. And though he grows to accept such border-erasing accommodations, Sam never rests easy, finding his ingrained idealism makes continuing as sheriff in Frontera onerous, begin-ning with his reasonable opposition to an expensive and unneeded new jail—opposition that arouses the town's boosters to thwart his reelection.

That recurrent clash of idealism with pragmatism is echoed in Colonel

Payne's handling of the shooting at Big O's roadhouse, in his interrogation of the shooter's ex-lover, Pvt. Athena Johnson (Chandra Wilson). Mystified by her soberly realistic assessment of the army, Payne nonetheless listens, transforming him from stiff-lipped martinet to mildly more judicious leader, explaining his dismissal of her without penalty. This malleable view of social life was earlier articulated by his father, explaining his saloon's appeal to young army personnel: "There's the Holiness Church and there's Big O's place . . . a lot of 'em choose both. There's not like a borderline between the good people and the bad people—you're not either on one side or the other." And that vision of concord is shared by the prison trusty Pete, who dismisses Sam's overly upright civic principles by endorsing Buddy's decision to conscript him for private work, if only because it improved his own life (better lunches, time outdoors) and cost the city nothing. Tensions elsewhere over minor legal infractions (drugs, adolescent petty larceny) are likewise acknowledged silently as acceptable costs for the price of local goodwill.

The opposite tack in such "frontier" skirmishes is represented by a hardening of lines, a refusal to listen, in clashes over Texas textbooks, or Hispanic holidays, or Native American deportations—all establishing the brash self-assurance and narrow vision that has long been the obverse of the Western hero's confident vision and egalitarian idealism. The bartender Cody (Leo Burmester) gives categorical expression to this characterization by insisting that "to run a successful civilization you got to have lines of demarcation between right and wrong, between this one and that one— your Daddy understood that. He was like the whatchacallit—the referee for this damn *menudo* we got down here. He understood how most folks don't want their salt and sugar in the same jar." If Cody's racism is sardonically marked by Sam's acknowledgment of him as a "redneck," he does express a view of borders manifest everywhere else: that they keep shifting capriciously; that our comfort zones need as often to be realigned; and that a perpetual change of frontiers is all we can ever expect. "You're the last white sheriff this town's gonna see. . . . This is it, right here Sam.

This bar is the last stand! Say *habla American* goddamn it." Of course, the paradox of this biased sentiment lies in its very lexicon, adopting Spanish to proscribe the speaking of Spanish, with the camera itself more forcefully rejecting Cody's claim by panning with Sam's glance to Cliff and Priscilla, white and black, while he presses her to marry him. As Mikey later chides Cliff about proposing to an African American, whose family has taken her unmarried status as proof she is lesbian: "It's always heartwarming to see a prejudice defeated by a deeper prejudice."[9]

Occasionally cultural borders are treated humorously, as in Sam's admission to his Chicana deputy Ray (Tony Plana) that "I'm going over to the other side," to which Ray responds: "The Republicans?" And Sam explains: "No—to Mexico." At other times, a perceptual melding takes place, exemplified in Otis's explanation to Chet that Native Americans have long mixed with African Americans: "These are our people." And at still others, the violence of racial tension manifests itself in the present, as Ray shoves the black suspect Shadow through the jailhouse, echoing Charley Wade's brutal admonition to Otis long ago that "this isn't Houston." The self-oppression of racism is elsewhere confirmed in Mercedes's threat to call the Border Patrol on Enrique's "wetback" friends. Individual scenes themselves as well as their strangely eclectic blend repeatedly remind us of various mixtures of people across frontiers.

Of course, the most culturally rooted "border" involves the film's central mystery: the unwitting incestuous relationship between Sam and Pilar. The prohibition against sexual relations between brother and sister, after all, is among the most severe taboos, far stronger than that against miscegenation.[10] Yet this transgressive breach is not hinted at in the film's first hour, and only begins to emerge as Pilar recalls to Sam how Buddy stared at her on the playground, with her not realizing he was her father, with a father's affection. That night, Sam stays up pursuing questions apparently kindled by this recollection, reviewing real-estate transfers, autopsy reports, police and calendar records, ending with a notation that Mercedes was hired as cook at the jail in 1957, leading to his string of added question marks. Later, in flashback to a 1972 drive-in scene with teenage Sam and Pilar in a car being rousted, we assume Buddy is acting out of nothing more than overly protective paternal anxiety, even as we also realize their mixed relationship challenges other limits. As Pilar observes, "That's who we were. Children," confirming as well (and once more) the borderline between adolescence and adulthood.

Conversely, the death of her husband Nando leaves Pilar on the border of the rest of her life, profoundly uncertain about how to continue. Not until she falls into bed with Sam, however, do we realize subliminally that the issue has been one of issue itself, as Sam asks her to tell him the name of her father. The final piece of the puzzle emerges at the roadside stand of Kickapoo Wesley Birdsong (Gordon Tootoosis), who in finally first revealing Buddy's "other woman" prompts Sam to visit his own ex-wife for Buddy's cache of letters from Pilar.[11] Knowledge of incest has been delayed until the film's very end, though that placement only confirms its lack of importance as we come to appreciate its lack of consequence. In this, Sayles registers problems that reside ineluctably in all such border divisions, in all the mixes we take to be impossible or otherwise scandalous. This is not to agree with Kim Magowan, who declares: "Not only is the miscegenation taboo relaxed in Lone Star, but this very relaxation serves as a vehicle for legitimizing incest" (2003, 21). On the contrary, far from either defying borders or legitimizing transgression, the film repeatedly signals how often and variously we live amid intersections, always with the need to balance and regulate the tensions involved.

CINEMATIC

Clearly, border issues of all sorts—social and geographic; gendered and familial; literal and figurative—lie at the heart of Lone Star. It comes as no surprise, then, that Sayles translates that self-consciousness formally, cinematically, in acknowledgment of the ways in which Westerns often have framed their subjects. Consider the opening and closing images of The Searchers, with Ford's celebrated use of the framed cabin door as a threshold between two worlds; or the intense close-ups of Gary Cooper's face in *High Noon*, as a border between anguished psychology and external threat; or the opening epic landscape panoramas of so many other Westerns, announcing the viewers' entrance into a cinematic space beyond conventional frontiers. Sayles's fragmented narrative, crossing borders and making historical loops, all but demands a fragmented cinematic style that at once compels and deters the viewer in comprehending his story or in piecing together the plot in ways that depend on generic patterns. It is not that his presentational style is an afterthought merely augmenting a thematic focus, but rather that only through a cinematic treatment so self-consciously liminal itself can the film's deepest logic be enacted. Episodes appear disarmingly nonsequential, sometimes arbitrary in their progression, with unrelated characters engaged in dramas having little to do with one another. And transitions between episodes vary immensely, as if signaling by their difference the need for adjusted interpretations of narrative borders themselves.

Consider again the opening sequence of scenes: army sergeants Cliff and Mikey stumble upon a buried skeleton; then we shift to Pilar in her classroom discussing student groups with Celie Payne (Oni Faida Lampley); next we veer to Pilar's son being hauled in by Sam for petty theft; the focus shifts in turn to Hollis and Sam discussing Buddy Deeds, interrupted by the first flashback, of Hollis's account of Charley Wade confronted by Buddy; at last, we turn back once more to Cliff and Mikey, now standing in formation listening to their colonel discuss the unit's recent assignment to Frontera. Nothing in any individual scene links to anything else as we strive to discern connections among parental anxiety, casual hobbies, filial disquiet, petty crime in the present, and police malfeasance in the past. Further fragmenting this disorienting mixture, the film veers among Hispanics speaking (in Spanish) about crossing the Rio Grande to a large murder mystery looming out of the past, to ongoing and contentious civic concerns, all melded bafflingly together.[12] Sequences themselves are broken up, as in the official installation of Buddy's commemorative statue interrupted by Cliff in Mikey's workshop discussing bullets they have collected. This dislocation of scenes has, of course, become part of contemporary cinematic practice, though in a film whose semantic elements are so clearly Western (Texan landscape, racial tensions, high-hatted lawmen, and small- town solidarity) we tend to become more aware of the generic patterns that help us sort out our narrative way.

In fact, very little binds divergent scenes together until nearly the end when racial, ethnic, political, civic, and sexual borders all gradually begin to reveal a common misalignment. The disjunctive sequence begins with Pilar in her classroom thinking of Sam, then shifts in flashback to the 1972 drive-in movie, with two women running through the field towards the viewer, trying to escape a threat of something we can neither see nor fathom.[13] That recollection, ending with Sam and Pilar dragged from the car, shifts to the present, but now with Sam at the drive-in sadly remembering the impassioned encounter. More often scenes are simply misaligned, as in the strangely evocative moment of old photos presented in close-up, with the camera then pulling back to reveal Sam examining them—though oddly (once again), this occurs right after Del has been lecturing his troops. Or the 1990 Texas A&M football game on Bunny's TV that immediately follows Enrique consoling his girlfriend, in a transition that also baffles us. Or the flashback of Charley Wade shooting Eladio as Sam contemplates the remembered scene, followed by Pilar being teased by a coworker: "Steve called for you." Earlier, Chet entered Big O's roadhouse pulling something unseen from his pocket (a pistol? no, a photograph) moments before shots *are* actually fired, with his gesture eerily anticipating the unsettling event to come. And this episode ends with a screaming young woman just as we transition through a quick cut to a heated parent-teacher meeting: "tearin' everything down! Tearin' down our heritage, tearin' down our history."

Accentuating how fully we are encouraged to be self-conscious about generic patterns, the film is edited in ways more random and fragmented than the screenplay itself suggests. After Sam and Pilar end up in bed, Sayles's script cuts silently, sequentially to the next morning, with Pilar's daughter Paloma inquiring playfully about the night before. But the film actually punctuates the love making with a scene of Chet stopping by Otis's house in order to ask about native American photographs, in turn followed by Sam at the café announcing to Hollis, "I think Buddy put a bullet in him." Only at this point does the morning-after scene occur, of Paloma addressing her mother. Again, the effect of so dissociative a method is initially disorienting, compelling the viewer mentally to rearrange temporal sequences but also enforcing the film's larger thematic strain: making us aware of narrative intersections as they weave disparate moments into a heterogeneous plot that reminds us of the cross-border logic underlying all meaning-making activities. The balance among oppositions is always being negotiated in the film, leaving us alternately unsettled and exhilarated, slightly baffled in the absence of familiar narrative signposting and yet (by the very process of doing the mental gymnastics ourselves) gratified at the unifying insights that emerge unexpectedly.

Compounding this fragmented style are the actual cuts *between* scenes, compelling attention to the border crossing involved in cinematic sequence. Sometimes, transitions are made via traditional straight or contrast cuts (the least self-conscious method), or through L cuts (or split edits) where audio and visual images misalign. But as well, fade-ins and -outs, dissolves and wipes, all punctuate *Lone Star*, as do a series of panning morph shots; each may seem at first arbitrary but collectively they further reinforce our self-consciousness about cinematic borders themselves. Simple straight cuts introduce the film by establishing a baseline against which to measure later transitions, among the first of which is the fade-out to black screen that follows Sam's efforts to release Pilar's son from jail, as he fondly watches her leave the room, then transitioning abruptly to sweaty Mikey, Del, and Cliff running an obstacle course. Soon after, a more complicated and gradual transition occurs, as elderly Minnie Bledsoe slowly recalls Big O's saloon back in 1957: the camera dollies close in on her before a crossover dissolve projects her fading face on dancers at the roadhouse, where a young, handsome Otis Payne appears serving Charley Wade a beer. Why is Minnie's face sustained in this fashion as she tells in voice-over about Wade, the "Grim Reaper"? Is it simply to register that this is *her* memory, or is it something more? And why should this segue differ from other flashbacks in the film? At other times, adjoining scenes are presented as parallel images, for example, in the shift from young Otis on his knees at the roadhouse to his older self walking into the same room, without a slide or transition.

The questions mount up as scenes blend together and as we mentally shift among expectations for convergent genres, from the Western to those for noir or mystery. But consider further the effect of Sayles's fade-outs to black screen, as when Sam stares after Pilar (described above), or when Enrique admires his boss Mercedes in her expensive automobile before the scene shifts to Delmar on the army base. In each case, the blackout seems intended to define a complete separation of two distinct episodes, drawing attention to itself *as* a cut, a transition or border between scenes that becomes dramatically inflated to register their difference. Later, after Pilar admits Eladio Cruz was her father, Sam stares back at her before a fade-out to black screen once again, as the next scene follows Chet wandering into Big O's to look at Indian photographs on the wall. The lovers' discussion of fathers will switch to Otis's discussion of patrimony (Native American, but also his own with Del and Chet), though this similar theme is hardly apparent at first, requiring a deliberate dark pause between scenes to alert us. When Sam leaves Big O's roadhouse after finally hearing about the actual account of Charley Wade's death, the transition to him sitting the next day at the drive-in is presented once more through a black screen fade, causing us again to pause—though in this case, presumably giving Sam as well a night to ponder all he has learned. Each of these fade-out cuts makes sense in context, though each has a slightly different effect on our understanding. Moreover, it is clear from these examples that the black-screen transition introduces a psychological tension that is not otherwise released or resolved.

After all, transitions in the film are sometimes made without a cut but simply as a continuous pan in space that can suggest either continuity or tension. Recall the slide from Cody talking of "coloreds" with Sam at the bar to Cliff and Priscilla sitting together, a conversation that forms at once an extension of Cody's visual field and a denunciation of his rant. The harsh racial border nurtured by Cody is dissolved in the very panning shot itself as it sweeps us into a sympathetic pairing that newly defines other borders, between army and civilian, still active and retired. At times like this, the film's very aesthetic compels an interpretation mildly yet persuasively different from its declared themes. By contrast to this visual pan, Sayles offers an acoustic equivalent with a different effect in the straight cut that divides Enrique knotting rope for his girlfriend from Pilar musing in her chair, as both listen to the same music across the cut. Later, a less resonant acoustic transition occurs when Sam and Pilar dance in the café to a Freddy Fender song that bleeds across the cut to them then making love in bed.[14] The sound track itself links characters as fully as any visual sequence, perhaps more so, given the psychological links suggested by musical transitions.

Of all the cuts between scenes, Stuart Dryburgh's morphing pan constitutes what many agree is the film's most interesting cinematic transition.[15] "I used theatrical transitions so that there would be this feeling [that] there wasn't a big seam between the past and the present," Sayles himself admitted. "Basically, you get a background for your tight shot from 1996, you pan away, and when you pan back to where the guy telling the story was, it's somebody completely different, and it's 1957. There's not a cut or a dissolve. I wanted to reinforce the feeling that what's going on *now* is totally connected to the past. It's almost not like a memory—you don't hear the harp playing. It's *there*" (Carson 1999, 204). This pan—the first in the film that is not a straight cut, indicating its importance—occurs with Hollis's initial account of Buddy's confrontation of Charley Wade, sliding us back from the present, pivoting on a tortilla basket, revealing the café now less spotless as lighting shifts from day to night. Following the emotionally fraught standoff, Buddy's "Mas cervesa, por favor" is echoed by Hollis in the present, with the camera panning from Buddy's face to

Sam's staring gaze. This species of morphing pan occurs half a dozen times in the film, each with dramatic effect, drawing attention to the fractured elements separating temporal borders and yet to the porous process by which past and present intermingle, each shaping the other. We have no reason this early to doubt Hollis's constructed narrative, though similar efforts by others will prove inauthentic, making us later wonder at this early account. And the morphing pan lends a signature style to these moments of reconstruction in the teetering balance between a present that actively configures the past, and a recalcitrant past that continues to have untimely consequences in the present.

Once more, Sayles compels us to reconsider the way history has been forged in the Western, reminding us of the recurrent theme in John Ford's films at once celebrating and exposing those views of the past that distort what actually occurred. The distinction is famously enunciated in *The Man Who Shot Liberty Valance*: "This is the West, sir. When the legend becomes fact, print the legend."[16] Yet one might also agree that Sayles's simple crosscuts in the film generate a different psychological effect from its morphing pans, as Jack Ryan has argued: "The harsh cutting into and out of the past underscores Sam's feelings. The glides into the past serve as a visual metaphor representing the memory of the speaker; the edits, which are abrupt, announce a memory that a character has internalized, something he or she is unwilling to share with others" (2010, 230). The cinematic transitions alert us to psychological tendencies and emotional responses, with cuts brusquely isolating characters within their own consciousnesses, while morphing pans suggest something of a shared, borderless agreement.

Sometimes that transition works in only one direction, as when Minnie describes Wade as a "Grim Reaper," followed by the dissolve *into* Big O's roadhouse saloon. The camera immediately focuses on Wade threatening Otis, shooting the bar up after closing it down, followed by a pan morph from Wade walking out the door to an older, present-day Otis now recalling his youthful self as he cleans and tidies up that same bar—almost as if he were repairing damage from decades before: "Course I was young and full of beans then." Not only do we return to the present with Otis, not Minnie, but that sequence underscores her claim for a psychopathic Wade. As well, the scene obfuscates the disarming lie Otis persists in telling, that Wade was never seen again in Frontera. This form of cinematic transition may suggest a truthful (or at least fully believed) account, but the account is not in fact confirmed, contrary to Davis and Womack's claim: "At each point in the film when Sayles shifts, through ellipsis, from the present into the recounted past, he purposively demonstrates that what we are receiving is a 'version' of history" (1998, 475).[17] On the contrary, what links the two time periods in these morphing pans is simply a cross-border identity, a fusing of past and present that occurs physically on screen, but that could be a "version," a deliberate lie, or possibly actual history. Sayles again keeps doubt alive about popular constructions of the American past, which in the West perhaps especially has so often shrouded or buried ugly facts within the grandly idealizing template of the Western.

Notably, this fusion occurs along the Rio Grande when Pilar leaves Sam after their talk, and Stuart Dryburgh's camera glides over the river to a scene of them also talking there in 1972. Young Pilar refuses to agree that what they are doing is wrong, and the morphing pan then continues at the end of *this* scene in the same direction (right to left), back to an older Sam with his muttered "Me neither." The sequence enforces the persistence of his feelings over time, seeming to stretch his agreement with young Pilar (in her rejection of their relationship as a "sin") over nearly a quarter century unabated. That transition into and out of the past, which looms so ponderously, is confirmed by the next morphing pan that begins with Chucho Montoya conversing with Sam, who has traveled to Mexico to find out about the death long before of Mercedes's husband, Eladio Cruz. The camera turns left from a close-up of Chucho's face, past a billboard to a road, as his voice describes Eladio in 1957 changing the tire of a battered truck. After Wade executes Cruz, we watch Chucho under the arroyo, hiding as approaching steps anticipate his discovery. Yet in the slow pan upward, we realize it is not Wade in the past but Sam in the present, oddly suggesting that he is taking Wade's place, standing in his stead, stepping into murderous possibilities as the film itself denies that sliding conflation.

Later, a different morphing pan does in fact conjoin present and past, compelling Mercedes to recognize her responsibility for herself and others. The scene begins with the sound of rapids as young Mercedes is saved from the turbid Rio Grande by a charming Eladio Cruz. Panning left, the camera then evokes her in the present reminiscing about that crossing, as Enrique's partner Anselma (who uncannily resembles the younger Mercedes) is saved by him. Mercedes's present has emerged from a past that is embodied in front of her eyes (and ours), while her resistance to accepting that transition is undone by the pan itself. The border she has erected in her life dissolves with the morph, which is confirmed by her changing her mind, refusing to call the Border Patrol against her own avatar.[18]

The most compelling morphing pan is suitably the last, when finally the film's mystery is unfolded and revealed, or so we presume. This version of the killing of Charley Wade follows a by now predictable pattern, of Otis acquiescing to Sam's desire for truth, with the camera closing in on his face in 1996 then to turn towards the door as Wade enters the café accompanied by Hollis in 1957. Wade brutally beats Otis, only to be interrupted by Buddy, who enters and appears to shoot him. This final retelling, however, depends on the camera withholding a view, first focusing on Hollis having drawn his weapon to lend his support to Buddy, but only belatedly panning down Buddy's body to reveal his own pistol still holstered. The effect of this uninterrupted pan is to keep the past alive, first as myth, then as corrective fact, but all as an extension of the ongoing present, figured convincingly if misleadingly in memory. As well, paradoxically, the sliding pan lays the past to rest, pushing it almost literally (or rather, visually) aside, finally allowing it to be forgotten. The whole series of pan morphs has prepared us for this sequence, where the weight of the past and its ramifying effects are at last made clear.[19] Yet if the film's formal features expose how easily past and present can be elided, they also clarify how much of a two-way street that elision finally proves to be in allowing the present to transform the past as fully as the past has determined the present. The film offers less a critique of the casual idealizing assumptions so often found at the heart of the Western than it sharply reveals what is actually at stake in holding them. And its morphing pans suggest how fragmented our achieved knowledge continues to be, with no one in command of a comprehensive view, leaving us with simply a collection of separate perspectives and differing bases of knowledge.[20]

CONCLUSION: "FORGET THE ALAMO"?

Part of the reason that Lone Star repeatedly troubles easy transitions among borders—between racial or ethnic groups, between parent and child, between men and women, between civic and social factions, and perhaps most importantly, between past and present—is to define the elisions the Western so often makes in moving toward its enforced resolutions. Sayles actively wants to confront us with the deep conventionality of borders, their arbitrary distinction among a set of values, experiences, languages, temporalities, and landscapes. That has, after all, been the province of the Western, a genre based on weighted contrasts between farmer and rancher, East and West, masculine and feminine sensibility, civic restraint and individual liberty, but it is also a genre that in its conservative tendencies has tended to confirm the supposedly innate configurations of those borders. Sayles, in other words, uses the materials of the genre to undo itself, exposing not only its functional terms but the premises by which we more generally comport ourselves in an uncertain world. And his cinematic cuts are there to provoke us into wondering at time-honored boundaries, to realize in the differences between them how powerfully formal borders work, provoking divergent responses with diverse cues.

The film notoriously ends with Sam and Pilar recognizing their ongoing love of each other under the shadow of incest. Sitting in front of the dilapidated drive-in, Sam has finally told her of their father and about how fully each felt overshadowed by him, needing to strike out on their own. The suspicion of racism (which both had assumed was their parents' reason for wanting to separate them) has been "defeated by a deeper prejudice," in Mikey's words. Still, the consequences of their knowledge are far from clear, and their willingness to ignore this deepest of cultural borders seems at once liberating and evasive, part of a much-traveled course in American culture of trying to escape the past, lighting out for the territory ahead of the rest. Pilar, the devoted history teacher, seems almost nonchalant in her willingness to ignore what has occurred, to treat it as inconsequential: "All that other stuff, all that history, the hell with it, right?" And her (and Lone Star's) final words—"Forget the Alamo"—seem deeply ironic in the aftermath of a film that has shown how little we can forget, how pliable but finally insidious all borders are, recurrently reestablishing themselves despite the toll they inevitably take.[21]

The closing shots of the ramshackle drive-in before the credits roll suggest that even with a rickety screen, its panels worn and tumbled down, with an audience long since departed, borders still prevail. We might well wish the various intersecting histories of the film, with all the consequences we have seen (both collective and individual), could somehow be ignored, forgotten, simply swept aside. Sam has already expressed this feeling in bed with Pilar when she comments on the absence of photos in his room— "it's nothing I want to look back on"—to which she rightly, dismissively responds "Like your story is over!" The entire film has shown us the futility of trying to escape history or otherwise to ignore its effects—in short, to assume our stories are ever finally "over."

The ending lends a resonance to Sam's efforts to uncover the mystery of Charley Wade's death, in his intense investment in revealing a Texas history that has remained silent, indeed that has been deliberately hidden (and requiring the film, in the process of bringing it to light, to mingle its Western materials with noir and mystery, both powerful genres tilted towards the past). Still, this is not to agree with the claim advanced by Todd Davis and Kenneth Womack: "By letting Buddy's legendary deeds on behalf of Frontera survive, Sam embraces, rather than disavows, the border town's ethnically beleaguered past" (1998, 480). The border to the past is never so easily traversed, at least as Sayles imagines it, nor can we be secure in either hewing to knowledge or casually putting it aside.[22] Sam's sardonic farewell to Otis and Hollis, that "Buddy's a goddam legend. He can handle it," seems not so much a testament to either pragmatism or idealism but rather a sober recognition that some knowledge is neither welcome nor salutary. Knowing will change little. Which thus makes Pilar's greeting to Sam as she joins him at the drive-in at the end, "When's the picture start?" a mildly ironic if self-conscious reference to the film we are watching, here as the closing credits are about to roll.[23] For as the two stare up at the derelict screen, admitting to having long felt "connected," they nonetheless acknowledge even in verbally abandoning the past ("We start from scratch") that, as their sober looks affirm, some borders are obdurate, not easily traversed.[24]

4

ALTERNATIVE FACTS IN
THE THREE BURIALS OF
MELQUIADES ESTRADA

Dramatically reinforcing the pattern traced in previous chapters, *The Three Burials of Melquiades Estrada* confirms the enduring power of genre in a Western that barely appears as such until midway through. Even then, the signs are unclear. True, once again we're in Texas with tall hats and high-heeled boots, but those semantic vouchers hardly persuade us that this is more than just a film set in the West. The opening sequences are discontinuous, as in *Lone Star* (though as well, of course, in many other recent popular films), shifting between past and present, domestic and public scenes, real-estate sales and job-hunting, even a burial. What emerges is a series of apparently random efforts to cope with a murder, beginning with an autopsy and the victim identified, though an interested party inexplicably persists in wanting to know ever more. Indeed, like *Bad Day at Black Rock*, that central figure holds back the rationale for his obsession in a plot that remains a mystery well into the first hour, leaving us unavailingly ignorant of determining causes driving the narrative.

When things do begin to become clearer, the film still hardly appears syntactically a Western, with neither nostalgia for a simpler past, nor investment in the triumph of law and order, nor contemplation of the redemptive power of violence, nor (perhaps more importantly) attention to appropriate forms of masculine behavior. All those familiar aspects seem absent, though Jones does introduce gestures that remind us fleetingly of generic demands at the same time that his characters appear more inscrutable, less forthright, with backgrounds unfamiliar and motives that remain obscure. Such characterization itself seems mildly alien for a Western (as opposed to spy films or mysteries or noir), since the genre has tended to celebrate a certain individual transparency. Figures, male and female, generally are what they seem in the common fashion of western decorum, at least of an earlier social era. And any review of the history of Westerns confirms plainspokenness as a regional virtue, with tight-lipped manners expressing what is genuinely felt, making others generally transparent. Yet character for Jones appears oddly enigmatic, slow to emerge, just as the meaning of the central event, the shooting of Melquiades Estrada (Julio Cedillo), likewise seems indeterminate, with little disclosed to help the viewer understand what has occurred. We submit to nearly half the film without knowing what has led to Melquiades's homicide, or able to make a surmise, and not until his best friend, the rancher Pete Perkins (Tommy Lee Jones), seizes control of these disparate scenes does the narrative begin to coalesce.

Only after Pete abducts the guilty border patrolman responsible for Mel's death, and compels him to return the corpse to its Mexican home for proper burial, do the disconnected materials (semantic as well as syntactic) of the film's first half come together as a resurrection of the Western itself. Those "materials" include the epic, west-Texas landscape; the conflict of lone rancher and western lawman; and the stalwart effort to restore justice to a scene of ruthless murder. In this, the film differs only marginally in themes embodied in Sayles's *Lone Star*, though it offers a more vehement (if seemingly convoluted) reassessment of stock gestures long since drained of imaginative life, thrown back at us in unexpected sequences. Jones, in short, presents a meta-Western meant to question bona fides, boldly testing the genre's assumptions, offering a cinematic arrangement that proves itself appreciably more fragmentary and disjointed than Sayles's. In the process, it affirms more forcibly how fully genre conventions themselves effectively appear to create the facts that confirm its informing myth.

CORPSES AND QUESTIONS

Following the credit sequence, the film opens with the stark view of an autopsy table, a corpse already laid out, which we gradually learn is a man named Melquiades, killed violently for what seems no reason at all.[1] The premise is not unlike that of *Lone Star*, pivoting on the urgent need to understand why a murder has taken place, though that conceit is hardly characteristic of the Western (any more than of noir or mystery or thriller). Yet Jones resists focusing a mélange of scenes into a predictable plot and instead scatters accounts so as to seduce the viewer into projecting generic assumptions onto his plot. Isolated events become shaped willy-nilly by assumed formulaic conventions, in this case into a more or less familiar Western trajectory. Surprisingly, however, we belatedly discover how fully expectations have been upended by facts in the process of fulfilling a solemn Western vow to return a dead body home, thus validating ritual codes. For despite ways in which the film encourages viewers to "read" it as Western, as part of a generic pattern (however muddied and impure), Jones nonetheless suddenly swerves at the end to cast doubt on the alleged "home" to which Westerns so often return, and thereby swerves away from all we have seen and understood. We are left to wonder at what has occurred, since despite multiple burials of Pete's friend Melquiades, his identification of the town of Jiménez and the family life he lived there seems to have been a complete fabrication. Among the mysteries that remain is whether this "return" to a place that everything suggests is not actually Melquiades's home is in fact a testament to our own insistent desire to believe in him and his account despite the emergent facts.

The film itself tends nonetheless to resist such scrutiny, distorting the facts so fully in its first half that questions seem to multiply like rabbits unwatched, with bewildering flashbacks and fractured scenes observed from diverse angles defying us to ascertain what holds it together. Unexpectedly, midway through, *Three Burials* abruptly shifts into a more familiar chronological flow, with the prospect of a viable narrative all of a sudden appearing mysteriously.[2] Partly this seems attributable to Pete's commanding decision to honor his vow to his friend, returning Mel's body home and thereby dictating a narrative thrust that will not be denied. But as well, in a pattern recognizable from other late Westerns, we realize that the syntactic fragments of the Western that emerged earlier have unpredictably prompted our own residual faith in the genre, which finally brings it alive once again. Melquiades Estrada's actual body, like Charley Wade's remembered one in *Lone Star*, has come to represent the very conventions to which the film pays homage, in first being simply covered up, then officially interred, and finally invested with a mythic resonance through restoration to native soil. Both films, in other words, offer a sustained rumination on the Western that reminds us of nothing so much as *The Man Who Shot Liberty Valance*, which ceremoniously presented the coffined dead body of John Wayne as the very emblem of a merging of Western fact and legend. Ford followed Sturges and Daves in reconsidering the genre he had long extolled, but did so more dramatically by selecting noirish monochromatic lighting; by heightening theatrical melodrama with clearly fabricated, back-lot Hollywood sets and frenzied acting styles; by focusing on shadowed interiors; and by selecting middle-aged actors who reinvent themselves as youthful figures. Variously, in all these cinematic choices having little to do with actual narrative pacing, Ford anticipated questions about the genre that would transform it in its later stages.[3] In the coffin holding the dearly departed John Wayne that stands at the center of *Liberty Valance*, the death of Western heroism itself is represented, just as it is also resuscitated in the long flashback that forms the film's central narrative. Four decades later, and a decade after Sayles, the corpse of the Western reappears in the very body of the film's titular figure.

Yet our realization in *Three Burials* that this is occurring fails to happen immediately, despite its opening with the corpse of Melquiades. Only gradually—that is, about midway through—do dislocated scenes pull together (almost despite themselves), enforcing a generic structure not quite warranted by the sequence presented to us: west Texas landscapes posed against small- town civic tension; celebrations of male camaraderie clashing with challenges to loyalty and honor; frustration with justice in the absence of legal remedy. While such staples of the Western seem unintelligible in this film at first, the forced march of its second half defines a narrative trajectory that elicits meaning from incoherence, replicating Ford's triumph in celebrating a genre he simultaneously deconstructs. That is more or less true of each of the films discussed so far, though each achieves its ends differently. The mystery that prevails through much of *Bad Day at Black Rock* is sustained through *Lone Star* and *Three Burials*, though Jones's film is more splintered than Sayles's, more destabilizing as viewing experience, frustratingly open-ended and even inscrutable by the end. Our gradual acceptance of *Three Burials as* a Western is finally challenged and undercut, making us wonder at how the deception has been set in motion.

Unlike the structure of Elmore Leonard's story, "3:10 to Yuma," which offers itself to being adapted cinematically in relatively straightforward versions, Jones's film defies the viewer to know quite what has occurred. In the process, customary Western ideals of loyalty, honor, fidelity, and restraint find themselves undercut in the very ambiguity Melquiades provokes as a figure. Pete's fervent dedication to him proves devotion to what increasingly appears a delusion, which renders his allegiance to Western standards (for promises, for burial, for extralegal solutions) at best somehow misplaced and, at worst, thoroughly inimical to civic ideals. The genre's long-standing focus on the legitimate obligations of masculinity comes under suspicion throughout *Three Burials*, where accountability itself seems shadowed by doubt, and where presumably fitting behavior (so otherwise clear in the genre's syntax) seems undermined by the facts as they are adduced. Against logic, however, viewers are lured into accepting a generic view of the film. In the absence of any confidence that Melquiades has been finally buried at "home"—indeed, that Melquiades is actually the man, husband, and father that we and Pete had presumed—we are left to wonder at a narrative that has convinced us of a resolution based on little more than a handful of generic constraints themselves.

It should come as little surprise that Jones delighted in his film's defiance of narrative structure: "If you turn the movie sound off and just watch the movement of it and try to look at it the way a dog or a bird would, not recognize any shapes, it's quite pleasing, it's a balletic event. It moves beautifully, the shapes, and colors have an abstraction" (T. Jones 2005). Yet even with sound on, the "beautiful delicate colors" that he admires are drained of meaning by the film's disruption of straightforward sequence, including multiple flashbacks and the maddeningly varied perspectives devised by screenwriter Guillermo Arriaga.[4] This is characteristic of *Three Burials* more obviously than *Lone Star*, suggesting that a decade after Sayles's script, the means of both disrupting a viewer's expectations and enforcing them generically had escalated, just as discontinuities in other contemporary films had become de rigueur. Douglas Pye observes of the film that "the fragmentation of our experience (39 scenes in 54 minutes, with constant movement between past and present) provides brief snapshots of a society that lacks any cohesiveness. We see several locations but have no sense of their spatial relationship to one another" (2010, 3). And he adds that a "further effect of the fragmented and elliptical first half is to enable the film to restrict access to context and motive without obviously doing so" (2010, 3). Pye's shrewd assessment of the film's sleight of hand is worth pursuing more specifically with Melquiades's first appearance at Perkin's ranch, followed by the brief five-second scene of the killer, Mike Norton (Barry Pepper), burying him the first time. Yet we are unaware that this is Norton since the figure is seen from behind, nor are we aware that these are the remains of Melquiades (although the film's title should clue us in). Immediately, Pete appears in front of the hospital after viewing the corpse (though that temporal progression is also not at first clear), causing us to wonder whether this "first burial" (as the onscreen intertitle announces) is only Pete's memory since he appears right after (though again we soon realize this could not have been). In short, as the parentheses here suggest, we keep being shifted back and forth. Forced to pause, stymied by the exchange with Sheriff Frank Belmont (Dwight Yoakum), we can only begin to grasp the intense emotional effect the death has had on Pete, without understanding why this should be. The film simply seems to delight at this point in moving the viewer around, disrupting expectations.

Soon after, possibilities clash as the stakes seem to rise, with Arriaga shifting from mildly disquieting sequences to actively misleading ones. Pete walks into the Sands Motel Restaurant to query a border agent about his favored rifle round, only to be followed by Norton walking out of that same restaurant prior to killing Melquiades. Later, a simple one-second flashback occurs when Norton watches his wife strut into the Odessa mall, as he recalls the dead Melquiades. In each case, narrative continuity is sacrificed for a sequentially disruptive scene.[5] Moreover, the meanings of these scenes are eerily transformed by the frequency with which they are shot in close-up, often gradually intensified (whether Norton, Pete, or Belmont), intimating (however misleadingly) that just such a focus on faces might offer a passing clue to character, in expressions of regret and intent, of decisiveness or impassivity. Occasionally, we are simply bewildered by such cinematic facial scrutiny, as in the strange two-shot of Pete and Lou Ann Norton (January Jones), after he has abducted her husband and bound her, both now facing the camera in an arrangement that seems as much kind hospitality as admonitory threat.

Had Arriago wanted to settle for a more conventional screenplay, he could have simply unraveled the knotted chronology of the film's first half, beginning instead some months before the killing and alternating in a customary chronological progression from Pete's first meeting of Melquiades and the Nortons' arrival in the Permian Basin town. The budding friendship between rancher and Mexican hand might have played out against the gradual estrangement of the displaced Cincinnati couple, while the side story of the waitress Rachel (Melissa Leo) and her running affairs with Pete and Belmont would have woven through the narrative. But contemporary films themselves have more generally become more "knotted" as part of the way nearly all genres have evolved, and Westerns are hardly exempt.

Still, Arriaga is not simply hewing to popular pressure in structuring his screenplay as he does. He actively adopts this typical strategy for thematic and generic reasons in a calculated effort to drain away the cumulative investment we might otherwise feel in these separate relationships. He seems to want to counter the normal course of understanding by isolating characters from the sequence of their lives, attenuating any insight into personalities by focusing on isolated moments plucked from a larger experiential or interpretive order. That offers an important advance (or at least, divergence) from earlier Westerns and differs from the effect achieved in Sayles's own self-consciously fragmented screenplay. The swelling arc of Pete and Melquiades's friendship, like the gradual dissolution of the Nortons' marriage, does not quite refuse to matter in Arriaga's screenplay, though it does seem less compelling narratively than other patterns and moments. That helps explain why scenes are so often repeated or later filled in, offered from different perspectives or otherwise redacted.

Take the tabloid television show of Johnny confronting his wife about their fraught marriage, which appears a few days before Melquiades's death and then once again three weeks later in a rebroadcast south of the border. In the first, Norton is unaware, mounting his bored wife from behind as she aimlessly watches the estranged couple; in the second, attending to the show with amused Mexicans alongside the road, Norton breaks into tearful emotional sobs. The doubling of this television scene seems to reflect a crucial difference in Norton as somehow transformed by the woeful experience of being kidnapped, then forced to walk south to Mexico. Yet in fact, Norton's changed response can also be viewed as little more than silly and sentimental, part of pop cultural inanity, and certainly revealing nothing of changed psychology, before or after.

Other actions in the film resonate with similar ambivalence, often replicated by different characters at different moments, sometimes lending a certain recognizable pattern to events without furnishing any greater insight into motive or intent. Early on, Mike Norton races after two border crossers, beating them brutally into submission in a scene echoed later by

Pete, riding after Norton himself, tracking him down. At one point early in his own pursuit of them, Sheriff Belmont carefully takes aim at Pete riding off with his captive, only to decide not to pull the trigger—again, a scene replicated almost exactly in Pete's subsequent decision not to shoot Mike as he scrambles to escape. Earlier, Pete callously slams Norton's face against his truck, then again later whacks him in the nose when commandeering his boots, both of which correspond to Norton's initial breaking of a desperate Mariana's nose as she tries to flee from the border patrol—and her own calm smashing of a coffee jug into his face as reprisal. In each exact repetition, behavior is revealed as somehow derivative, even clichéd, exposing a crudely impersonal aspect to events that simply reproduce an earlier pattern.

These deliberate scenic cleavages and selective repetitions in Arriago's script have the effect of draining interest in the customary developments of relationships, since neither characters nor affiliations ever seem to change or evolve. Instead, the various reiterations of the plot tend to concentrate our attention on the central death itself, anticipating it, recalling it, trying to make sense of it, with the actual killing presented onscreen only forty minutes in. A brief earlier flashback to Norton bending over Melquiades's bloodied body with his own bloodied hands (the flashback that torments Norton at the Odessa mall) occurs immediately prior to a sequence of Lou Ann a week before as part of a foursome with Melquiades, happily dancing in his arms to a Freddy Fender song. Again, the scene emphasizes less loss of affection for Mike than simply the presence (and absence) of Melquiades himself.

More importantly, such scenes expose the stark chasm that lurks just beneath the surface of relationships, adding to the weight of Melquiades's death. Tommy Lee Jones observed that "If you read this script, really it doesn't look like anybody's saying anything that actually matters" (T. Jones 2005). And the dialogue endorses his assessment, via the strained exchanges and alliances in which basic understanding goes unacknowledged. Notably, Sheriff Burnett and Pete never concede their mutual involvement with Rachel. More eerily, Pete refuses to reveal he actually knows Lou Ann, having spent convivial time as a foursome with her, Rachel, and Melquiades. When he finally breaks into the Norton's trailer to drag Mike away, his declaration to her is mercilessly blunt: "You scream again I'll kill you." And the strange ruthlessness of this long scene is compounded by being filmed almost entirely in close-ups, shifting abruptly from face to face inquiringly (first Pete, then Norton, then Lou Ann, back and forth) as it becomes clear how little they actually know of one another. Or as Pete queries Norton—"You tell her what you did?"—before then announcing to Lou Ann in Spanish ("él mató Melquiades Estrada"), though he is clearly aware she speaks no Spanish.

In fact, the Nortons' ignorance of all things Hispanic reinforces this dearth of mutual curiosity or knowledge registered in the film, perhaps mirrored by Melquiades's own broken English. Pete alone is perfectly bilingual, at home in both linguistic worlds, though the film suggests that such competence is hardly essential to cultural acknowledgment, much less sympathy. As the blind old man (Levon Helm) explains to Pete when they arrive at his desert homestead on their trek south: "I like listening to this Mexican radio station. I can't understand anything, but I like the way Spanish sounds, don't you?" Later, again in a scenic repetition, this sentiment will silently be endorsed by four Mexicans on the trail watching reality TV, not understanding a word they hear but enthralled by the drama nonetheless. In accord with Jones's larger claim that nobody is "saying anything that actually matters," language itself seems to serve little purpose (contrary to the view Sayles more conventionally advances in Lone Star). Instead, the repeated exchanges that occur through the film seem to match the effect of its recurrent encounters: leaving us focused on simply the death of Melquiades itself, without really moving closer to understanding it.

Granted, the film itself seamlessly alternates between English and Spanish (via subtitles), which would seem to contradict the unavailing quality of verbal exchanges. Yet while that alternation draws attention to language, it has the effect nonetheless of reinforcing border constraints (constraints it also questions) and augmenting more generally the film's investment in the resolute inscrutability of character. Instead of granting us fuller knowledge of motives or emotional commitments, *Three Burials* regularly configures characters as largely formulaic and fixed, if no less intriguing for the ways in which they nonetheless behave. They seem themselves to embody the very constraints of the Western, with the plot's discontinuities and their ineffective expressions tending to focus our understanding according to generic prescriptions.

Lou Ann may best embody this aspect of the film, in what Douglas Pye identifies as the "difficulty of knowing other people" (2010, 4), not only as isolated outsider or as a figure limited by language but more importantly as someone unclear about her own nebulous desires. Despite the film's dislocations, her evolving consciousness gradually emerges via muted expressions, as she eyes an overweight woman in a two-piece bathing suit squeezing into her trailer. That explains her earlier comment to Mike that she feels fat "a little bit," as we suppose her imagining herself in west Texas twenty years on. Afterwards, sitting with Mike outside their trailer at dusk, she wordlessly reaches out with a mournful look, unaware that Melquiades is dead, or that her husband is the killer. Two scenes later again, the waitress Rachel nods to Lou Ann in the restaurant in silent assent about the strains in her marriage to Bob. All this is meant to explain why she might be willing to stray in her marriage, though not quite enough to explain why she accompanies Melquiades to a motel on a double date. After Mike is abducted by Pete, Lou Ann disappears from the film for half an hour only to appear briefly in the restaurant to inform Rachel that "I hate this place." Next, she is seen leaving town on a bus, heading back north to Cincinnati as Mike is abducted south to Mexico. The transition from initially content home buyer to disaffected ex-wife only a few months later is presented as at once strange and predictable, with Lou Ann unable to articulate her feelings or otherwise to understand her life.

It is worth reiterating a point made elsewhere in this book, that as much as any genre, the Western has over the course of its history energetically focused on domestic concerns, with threats of violence often presented (unlike noir or mystery or action-adventure) as affronts against the nuclear family. In *Three Burials*, such concern is pointedly absent, though the very failure to achieve a sustained relationship becomes itself a significant gauge of its generic inclinations. Lou Ann's ruptured relationship with Mike, Rachel's unapologetically adulterous liaisons, Pete's somberly solitary life are each a reminder of what might have been, with the tabloid television complaints of Johnny and his wife giving fulsome expression to a more generally felt absence of affection or domestic unity. By contrast, Melquiades's idealized vision of family life, articulated in his rhapsodic account to Pete, stands as something like a testament to more familiar Western aspirations, from Ringo's expression to Dallas in *Stagecoach* ("I asked you to marry me, didn't I?") down to the present. That such a vision may have been fabricated does little to deny its generic centrality.

Yet part of the failure of that vision in *Three Burials* is due to how little characters reveal, seeming inscrutable or otherwise mysterious to each other as well as to us, with the semantic and syntactic aspects pointing to a generic Western cross-fertilized by noir and mystery components (once again, as in *Bad Day* and *Lone Star*). Here, characters act out of inexplicable anger (helping explain Mike's life) or petulant boredom (Rachel's) or some deep sense of nostalgia (which appears to explain Pete) but otherwise remain largely unknowable. And the most dramatic enigma is represented by Melquiades, who claims to have left his wife and children five years before he glowingly describes them to Pete (though again, we later discover he may have had no family at all). History appears to have become irrelevant, with memory fabricated out of nothing but sheer desire, for reasons never made clear. In this regard, Arriaga differs dramatically from writers of other late-Western screenplays in the intensity with which he focuses on fake facts unconnected to each other or to conventional history but simply alluring on the basis of their independent narrative fit.

Melquiades at last seems only a more extreme version of nearly everyone else in a film that offers character types we recognize, in a plot whose lack of sequence compels us to register scenes as simply a series of discrete moments and distinctive gestures. The fact that those gestures are largely generic, familiar from countless Westerns before and bolstered by other genre syntaxes, only induces belief in a reading that has not actually been borne out by the plot. Jones's film reminds us of nothing so much as the classic Western—of gunfight exchanges and transcendent landscapes, of fraught encounters with law coupled with issues of masculine self-construction—a reminder that becomes itself the film's most distinctive and ingenious premise.

GESTURES AND SCENES

The Three Burials of Melquiades Estrada brilliantly engages the essential features of the Western genre by inventively avoiding a narrative sequence we might recognize *as* Western and instead presenting a series of gestures and scenes that lure us into imposing a mythic plot on materials. The film introduces this deconstruction initially through framing itself, like other late Westerns: following a series of unremarkable scenes that begins with the credit sequence of a coyote being shot as it feeds on something half-buried, we are suddenly confronted with a gray-lit autopsy of a corpse, followed by the Nortons' bland encounter with a realtor selling them a trailer home, and then a brief encounter between Pete and Sheriff Belmont outside the hospital. These scenes seem random (disconnected, juxtaposed, unexplained) before the cinematographer, Chris Menges, frames the first encounter of Pete and Melquiades in a sequence that quotes the famous opening and closing shots of *The Searchers*: Melquiades on a horse viewed from a dark interior out beyond the frame of barn doors. Simple cinematography establishes the classic prism of the Western through which the scene needs to be interpreted, of natural landscape outlined by domestic structures that serve as barrier to the archetypical lone horseman, a space into which he cannot enter. In Menges's self-conscious framing, the entire weight of a genre tradition is quoted, made unavoidable, almost as if a musical score were suddenly heard announcing the Western's appearance. Jones himself indirectly drew attention to this moment, though intriguingly from a source more attuned to dance than sound, when he admitted: "I told people that the visual life of this scene comes from the Kabuki theater" (T. Jones 2005).

Following this revealing scene from Pete and Melquiades's past, the perceptual prism of the Western is reiterated in different forms, shifting from framing to color and back. Jones himself observed this in admiring the balletic quality of the film's abstract beauty, which is accentuated in the contrast between leaden interiors and vibrant, epic landscapes, New West and Old. Repeatedly, Chris Menges lights indoor scenes with a fluorescent sheen that imparts a cold, blue, stark sensibility, amplifying the transition from wide-open landscape to shabby double-wides and cinder-block motels where lackluster lives persevere. As soon as one ventures out, however, the camera captures the rich hues of the trans-Pecos panorama, its luminescent sunsets and redemptive scenery.[6] The film, punctuated and broken this way, reminds us of the scenic stamp of the genre after which such landscape is named: whether it is Pete and Melquiades holding the photo of his family against an opulent natural backdrop or Sheriff Belmont ready to pursue them as he gazes across the ridged horizon. Billowy cumulous clouds hover above green mesas, held in panning long shots that remind us of William Wyler's *The Big Country* (1958) or the transition from sepia into full-color landscape in the opening of *Butch Cassidy and the Sundance Kid*. Dazzling white sand dunes recall *The Wild Bunch* not simply as wide-screen spectacle of resplendent desert southwest but in a direct quotation of the scene in which Freddy Sykes (Edmund O'Brien) spooks the horses and sends them cascading down. Norton escapes from abduction through a field of piercingly yellow sun flowers, and later a drunken Pete surveys a sunset glowing beyond an outdoors cantina in Mexico, smiling drunkenly at all he sees. Each of Menges's lingering images registers the enduring appeal of Turner's supposedly empty frontier, reminding us that even when generic materials of the Western seem hollow, they still have power

Fig. 10. Melquiades Estrada introducing himself to Pete Perkins, inquiring about a cowboying job, in *The Three Burials of Melquiades Estrada* (Sony Pictures Classics).

Fig. 11. Ethan Edwards appearing at his brother Aaron's homestead, eager to see his sister-in-law Martha, in *The Searchers* (Warner Brothers).

Fig. 12. Driving cattle as workmanlike camaraderie, recalling *Red River,* updated in *The Three Burials of Melquiades Estrada* (Sony Pictures Classics).

to evoke a sense of personal transcendence without necessarily needing to be linked to a larger narrative sequence. These scenes—regularly sustained in extreme wide shots in direct contrast to the close-ups and two shots that offer a tight, even cramped visual frame—register a tradition of landscape celebration associated with the Western (as with no other genre), and their representation alone helps bring the genre alive once again.

Landscape aside, a host of other generic echoes are heard and seen to similar effect. A sustained, wordless episode with Pete and Mel driving cattle is framed as evocation of an identical scene in *Red River*, the Western that has most glowingly celebrated this iconic cowboy experience.[7] And Marco Beltrami's music takes its lead from Dimitri Tiomkin's exultant score for Hawks, likewise endorsing a joyous nostalgia through lyrical rhythms, investing the experience with a pathos that exceeds its status as simple cattle herding. Later, in a different key, a boy races his bicycle past the Nortons' trailer screaming "You goddamn son of a bitch" for no discernible reason, recalling the feral urchins who open *The Wild Bunch*, jaded before their teens. January Jones, as the bored baby-doll wife of a frustrated lawman, glows on-screen as a silent reminder of Grace Kelly in *High Noon* or Joanne Woodward in Fielder Cook's *Big Hand for the Little Lady* (1966), each with a blonde allure and deflated gaze that reflects their status as married women ill attuned to small-town western life. And of course, the film's opening focus on Melquiades's corpse forms a wry quotation of Wayne's dead body in *Liberty Valance* as the central enigma to be unraveled, the dead figure around which the film revolves. It may go without saying that nearly all Westerns are obsessed with the masculine body, perhaps nowhere as much as those moments when rigor mortis sets in. And given that burial itself is generically coded for the Western, the very title of Jones's film self-consciously fetishizes the process, all but declaring its generic bona fides.[8]

As well, a more characteristic generic strain emerges all but imperceptibly in the tensions associated with civic life, dramatized in the Western's recurrent contrast of riven Texas towns and supposedly more integral communities south of the border. As discussed in the last chapter, Ford's *Stagecoach*—widely supposed to have revived the genre after more than a decade in decline—concludes with the Ringo Kid and Dallas being "saved from the blessings of civilization" by fleeing to his Mexico ranch. Three decades later, *The Wild Bunch* embellishes that endorsement of border crossing, investing the fording of the Rio Grande with a powerful emotional impact. And following a long interlude in "my village, Mexico," as Angel (Jaime Sánchez) announces, the Bunch spends an evening celebrating with music, carousing and dancing before being given an idyllic farewell by the villagers to the nostalgic strains of "La Golondrina." More recently, Billy Bob Thornton's *All the Pretty Horses* (2000) offers a similarly idealized vision of Mexican fellowship and civic harmony.

This legacy might almost be said to have inspired Arriaga's script, in the central conceit of returning to paradise, burying the mistakenly murdered Melquiades in the land where Western dreams (at least, many of them) still reside. And Mel's plea to Pete to bury him in his hometown, far from "all the fucking billboards" north of the border, is matched by his later

Fig. 13. On the road south through Mexico, encountering the generosity of local ranchers, in *The Three Burials of Melquiades Estrada* (Sony Pictures Classics).

tribute to Jiménez as a surpassingly beautiful, almost magical setting. Pete accordingly shares this vision, expressed in his drunken phone call from an outdoor Chihuahua cantina for Rachel to join him: "I want you to come to Mexico. . . . Marry me, be my wife." The scene ends as they both hang up, each looking mournfully off, aware of the fantasy's conjoint lure and impossibility. Earlier, the film has occasionally aligned itself with this view of life south of the border, most obviously in the generosity shown by the Mexican ranchers that Pete and Mike meet on the road, sharing their meat and drink without thought of recompense. Still, this is a fleeting gesture, and the film finally resists any truly sustained distinction between Mexico and Texas, insisting on abstaining from Peckinpah's or Thornton's glorified Hispanic idyll.[9]

What does remain clear is that Anglo relationships are rendered largely meaningless and thinly two-dimensional, characterized by a lack of any deep-seated affection or even of basic kindness and minimal loyalty. That is admittedly part of the constellation of values assumed in the Western, where larger contemporary anxieties (as reflected in many other genres as well) are reflected in supposedly small-town crises. Like the townspeople of *High Noon* (along with countless other Western examples of civic inadequacy) who are exposed by their fear as craven and feckless, the figures in *Three Burials* are coldly mean spirited. A border officer snaps back at Pete; a realtor carries on an inane phone conversation as he advises the Nortons; self-centered neighbors kiss their pets or fiddle with umbrellas or drink their coffees without ever so much as acknowledging one another. Sheriff Belmont is as aggressive and thin skinned as Mike Norton, while Pete (as characteristically acted by Tommy Lee Jones) masks his feelings with an inexpressive demeanor and rudely abrasive demands. Belmont salaciously strokes Rachel at the restaurant in full view of others, calling her "You dirty bitch," arranging to meet "tomorrow" in a scene followed shortly by Mike Norton mechanically screwing his bored wife from behind as she watches the tabloid television show of a marriage gone bad. Norton arches his back and Lou Ann looks off, as the husband on TV is heard complaining "it's always the same, always the same," until his wife asks if he recalls "River Valley," to which he sentimentally responds: "Yes darling, I remember River Valley. And we were happy then. And we'll be happy again. I know it. Please, don't cry. There will always be a River Valley for us." His wife then intones, "I hope so, Johnny, I hope so." The mawkishness here registers not only the thin instability of the relationship but the lack of any emotional kinship at all, for either the TV couple or the Nortons. The sole exception to this brittle state of self-centered apathy is the friendship that develops between Pete and Melquiades, whose death prompts Pete to speak of him as "my son."

In short, *Three Burials* brings together however chaotically a wide assortment of gestures, scenes, and themes that have long burnished the Western. The central narrative itself, of accidental death and long journey to burial and redemption, though not itself an overly familiar plot, is anticipated by Anthony Mann's *The Naked Spur* (1953) and Budd Boetticher's *Ride Lonesome* (1959), along with *3:10 to Yuma*, each of which narrates the perils of an unstable group escorting a captive to justice. In that regard, the film invokes conventional genre moments—thematic as well as visual—without itself actually seeming to be a Western, inverting the process by which we understand the genre as emerging from plot rather than vice versa. In this case, the concentration on only one normally limited aspect of the Western (burial), repeating it multiple times in an effort to get it right, seems mildly idiosyncratic, in the need simply to place a body appropriately into the ground. Yet that very imperative, elaborated through signature generic facets, ends by enforcing an interpretation that the film would at first seem barely to support.

CONCLUSION: THE JOURNEY TO JIMÉNEZ

Only in the film's second half, beginning with the third of four sections ("The Journey"), does a straightforward narrative finally begin to emerge with the trip Pete Perkins demands Mike Norton make becoming the means by which significance is imposed on an otherwise meaningless death. Curiously, Pete could be considered a constitutive figure for this very book, in his willingness to wrench a series of disparate events into a narrative, and finally into a Western. But consider as well how eerily Arriaga's script resembles the tenor of Faulkner's *As I Lay Dying* (1930), which recounts the seemingly lunatic venture of the Bundren family to bury their mother, hauling Addie's stinking corpse forty miles across backwoods Mississippi, enduring flood, fire, and other adversities simply to fulfill a promise made to her long before. And the very senselessness of that promise becomes a strange testament to its regenerative power, uniting a dysfunctional family and keeping Addie's memory alive.

Three Burials traces a similar arc in Pete's demand that Mike help fulfill Melquiades's fervent wish to be buried in Jiménez, his avowed hometown. Mike is humiliated, beaten, and repeatedly threatened in a journey that slowly transforms him, bringing about a singular redemption. We know he has already regretted killing Melquiades, confirmed by his silent expressions of anguish before being abducted, dramatized in particular in his troubled recollection as he sits in his truck at the Odessa mall. Yet regret alone is insufficient, given his resurgent anger, his characteristic emotional violence that continues to erupt well after Melquiades's death. The process of unlearning such behavior constitutes the film's second half, as Pete strips Mike down psychologically in a series of indignities and violations that remind us of the Western's familiar fascination with forms of masculinity. Forcing Mike to inhabit Melquiades physically—to sit in his chair, drink from his cup, don his clothes—Pete begins to foster a modest change that continues in the long excursion south as Norton becomes effectively the unauthorized immigrant he once hunted and harmed. That traumatic passage is marked by beatings, snakebite, retribution from those Mike abused, encounters with those he scorned, until his sensibility gradually alters to the point where he prepares food with those who have saved him. As villagers shuck corn, one asks "You want to help us?" and he agrees, signaling his metamorphosis.

It is clear by now that the very suffering involved has transformed consciousness, and that the anguished process of journeying south has itself altered our own assumptions as viewers, making us reluctant to relinquish the idea that has propelled the journey. Pete's belief in Mel's assertions, false as we find them to be, has led to our understanding of their journey as a Western. It may have been delusional, but it has become by this point our shared delusion, drawing on generic assumptions that recreate the Western we think we already see. Pete and Norton each foster a growing respect for each other mixed with shades of incredulity as they try to locate the promised Jiménez. This unexpected modulation in their relationship occurs, however, just as we begin to have second thoughts about Melquiades ourselves, wondering whether his account of his family is a sham. First, we learn from a man at a Mexican cantina that Evelia Camargo, whom Melquiades claimed was his wife, is actually named Rosa, and that no one has heard of Melquiades, much less met him. When Pete finally tracks Rosa down, she is amazed at his account, having no idea how he has come to possess a photo "of me and my kids." Adding marginally to the mystery, Pete refuses to switch to Spanish when she initially claims to speak little English ("Poquito").

Following multiple scenes of Pete vainly trying to locate Melquiades's widow and children, then simply his town, we grudgingly come to realize that none of these may in fact exist. So that when Pete at last asserts they have actually found Jiménez, the declaration seems as arbitrary and capricious as anything else—possibly true, possibly not, but who knows? The culmination of the film consists, then, of what seem like shimmering lies and half-truths about Melquiades's past, compelling us to wonder whether he was ever actually married. After all, Rosa denies everything, faltering at the very pronunciation of Melquiades's name, suggesting she is actually hearing it for the first time, as if to confirm her disavowals. Conversely, perhaps she is prevaricating for understandable reasons, misleading Pete out of fear of her present husband's jealous anger. Still, no similar reason can be conceived for why Don Casimiro, the local authority, should likewise deny knowing Melquiades or a town called Jiménez. Adding to the confusion is our view of the photograph that Melquiades shows Pete, with Rosa hovering over three children and Melquiades oddly aloof in the background, visibly cut off from "his" supposed family, perhaps simply passing by. What might all this mean, and how could he have gained access to the photograph? Moreover, when he in Pete's recollection of their conversation says "And this is Evelia. Evelia Camargo, my wife," the distant look in his eyes suggests a range of emotion from actual reminiscence to fantasy desire to pure invented memory. As Matthew Carter observes, "So Pete rides off, betrayed by a mythic identity that did not exist as surely as Mel's professed identity did not exist either" (2014, 178).

Near the close, as Pete and Norton wander further afield, with Pete all but delusional in refusing to accept any skepticism about his rationale for returning to Mexico, and Norton fiercely rationalizing his shouted disbelief, we are presented with a flashback to Melquiades's plea to Pete, describing in sentimental, mildly saccharine tones his vision of his hometown: "Jiménez is a beautiful fucking place. It sits between two hills. The air is so clear there you feel like you can hug the mountains with your arms. A stream of clear clean fresh water bubbles up right out of the rocks there.

Fig. 14. Melquiades's mysterious photo "of me and my kids" that has propelled the journey of *The Three Burials of Melquiades Estrada* (Sony Pictures Classics).

If you go to Jiménez, I swear to you your heart will break with so much beauty." The inflated accents of this description make it appear a dream vision too peerless to be true, and yet as viewers we have no assurance the family and Jiménez do not exist.[10] In the DVD commentary, even January Jones (having spent weeks on set acting the part of Lou Ann) asks: "Is there actually any Jiménez?" To which Tommy Lee Jones acknowledges, if rather cryptically, "That's a very good question." As he adds (at the point where they finally arrive at Melquiades's presumed home): "I think what's under consideration here are the mechanics of faith, how does faith work, how does it change the world. . . . Yeah, from our point of view you couldn't say that seeing is believing, but you could say that believing is seeing" (T. Jones 2005). The film's deconstruction of the Western occurs in precisely these terms, not of seeing a narrative that then allows us to interpret materials in terms of the genre but of believing first in a set of generic features and codes (as part of our cultural, cinematic experience) that then allow us to accept against all odds a reading of strangely disparate materials *as* a coherent Western.

Among other mysteries in *Three Burials* is the opening credit sequence itself, of two border patrol agents shooting a coyote feeding on what appears to be Melquiades's corpse, since the scene precedes (and thereby seems to instigate) the autopsy that generates the film. Is that the same coyote, we wonder, that prompted Melquiades's earlier effort at vermin control, with shots that themselves bring about his own death? Moreover, the scene hints at a verbal pun, of "coyote" as vernacular for those who smuggle immigrants into the United States, the figures Norton combats at the film's beginning and who later help Pete and him escape into Mexico. The implied circularity of the opening scenes becomes once again emblematic of the way meaning is generated in the film, beginning not with facts that lead to interpretation but with expectations that define what the facts must be. Strange as it seems to contemplate, the power of the Western's continuing hold on our imaginations is measured by the persistence of our engagement with the film's very lack of determinate meaning. For we are left feeling more bewildered as we proceed rather than intellectually more in control, aware at last that logic does little to help explain our fascination with a genre that by all rights should be dead: a genre here exemplified in a film where motives are inscrutable, where memory is flawed, where history proves unrecoverable. Yet the film's very attention in fleeting form to the Western's traditional concerns—its allusion to versions of manhood, to questions of civic duty, to the reach of the law, and most of all, to belief in some myth of a trans-cultural West—drives us as viewers to contemplate Melquiades's burial in generic terms, reviving a set of conventional understandings of gender, community, and nation in terms of our most distinctive national narrative form.

The scene of Pete Perkins and Mike Norton sitting among the ruins of Jiménez, tired from shared labor, guzzling whiskey together, seems finally revitalizing, offering the only comfort we can garner from the film in the camaraderie they both feel. Still, Pete will have to draw his gun, scaring Norton into asking forgiveness with shots fired—replicating the five shots that ended with the death of Melquiades himself—reducing

Norton to sobbing remorse: "It was a mistake. . . . I didn't want it to happen. That hurt me. I regret it, every single day. Forgive me. Forgive me, Melquiades. For taking your life, forgive me, forgive me." The corpse of Melquiades Estrada, now three times interred, has taken on significance not for anything he happened to do or be but through the very process of others taking responsibility for an accident unintended. And in that, the scattered materials of the Western find an analogy, coming together through the very process of signification itself. The triumph of *The Three Burials of Melquiades Estrada* lies once again in its turning away from conventional generic rhythms (something true all along of the genre's formidable successes) as a means of restoring its supposed inaugural power. Rejecting traditional materials and configurations, borrowing from other generic strains and non-Western modes, Jones confirms the ongoing vitality of a cinematic form that its premier director, John Ford, had himself begun to think lifeless, finally ready to be laid to rest, but prepared nonetheless to imagine its revival.

5

DEFYING EXPECTATIONS IN
A HISTORY OF VIOLENCE
AND *BROKEBACK MOUNTAIN*

The appearance in 2005 of both Ang Lee's *Brokeback Mountain* and David Cronenberg's *A History of Violence* was met by unusual popular enthusiasm and marked critical esteem, though strangely neither film was quite what it seemed. Lee's proved the more scandalous, given a same-sex affair that challenged presumed Western ideals, though most allowed it otherwise fulfilled generic requirements with spectacular scenery, a Wyoming location, its focus on cowboys (though temporarily reduced to the status of shepherds), and its de rigueur celebration of horsemanship and masculine reticence. By contrast, Cronenberg's film lacked any hint of scandal (other than to cinéastes upset at its marked departure from the director's celebrated "body horror" style). But it also seemed to share little with Lee's genre choice, set as it was in an Indiana small town with a single horse viewed briefly and its explosive violence appearing more Mafioso than Western, occurring in motels and diners, suburban front lawns and finally a Philadelphia mansion. The surprise revealed in any contrast of the films is how fully generic considerations defy first impressions, with *Brokeback Mountain* (despite its setting, characterization, and costuming) seeming to owe less to John Ford than Douglas Sirk, as less a horse opera than a romance melodrama, while Cronenberg's film slowly comes to seem less a crime thriller than a Western.

Keep in mind that, as much as any genre, the Western is powerfully committed to the dynamics of family life, though it often portrays men leaving home, riding the range, enjoying a homosocial experience with other men. Yet in an unusual percentage of Western films, family encounters persistently crop up, whether educating the young about gender roles, or posing versions of manhood against each other, or testing the conventional boundaries of marriage and commitment, or concentrating on the tensions arising in communities refocused on the very family values that brought them together in the first place. Unlike screwball comedy, say, or melodrama, thrillers, or film noir, the Western clarifies familial conflict through the violence that invariably threatens. In fact, as this book argues throughout, so strong are generic conventions of character and plot that we increasingly come to read some films *as* Western despite the absence of such semantic markers as cowboys and horses, period costumes and historical crises involving ranchers and farmers—in short, despite nothing other than the film's syntactical concern with borders suggesting it *is* a Western. By the same token, for all their appearance *as* Westerns (with the requisite boots, pistols, and hats, the horses and herds), numerous recent films seem more forcefully predicated on a somewhat different generic dynamic. This is, of course, not to deny the ways in which genres necessarily intermix, and always have; but it does raise the provocative question of what the presumably dominant generic construction of a particular film might be.

As arbitrarily paired films, *Brokeback Mountain* and *A History of Violence* offer an exemplary demonstration of this intermixing and of the ways in which genre conventions sometimes fail or alternatively succeed despite what seem to be a film's ostensible materials. In the process, they help reveal how the Western's commitment to issues of family solidarity emerge in forms not always obvious. Both films, moreover, self-consciously address the dynamics of social identity, dramatically exploring scenarios of those who happen to hide who they are from others or even from themselves. Each shares an intense narrative engagement with the expectations entailed by conventional domestic obligations, though they manifest it in ways so different that our own assumptions about their generic allegiance becomes thoroughly tested. In the end, *A History of Violence* emerges as a distinctly Western example, perhaps surprisingly so—offering a profound reconsideration of values traditionally associated with the genre—while *Brokeback Mountain,* for all its semantic earmarks as a bona fide Western, is structured syntactically in ways that defy that identification.

FAMILY LINEAMENTS

Before turning to that contrast, it might help (even late in this book's overall argument) to review the Western in its genre configuration, which frequently tests masculine assumptions that emerge in the contest between bullied farmers and hired gunslingers acting on behalf of ranching interests. Scenes are set in small towns, where law-abiding citizens helpless in the face of violent threats confer as families about appropriate responses. The emphasis rests squarely on teaching children gendered roles as well as testing marital unions, often posing an ethical feminine logic against high-testosterone action. The supposedly "classic" exemplar is *Shane,* in which farmer Joe Starrett (Van Heflin) defies brutal ranchers eager to drive him from his land. Shane (Alan Ladd) appears as a capable alternative to capitulation and as someone who "fathers" young Joey in stalwart masculine skills as well as offering a quietly adulterous fantasy to Marian Starrett (Jean Arthur). The informing premise of the film (as of the Western more generally) hinges on the contrast of Shane and Starrett, each of whom shares aspects of the other's personality. Revealed in dramatic scenes of the stump removal, that contrast is made even more dramatic in their resistance to the villain Riker (Emile Meyer) and his vicious hired gunman Wilson (Jack Palance). Shane's reserved demeanor is matched by Starrett's voluble defense of the rule of law, as if each represented aspects of some more complete version of exemplary masculinity. Finally, however, the ranchers' threat to the Starretts comes to seem less central to plot (however determinative) than the various interactions between the family and Shane in negotiating a reasonable response to the chaos Riker embodies.

That pattern recurs in countless other films, which vary according to plot but cumulatively establish a central strand in the genre's syntactic weave. John Ford, for instance, returned repeatedly to the intertwined aspects of family dynamics, whether in *My Darling Clementine* with an older Wyatt Earp (Henry Fonda) as the elder sibling guiding his brothers; or in *Fort Apache* (1948), with Lt. Col. Owen Thursday (Fonda again) conflicted between arrogant ambition and his daughter's more judicious insistence on domestic values, including a subplot of Sgt. Maj. Michael O'Rourke (Ward Bond) as proud father and Lt. Michael O'Rourke (John Agar) as loving son; or in *Rio Grande* (1950) with now-promoted Lt. Col. Kirby York (John Wayne) visited at his western station by his forceful ex-wife Kathleen (Maureen O'Hara), who is at odds with him about the prospects for their enlisted son, recently flunked out of West Point. A half-dozen years later, *The Searchers* unsettles family life dramatically, with Ethan Edwards driven to track his niece's abductor out of an utterly obsessive love of Debbie's mother, his own sister-in-law. But consider other directors' celebrated examples: *High Noon*, with town marshal Will Kane represented as both newly pacific (ready to retire to marry his Quaker fiancée) and militant on behalf of his town ("Seems to me I've got to stay"). Or *Red River*, posing a compassionate stepson against an eager martinet in different versions of masculine (and ultimately family) configurations. More recently, the theme has been compounded to the point of parody: Clint Eastwood's *Unforgiven* repeatedly stresses the looming presence of Will Munny's dead wife, dead for ten years but still clearly governing his behavior. *Lone Star* offers a strange twist to family relations in the incest that lies at the heart of a plot about rediscovering parental values. *Down in the Valley* focuses on paternal tyranny and the deadly effects of an interloper, while *Don't Come Knocking* presents a backward-turning narrative of a cowboy hero's efforts to learn how he failed his own family obligations (with an unknown son, a discarded wife, a daughter he never knew). Throughout these and other films, early and late—and despite significant alterations of costuming and setting, of plot conflicts and genre intermixing—the role of the traditional family has remained despite divisions and conflicts the central, dominating theme.

Granted that Westerns frequently (all but necessarily) focus on family dynamics and gender roles, it is clear that many other instances of classic Hollywood cinema do so as well, most unrelated to the genre. Thus, one way of measuring the strength of generic expectations is via the reception of films *not* obviously Western, where no conspicuous semantic earmarks are apparent (setting, costume, period identification)—films that still for syntactical reasons remind us of genre and then demand to be read as Western. The shape of a film, its scenic pacing as well as its cinematic style, is identifiable within certain recognizable generic constraints, and those constraints in turn tend to reinforce the film's identity. Given the ubiquitousness of family considerations in the genre, that particular thematic component might well tip the scales.

A *History of Violence* forms a perfect example of this interpretive suasion if only in appearing at first hardly a Western at all. Yet its fundamental plot dynamics—its adumbration of the tension between opposed forms of masculine performance (placid small-town businessman; skilled martial combatant); its focus on a wife's strident ethical protest; its evocation of children's confusion at their own prescribed gendered roles—all coincide with the Western's preoccupations more than any other genre.[1] As well, the film begins with a threat to community and family well-being that corresponds to the opening of countless Western films, focusing in the initial four minutes on the indiscriminate brutality of two thugs. Cinematographer Peter Suschitzky offers a simple dolly shot of a motel exterior as Leland (Stephen McHatty) goes to check out, while we watch Billy (Greg Bryk) move their car, then wait for Leland to get behind the wheel before Billy goes back for bottled water, nonchalantly approaching the front desk where Leland's handiwork is evident in the vicious killing of a motel clerk and a maid. Violence seems to erupt through this slow tracking shot, making it seem almost intimate, ending with Billy's cold-blooded execution of a child stumbling in upon him as he casually surveys the motel counter.

That sequence of gratuitous violence announcing a film yet to come forms a further part of standard generic syntax, calling to mind, among other examples, *My Darling Clementine*, which opens with the eerily malevolent Clanton family confronting the Earp brothers, before ruthlessly killing the youngest, James; or the credit scene of *High Noon*, with Colby, Pierce, and Ben Miller meeting to ride into Hadleyville in order to commit havoc; or *3:10 to Yuma*, as the gang holds up a stage and Ben Wade brutally shoots the driver. Cronenberg and Suschitzky make a deliberate cinematic choice in opening their film this way, even down to their selection of lens. As Amy Taubin observes: "The scene is shot with the 27mm (wide-angle) lens that Cronenberg will use for almost the entire movie, and the slight distortion of the space, combined with the amped-up, abruptly edited sound effects (crickets, a snatch of rockabilly music), the slowness with which the bad guys move, as if they were underwater, and their disconnected, affectless conversation, has a nightmarish tone" (2005, 27). That disquieting effect is bolstered by adopting such a lens for medium and close-up shots, bringing the scene that much closer, immersing the viewer in violence.

What further dramatizes this opening is its juxtaposition with the scene that immediately follows, in the striking elision of witnessing the execution of a moaning, overwrought girl in a motel lobby, to watching a second girl in bed scream herself awake from a nightmare of "monsters." The suturing of these scenes as the gunshot explodes on the sound track—of savagery casually enacted in real time melding into the projected anxieties of Sarah Stall (Heidi Hayes)—disrupts our calm assumptions about what lies on and beneath the social surface. As Adam Ochonicky argues:

> A rapid tonal shift results from the combination of the lethargic long take, the jump cut, and the sound bridge. These elements lend the opening moments a certain degree of uncertainty as to whether the motel scene was Sarah's dream or an actual narrative event. The sound bridge somewhat suggests temporal continuity, but the spatial proximity between the gunshot and the bedroom is unclear. Are

these killers near the Stall home? Are they inventions of Sarah, and is the girl at the motel an imagined version of herself? This sense of ambiguity is furthered by Cronenberg's nearly parodic depiction of familial unity that ensues. (2015, 132)[2]

And it is precisely that aftermath, so fiercely stressing domestic unity, that is among the early reminders of the Western's usual contrast between calm domesticity and agitated evil, leaving the entire Stall family (first father, then brother, finally mother) patiently trying to calm Sarah down with soothing bromides. The reassuring effort continues over the Wheaties breakfast that follows, with each of the family members reviewing the commonplace moments of the day to come. That contrast continues throughout, sustained in scenes of family and community support that confirm traditional bonds, in the process reminding us of the genre most closely aligned with such encounters.[3] The celebration of small-town life extends to an early morning scene of Edie Stall (Maria Bello) dropping her husband Tom (Viggo Mortensen) off for work in what seems like a timeless mid-American town where the post office clock is permanently stopped at 1:15 (as we only later notice), making time actually seem to stand still.[4]

More than embodying an idyllic community of heartening traditional give and take—where neighbors politely greet each other, employers respect employees, and American civic virtues are burnished—the town reveres family life in particular, however untoward the strains may be (consider that at the Cannes Film Festival, the film was announced as a 'twisted look at family'" [Mathijs 2008, 233]). Following Sarah's nightmare, we are offered a series of encounters that stress how important domestic dynamics are, with fatherhood notably represented as an essential role as well as a predictable genre reminder. Tom repeatedly offers reassuring advice to his son Jack, and becomes ever more paternal with the appearance of gangster Carl Fogarty (Ed Harris) as looming threat to his loved ones if also to Tom's own authority. In fact, Fogarty chips away at the Stalls' self-assured contentment, as Ernest Mathijs observes of the film's shift to "a post-romantic critique of family life. Fogarty's insistent harassments and allusions to Tom's past as a gangster have caused a gradual breakdown of trust in the family" (2008, 230). Fogarty comes to represent precisely the egocentric male violence so often configured by the Western as a threat to domestic bonds, putting at risk the very prospect of ongoing family ties.

After Fogarty scornfully warns Jack on Tom's front lawn, the film continues to focus on domestic tensions rather than to make a more predictable turn towards revenge drama. Quick retaliation against external menace is revealed as far less important than easing household strains. Again, as Mathijs reminds us, "What is uncommon, however, is how the film does not move away from the troubled family" (2008, 232). Even with those imperatives—Tom Stall being required by generic demands to confront forces violently emerging from his past, forces threatening to destroy him and his loved ones—retribution lasts only the seventeen minutes in which his return to Philadelphia takes place. The more significant engagements occur in the private realm of Indiana, before and after the homicidal trip east, where the dark hazards entangling husband and wife, parent and child, are revealed as more painfully destructive than the perils posed by his brother Richie Cusack (William Hurt).

The contrast boils down to twin versions of manliness long familiar to the Western, though Cronenberg nicely encapsulates these "versions" in a single figure oscillating back and forth in his behavior.[5] Mortensen's performance as both Tom Stall and Joey Cusack brilliantly discriminates between masculine alternatives and does so entirely through subtle shifts in facial expression and bodily gesture that only slowly raise our viewing suspicions. As Stuart Klawans observes, "Cronenberg bets the movie on Mortensen's ability to bring depth to a face that you thought was all surface" (2005, 49). The actor's voice itself shifts between quiet-spoken, almost meek Tom Stall and the mildly menacing intonations of Joey Cusack that emerge imperceptibly midway through the film as Adam Ochonicky observes (2015, 133). Our first inkling of something strangely borderline occurs when Tom explosively kills the threatening gunmen in his diner,

Fig. 15. The diner killing, with Tom Stall seeming to transform (if momentarily) into Joey Cusack, in *A History of Violence* (New Line Cinema).

in a scene whose violence lasts seventeen seconds and ends with his look of wide-eyed concern mixed with what seems like uncertainty.[6] Leland's psychotic bellowing of "Coffee" has sparked the encounter as he sits at the diner stool; and the whole confrontation ends with the camera finally shifting to his mutilated dead face, all dramatized by Cronenberg's deft use of close-ups (Leach 2011). But Suschitzky employs close-ups here in part to mislead the viewer, who remains uncertain about Tom's agency as registered through Mortensen's hesitant responses. "He looks down at Leland," Liz Powell observes, "and then at the gun in his hand, seemingly taken aback by the violence of his own actions" (2011, 167). From her perspective, Tom undergoes a psychological "transformation," signaled in the following scene when he deftly handles a shotgun in calmly advising his son. Whether Tom is actually transformed here or not is unclear, though as he later admits to his wife, he thought the persona of "Joey Cusack" had been killed off and was surprised to discover "he" had returned from the dead in a moment of instantaneous violence.

In the savage scene at the diner, we remain ignorant of Tom's past and hidden skills, with Mortensen's performance in the hospital after that initial assault leaving us still unsure—an uncertainty that continues to linger after he returns home to recuperate. Not until confronted on his own front lawn, with Fogarty holding his son Jack hostage, does Tom seem to cross a psychological border, clearly altered into his persona as Joey, eyes widening, hands moving independently, suddenly cornered and compelled against his will into becoming his former self. "After the mobsters release Jack," Adam Ochonicky observes, "Tom calmly declares, 'I think it'd be better if you'd just leave now,' and this statement assumes the tone of a warning more than a polite Midwestern request. Here, Tom's Midwestern accent is barely perceptible, and Mortensen appears to be portraying Joey performing 'Tom.' Even as Joey asserts control of the body, a slight vocal trace of 'Tom' persists and reflects the tenuous nature of both identities" (2015, 135). The conversion is remarkable, confirming for viewers what had only been suspected before, even given Tom's remarkably quicksilver response to the thugs in his diner. As Edie states in the second hospital scene after his shoulder has been repaired: "I saw you turn into Joey right in front of my eyes. I saw a killer that Fogarty warned me about."[7] The eerie border between Tom and Joey has slowly begun to surface, emerging quietly before we have even suspected it.

Yet despite her accusation, our uncertainty lingers, so that even when Joey returns to Philadelphia at his brother's demand, Mortensen performs the role in a mild-mannered aspect, still more Tom Stall than Joey Cusack.[8] As Richie astutely taunts his brother: "You're living the American dream, you really bought into it, didn't you? You've been this other guy almost as long as you've been yourself. Hey, when you dream, are you still Joey?" The barbed query hangs in the air unanswered, though various critics have agreed with Richie's assumption that "Tom" is merely an impersonation adopted to disguise the past, and that Joey has remained the same all along.

Still, there seems equal evidence for assuming Tom is Tom, having actually transformed himself years before into the person he preferred to be. In matters of such cognitive fine tuning, any consensus is rarely forthcoming.

The question raised by these kinds of psychological borders may not finally be answered convincingly, but notably this condition of multiple personalities is hardly Tom's alone, having been reflected in nearly the entire Stall family—in his son, but also his wife, perhaps even his daughter at the end. For Edie, this becomes apparent in the first of two sexual encounters, dressed up as a cheerleader jumping on Tom in bed. "You're the best man I know," she confesses, and their lively enjoyment of each other confirms the affection binding them together. Yet the terms alter significantly in the second such scene, since Tom now realizes she knows fully well he lied to the sheriff, just as she lied in confirming his fabricated account. The episode is far more tangled amid mixed emotions—embodying a complex intersection of resentment and arousal as well as affection—than the earlier scene, with bodies acting in ways that unsettle the knowledge the two have of each other, or think they do. Edie's mixture of revulsion and desire adumbrates a more convoluted response, defying critics who see this as simple sexual assault. "It's not a rape scene," Cronenberg has bluntly declared. "People who are inattentive might think that. I wanted the music to address that. There's a moment where the music is telling you that this is a much more complex thing than a scene of rape or violence."[9] In the interaction between husband and wife, each discovers in the other a longing, a familiarity, and also an enticing if complex sense of identity they had not appreciated before. The scene, in other words, hardly reduces to the kind of straightforward judgment that Bart Beaty delivers: "The sequence drives home the point that, stripped of all the illusions, Tom is a mere fiction and Joey is the authentic personality. Reduced to primal urges in the face of sex and death, Joey is revealed to be no more Tom than Edie is still a cheerleader. The first sex scene demonstrates how people can agree to wear masks, while the second emphasizes that masks can obscure the truth only for so long" (2008, 108).[10] On the contrary, the second incident actually demonstrates how fully Edie and Tom desire the multiple versions of selfhood they have newly identified in each other, making them wonder as well at what those versions may reveal of themselves.

That very condensation of motives, identities, feelings, and knowledge helps explain why the second encounter between husband and wife has become the focus of so many varied accounts, often more revealing of the critics than the film. Consider Adam Lowenstein's claim:

> the sex scene between Tom/Joey and Edie condenses all the hatred, mistrust, desire, and need that exist between the characters into an ecstatically punishing fuck on the staircase of their home. Cronenberg films this encounter with stunning eloquence—the line between revulsion and arousal, rage and love emanates from the bruising twists and turns of their bodies on the stairs, attracted and repelled in equal measure. Edie knows Tom lied to her about his past as Joey, just as Tom knows Edie saved him from the law by lying about her knowledge of Joey. Nevertheless, their bodies *act* in ways that make what and how these characters *know* seem impoverished, one-dimensional. Their bodies speak the darkest ambivalences of their relationship. (2009, 206)

This assessment gets closer to the complicated series of emotions that have emerged as the initial conflict between husband and wife escalates and then becomes transformed by their recognition that what holds them together is a toxic yet intoxicating mix of emotions, desires, revulsions, and unintended arousal. What Lowenstein refuses to acknowledge, however astute his description, is how fully the encounter embraces a mix of responses in most good marriages, with individuals sometimes simply unaware of the personalities to whom they're attached, indeed unaware of their own inadmissible personas. And though the aftermath of this episode consists of Edie's angrily walking away from Tom, exiting the bathroom as she pulls her robe closed (denying him the intimacy of her body exposed), in fact the scene underscores the complicated tension that exists precisely because of so much that binds them together, if also newly dividing them.[11] The confirmation of this complicated relationship has already occurred in Edie's willingness to stand by her husband, knowingly to lie for him, when Sheriff Sam Carney (Peter MacNeill) confronts Tom with rising doubts.[12]

SHIFTING IDENTITIES

The film carefully pursues the complicated question of shifting identities, and of the disjunction between personas we project and the sometimes conflicted character that lingers beneath them. In high school, Jack suddenly transitions from adolescent nerd to outraged warrior. Threatened in the gym locker room, then again in the school hallway, he reveals a violently competent streak that resembles his father's own martial actions—indeed, almost replicates Tom in his sudden, all but miraculous ability to defend himself against two bullies. And given the family dynamics of the film, with Tom's repeated efforts to get through to his son, to explain how to act responsibly and effectively, we are led to believe that Jack's metamorphosis owes something to his father's patient efforts to help him mature.

These scenes cumulatively contribute to the larger question of what makes us up, of how identity is constituted. Are we the sum of choices made, or is it the actions we have performed? Can we choose anew, and by doing so set our lives on a new track? Or does the past create an iron rail of characteristics that finally become inescapable, returning to reassert themselves, establishing a firm border? The questions are unanswerable, of course, and the film nicely does not actually try to answer them, instead revealing how insurmountable they are as questions. More specifically, *A History of Violence* interrogates its own title in the response of both Edie and Jack to the secret past that husband and father has concealed. Was he lying to them, or simply dividing himself from a past that has nothing to do with his present? And from their perspectives, did love rest upon a relationship and a person who somehow did not ever actually exist, as Roger Ebert has claimed (Ebert 2005)? Repeatedly, the film returns to the Western's pivotal concern with family relations, and how they are meant to be constituted.[13]

In fact, the one place where the film most dramatically diverges from the genre is in its final four and a half minutes, when Tom returns home from the deadly mayhem in Philadelphia to a conventional dinner of meat loaf and canned corn where everything is once again muted, all remaining quiet. A tense atmosphere isolates the four Stalls as they sit at the dinner table unwilling to speak, with Edie refusing even to look up or acknowledge Tom (or is it Joey?), leaving the question of whether this family can be reconstituted to linger through the closing credits. Not a word is exchanged, as Suschitzky carefully shifts among the four faces, stressing how uncertain the status of Tom's marriage remains, as Jack and Sarah accommodate their father by setting a plate for him, silently passing him food. The film finally ends as a tear-stained Edie slowly gazes up at Tom, also in tears, with their future left in doubt. The power of this ending lies in its self-conscious questioning of the genre that structures the film: can the isolated Western hero ever be assimilated into community (town, family, church) and still remain the hero? Could Shane have obliged Joey in his closing plea to stay—"Shane, Shane, come back"—and still remain Shane? Doesn't the genre's syntax somehow preclude such a narrative accommodation, as tracked by the endings of so many Westerns from *Stagecoach* to *Unforgiven* in a strong dramatic line? Cronenberg himself understands the stakes involved in keeping this Western's conclusion indeterminate and, contrary to some confident readings, has argued that "this movie has quite an open ending because things are not resolved, nothing is really resolved. The relationships are not resolved, and even the question of whether Tom can escape the law is not resolved. We don't know there aren't some gangsters who will come after him, we don't know that he's managed to cover his tracks so well, we don't know any of these things" (Grünberg 2006, 175).[14] In short, the film's concluding equivocation is at once a tribute to the genre and a questioning of it.

Still, any confidence about the ending, or about earlier sequences, is delayed until we are allowed to view the film once again, with more secure knowledge of earlier scenes gained only retrospectively, and major questions only arising after the whole has transpired (much like the surprise reflections that emerge retrospectively in Night Shyamalan's *The Sixth Sense* [1999]). Take Tom's initial comforting of Sarah awakened by nightmares, which sounds at first like a bromide and only on second viewing serves as a quietly revelatory anticipation of the whole, as if he were speaking of his own interior space when he claims: "No sweetie. There's no such thing as monsters. You were just having a bad dream." Reviewing the film, we begin to wonder (as we could not the first time through) what it is that Tom is actually thinking when Carl Fogarty arrives at the diner backed by his henchmen. On first viewing, Tom seems innocent, genuinely confused, carrying the viewer as well with his apparently perplexed emotional state. Once we later realize that Carl is actually right in his contentions and that Tom has actually been Joey Cusack, the scene acquires a very different emotional resonance. Likewise, later we wonder at what he is thinking when Sheriff Carney first comes to the house to question him, seemingly bewildered, almost aggrieved at the officer's misidentification of him as a possible criminal, protesting that he is certainly not in the Witness Protection Program or in any other way under suspicion. Not until he finally, grimly admits on his own front lawn that "I should have killed you in Philadelphia"—eliciting a wry grimace from Fogarty—do we know for certain he *is* Joey, or at least once was. The rest of the film occurs as an erasure of that past in an effort to eclipse a presumed identity he has long since shunned. The subsequent killing of his brother Richie (and Richie's thugs) is a way of extinguishing that past, killing off himself at last as Joey Cusack so that he can return to his reborn life in Indiana.

In this, *A History of Violence* raises a crucial question about what constitutes a family that is rarely addressed in Westerns, or in any other genre: is family a traditional nuclear entity, or a more colloquial version of gang affiliation?[15] The pressures applied by Carl Fogarty are invariably towards the latter, of Mafia brotherhood and Cosa Nostra affiliations, introducing the idea that Joey Cusack cannot actually ever become Tom Stall because he is already committed to a fraternal "family" by blood spilled and a shared gang history. But Tom's silent assertion is that neither blood nor past behavior necessarily dictates identity, and that one can actively choose not only one's self but one's family as well—that it is possible to make a cultural choice rather than submit to a biological imperative. Unsurprisingly, Edie finds this an astonishing notion, at least at first, flustered and bewildered at discovering that the man she knows as husband and father to her children has simply reinvented himself. Her explosive response to that discovery, expressed in their hospital confrontation, is at once understandable and somehow misplaced: "What are you, like some multiple personality schizoid? It's like flipping a switch back and forth for you?" The recognition that Tom is not Tom, or at least has not always been, deeply unsettles her, as it should, even after her bewildered husband offers a calm and reasonable reply: "I never expected to see Joey again. . . . I thought I killed Joey Cusack. I went out to the desert, and I killed him. I spent three years becoming Tom Stall. You have to know this: I wasn't really born again until I met you. I was nothing."

That avowal speaks to the film's central consideration, of whether Tom is Tom or not. Richie and Carl, of course, refuse to acknowledge he might have been transformed, while his Stall family remains at least suspicious of the prospect. But the film itself seems, despite some critics' objections, to acknowledge the osmosis between personalities, the sliding over otherwise firm borders, the way in which certain personas bleed into others. Despite Edie's fear that Tom has simply reverted to being Joey, he does seem to remain largely Tom throughout, resistant to the suasions of his former persona, though willing to rely on Joey's skills when push comes to shove. Nothing suggests he takes any pleasure—as he once did—in killing or physical mayhem. As Cronenberg himself has said, confirming the instability of character: "When I look at a person I see this maelstrom of organic, chemical and electron chaos; volatility and instability, shimmering; and the ability to change and transform and transmute" (B. Gordon 1989, n.p.). In this sense, those who think of Joey as a creature lurking under the misleading mask of Tom Stall are mistaken.[16]

Instead of conceiving Tom as a recidivist figure, choosing to revert to a former personality from the one he has so carefully crafted for himself, it might be more appropriate to consider his reversion as simply momentary, compelled by untoward circumstances—in fact, not to consider it a "reversion" at all, but simply a matter of relying instinctually on earlier martial skills to save himself, his coworkers, and his family from death. Again, we return to the juridical issue that centers the Western, of the occasional need for violence to ensure that violence does not destroy us— as a means of restoring domestic order and the possibility of a rule of law when both are for the moment suppressed or deemed inadequate. And in the alternation between deferential Tom and feral Joey, part of the genre's syntactic scaffolding emerges as a way of clarifying how to interpret the film.[17] The restoration of civic order; the awareness of violence as temporarily unavoidable but now suitably past; the calm appeal of family ties renewed after renouncing a masculine dynamic celebrated by the film: all these constitute the interpretive generic grid that finally dictates our viewing. Without acknowledging this directly, Amy Taubin describes the lineaments of the film in terms that remind us of the hold the Western continues to have on our imaginations:

> One way of looking at A History of Violence is as a depiction of a marriage that begins with a shot of a happy family crowded together in the frame (as Tom, Edie, Jack, and Sarah were when Sarah woke up screaming from the nightmare which then erupted into their waking lives) and ends with the same four people around the dining room table, unable to look at one another, each of them locked away in a separate frame. The husband has confessed that he and consequently his entire family have been living a lie, but the truth has not made them free. In the course of the story, he has killed nine men and involved his son in killing another. And while he killed all of them in self-defense or to defend his family, the efficiency with which he dispatched them is, how can we put it, disturbing. On the dinner table

is a meal that could have been an illustration in *The Joy of Cooking*: meat loaf, potatoes, a yellow vegetable, and a green. The meal in itself is as close to social satire as the film gets. But the confusion and loss felt by the characters is heartbreaking. What we have here is cognitive dissonance, and it's the American way. (2005, 28)

In fact, the uncertainty of the film's conclusion—its measured four-plus minutes of silent interaction and indeterminate emotions—constitutes a potentially hopeful segue, as the gaze between husband and wife, parents and children, reaffirms however tentatively what the Western has always held dear: that family matters.

MISLEADING SEMANTICS

One way to clarify this pressure on generic expectations, from a film that hardly seems like a Western though it clearly performs like one, is through an equally successful example from 2005, *Brokeback Mountain*, that presents itself more obviously *as* a Western. Adapted from Annie Proulx's 1996 short story in a screenplay by Larry McMurtry and Diana Ossana, the film stays relatively faithful to its initial, self-consciously Western plot. From the outset, all the ingredients are there, in costuming, casting, setting, and not least in its engagement with notably domestic concerns. Taciturn, denim-clad men in cowboy hats sit astride horses as the film goes on to encompass the familiar vocations and diversions that have long been part of the genre (herding, rodeos, campfires, even line dancing). Moreover, Heath Ledger's signal performance of Ennis Del Mar as inflexible, tight lipped, classically taciturn matches the characteristic demeanor of Western icons from Gary Cooper to Clint Eastwood.[18] The plot circles persistently around (and self-consciously away from) questions involving wives and the problems of parenting that have long stamped the genre. From the beginning, in fact, the sound track gestures generically as Elsie Walker observes: "The very first sound of the film is wind, a common aural motif in westerns, especially in connection with vast, inhospitable landscapes.

Then comes the sound of a single guitar and a lone truck winding its way down the empty road. The guitar dominates Gustavo Santaolalla's original non-diegetic score for the film. It is an instrument much-associated with the western genre, but its usage varies widely: from traditional folk songs, to lyrical themes, to contemporary, fragmented cues" (2015, 5–6).[19]

Perhaps the most telling semantic barometer is Rodrigo Prieto's cinematography when Ennis and Jack Twist (Jake Gyllenhaal) finally ride to camp, filling the frame with lustrous mountain panoramas that go undescribed in Proulx's Wyoming story (though in fact Prieto filmed in the equally spectacular Canadian Rockies of southern Alberta). The simple process of traversing the landscape, riding horses across the mountains, celebrating scenery purely for its intrinsic, unalloyed attraction, lies as much at the heart of the Western as does any other signature semantic feature, confirming a generic identity that continues to inspire simply by letting the eye linger on uninterrupted trees and cirrus clouds, azure sky and glistening mountain ridges.[20] Yet as Jim Kitses observes, the film lures us into a glorious Western setting only to turn its back on it, foreclosing some of the very possibilities announced initially as distinctively Western: "The trick of *Brokeback Mountain* is to evoke repeatedly at the outset a vast and desolate frontier setting that allows the creation of a passionate relationship, but thereafter to leave behind that space and its possibilities" (2007, 26). As he provocatively adds: "Although there are brief returns to the wilds, the world of the Western that is created in the film's first forty minutes soon transitions into melodrama, both male and family varieties. Our wilderness types are instantly civilized on their return, cabined, cribbed, and confined" (2007, 26).

In short, *Brokeback Mountain* initially begs to be viewed as a Western, with Prieto deliberately inserting scenes much like the celebratory cattle herding in *Three Burials* that also cites *Red River*. And Prieto doubles down on the debt, repeating the scene early and late in an exultant rounding up of sheep that revels in the panoramic exhilaration of men at work in a glorious setting. Yet if genre semantics remain the same, evocative and memorial, the genre also depends on a syntax that alters over time in ways that can at once enliven our pleasure and yet lead to curious deviations from expectation. Genres are, after all (as I have repeatedly argued) always adulterated, invariably to their benefit; but what is significant about *Brokeback Mountain* is how the syntax of the Western seems to drop out all but entirely, leaving a film with Western semantic trappings that in fact turn out to be something else.[21] It may succeed as that "something else," but only becomes a Western as a wolf in sheep's clothing. None of the syntactical suasions that continue to underlie the genre—the feckless civic complacency; the economic conflicts of rancher and farmer (and in this film the cowboys are shepherds); the opposition of illegal violence and inadequate legal constraints; the harsh isolation of desolate landscapes in contrast to community values; the final showdown that paradoxically represents a triumph of social values over blustering anarchy—none of these features emerge in the film. As well, the genre's recurrent address of family values and conventional civic structures is notably absent if only in the casual nature with which wives are mistreated and abandoned, children forsaken, and men seen in flight from the customary domestic roles they have deliberately chosen.

Divergences from Western dynamics aside, the film does seize (like Proulx's story) quite brilliantly on one aspect of the genre celebrated from the beginning—the allure of male bodies, and of male-on-male sexuality. Owen Wister's establishment of the fictional Western in his best-selling novel *The Virginian* (1902) already introduced this erotic dynamic in the male narrator's glowing desire for the handsome cowboy hero he describes as "a slim young giant, more beautiful than pictures" (1902, 4). Or as Wister later adds of the hero's girlfriend, "the Virginian looked at her with such a smile that, had I been a woman, it would have made me his to do what he pleased with on the spot" (1902, 251). Ever since, that sexualizing gaze has constituted one of the genre's main appeals, perhaps especially in film, where beautiful male actors are regularly posed on screen (as I have argued elsewhere) "in a fashion that seems generically distinct" (1996, 156). [22] Yet the oddly antigeneric aspect of Lee's film paradoxically grows out of this strain, with its entire first third focused all but exclusively on the growing affair between two men removed from everyone else, from every kind of public or even domestic situation. Not until Ennis allows in a postcoital moment that "You know I ain't no queer," in response to Jack's assurance that "It's nobody's business but ours," does a larger world ironically open up. For it is then that he confesses his dutiful plan to marry Alma (Michelle Williams), followed immediately by a scene of their wedding.

The film hinges on excluding, as a rather strictly defined border, the entire social environment surrounding the relationship between Jack and Ennis, with civic obligations, social arrangements, family engagements all made to disappear in the thrill of their mountain romance. The reappearance of that world in ensuing scenes tracks what Daniel Mendelsohn rightly describes as the "psychological tragedy" (2011, 34) underlying Ennis's deep self-hatred coupled with Jack's bitter sense of rejection, both of which reveal emotional aspects of the Western never explored so intently before. Ang Lee, with McMurtry and Ossana, focuses on aspects of the traditional Western otherwise ignored or repressed, exposing psychologies and emotional possibilities flattened out by generic demands. The scene that most closely resembles Tom Stall's outburst of violence in the diner occurs at a Fourth of July celebration when Ennis erupts in anger at two drunken bikers swearing in front of his wife and children: "stunned and wide-eyed, they have witnessed a kind of fury in him that they have never seen before" (McMurtry and Ossana 2013, 41). Yet where Tom's violence seems to endorse a classic Western response, Ennis's (if for reasons we as viewers understand) seems the opposite; his adopting the role of bully suggests he differs little from vicious sadists in Westerns needing to be thrashed themselves: "How about it? You wanna lose about half your fuckin' teeth? Huh?" Later, after a postseparation Thanksgiving dinner, when Alma expresses her deep-seated resentment at his long history of alleged fishing trips with Jack, Ennis storms out and deliberately incites a brutal beating from two truckers. The pattern clearly reveals the pathology of sexuality long repressed, of an inability to engage his own feelings of affection for Jack, whose offer of a possible social accommodation is flatly dismissed. My point, however, is not that this angry, antisocial behavior is unexpected or inexplicable, but that it seems somehow misidentified generically, more noir than Western, more horror than noir.[23]

As well, that response finds confirmation in the relative paralysis of the film itself, reflecting the psychopathology of the characters, evoking the anguish of being so deeply closeted and bordered off from self-knowledge. The choices Ennis makes and the exchanges he has with Jack are again uncharacteristic of the Western's typical outward, active style. As Ennis reflects, for once willing to open up: "You ever get the feelin' . . . I don't know, er . . . when you're in town and someone looks at you all suspicious, like he knows? And then you go out on the pavement and everyone looks like they know too?" To which Jack casually responds, "Well, maybe you oughta get out of there, you know? Find yourself someplace different. Maybe Texas." At that point, Ennis closes down, immediately sarcastic and dismissive: "Texas? Sure, maybe you can convince Alma to let you and Lureen to adopt the girls. And we can just live together herding sheep. And it'll rain money from LD Newsome and whiskey'll flow in the streams—Jack, that's real smart." That abrupt, inward-turning resistance to change, to alternative possibilities, to simple travel or movement itself seems increasingly characteristic of Ennis, bound down by his own self-abhorrence. And the intensity of that emotional tightening becomes an inner claustrophobia less like the spatial constraints of *Bad Day at Black Rock* or *3:10 to Yuma* than the psychological repressions and coercions of a wholly different genre, one that does not allow for resolutions syntactically available in the Western. In short, the larger confusions of the film invite a different reading based on the romance genre, or perhaps more on family melodrama, which all but declares itself the obverse of the Western.

Among the more influential critics of melodrama, Thomas Elsaesser offers both a historical and formal assessment, particularly of the emergence in the mid-twentieth century of a cinematic mode commensurate

Fig. 16. "How about it? You wanna lose about half your fuckin' teeth? Huh?" The anguished violence of Ennis Del Mar in *Brokeback Mountain* (Focus Features).

with the fictional melodramas of a century before (Dickens, Balzac). And central to his thesis is "the restricted scope for external action determined by the subject, and because everything, as [Douglas] Sirk said, happens 'inside.' To the 'sublimation' of the action picture and the Busby Berkeley/ Lloyd Bacon musical into domestic and family melodrama corresponded a sublimation of dramatic conflict into decor, color, gesture, and composition of frame, which in the best melodramas is perfectly thematized in terms of the characters' emotional and psychological predicaments" ([1973] 2012. 443). Relying on films by Douglas Sirk (*Written on the Wind* [1956], *Imitation of Life* [1959]), and Vincent Minelli (*The Bad and the Beautiful* [1952]), Elsaesser poses their closed structures and camera framing against popular Westerns of the period, which:

> seem to find resolution because the hero can act positively on the changing situations where and when they present themselves. In

Raoul Walsh's adventure pictures, . . . identity comes in an often paradoxical process of self-confirmation and overreaching, but always through direct action, while the momentum generated by the conflicts pushes the protagonists forward in an unrelentingly linear course. The family melodrama, by contrast, though dealing largely with the same Oedipal themes of emotional and moral identity, more often records the failure of the protagonist to act in a way that could shape the events and influence the emotional environment, let alone change the stifling social milieu. The world is closed, and the characters are acted upon. Melodrama confers on them a negative identity through suffering, and the progressive self-immolation and disillusionment generally end in resignation: they emerge as lesser human beings for having become wise and acquiescent to the ways of the world. ([1973] 2012, 446)

Or as he adds about this difference: "In one case, the drama moves toward its resolution by having the central conflicts successively externalized and projected into direct action," say of a jail break, or a robbery, or a western chase. The very paralysis that both Ennis and Jack feel in their relationship and their lives is embodied in the integral structure of melodrama as a genre.[24]

In fact, one could say that the Western forms something like the inverse of domestic melodrama, emphasizing contrary emotional and behavioral premises, making us realize how fully any true merging of the two genres is impossible. As Elsaesser continues in elaborating the tenets of classic melodrama:

The social pressures are such, the frame of respectability so sharply defined, that the range of "strong" actions is limited. The tellingly impotent gesture, the social gaffe, the hysterical outburst replaces any more directly liberating or self-annihilating action, and the cathartic violence of a shoot-out or a chase becomes an inner violence, often one that the characters turn against themselves. The dramatic configuration, the pattern of the plot, makes them, regardless of attempts to break free, constantly look inward, at each other and themselves.

The characters are, so to speak, each others' sole referent; there is no world outside to be acted on, no reality that could be defined or assumed unambiguously. ([1973] 2012, 447–48)

Written nearly a quarter-century before McMurtry and Ossana's script, this interpretation would seem an apt appraisal of its structuring tensions—indeed, to be a prescient shorthand summation of the completed film itself.[25]

Yet identifying the dominant generic matrix of *Brokeback Mountain* is only the initial step in evaluating it. Alan Dale argues further that the film is deeply confused about the stakes raised by melodrama, often centered on a contrast between the stale dissatisfactions of conventional married life and the emotional intensity proffered by forbidden, often adulterous unions. Given that tension, "between licit love that is only dutiful and true love that is passionate but illicit," Dale contends that "Lee shoots the story as this kind of domestic romance. The structural problem with his approach is that the story can't function as a romance because Ennis and Jack fail in a quest—the object of which in their case would be the openly committed relationship Jack urges on Ennis—without ever attempting to achieve it" (2011, 168). In fact, Dale accuses Lee (and by extension McMurtry and Ossana) of sharing little sympathy for his male leads, or for decisions they make in the course of their lives.[26] This is partly revealed in the blithe disregard of domestic commitments that regularly loom so large for both melodrama and the Western. Ennis remains a selfish parent to his girls, only fleetingly concerned with their welfare and development; Jack foregoes any constructive relationship with his dyslexic son, leaving parenting to his wife. That shared disregard for family is displayed in back-to-back scenes, as both are about to depart for another "fishing trip," with Jack claiming he wants to simply abandon their families and start a ranch together, and Ennis resisting, but only out of anger at himself and fear of what the community will think. His response—"Two guys livin' together? No way. We can get together once in a while way the hell out in the back of nowhere"—is met by Jack's equally recalcitrant "I don't give a flyin' fuck about other people." That disregard for others is assumed in the film to offer a testament to their mutual passion, by which "the movie unrelievedly elicits a single-layered, patronizing sympathy" (Dale 2011, 170). As Dale continues, "by amping up the romance of the boys' impossible love, the movie implicitly justifies how they treat their wives. The problem becomes plainer if you imagine Ennis and Jack committing adultery with *women* they found more attractive than their wives. The main point is that lying and cheating don't make people sympathetic. (In my experience they further corrode character almost regardless of the reason a person resorts to them.)" (Dale 2011, 170). The very lack of accountability for their actions centers the film, which we as viewers are meant to accept because they supposedly have no choice in the matter.

In short, the passion that joins them seems distinctly antidomestic and unfamilial, an anguished defiance of their own conflicting needs and desires: Ennis, for Jack alone; Jack, primarily for Ennis, but also defined more casually by trysts with a Mexican in Juarez, later after a couple's dance with Lawshawn's husband Randall Malone (David Harbor), and earlier (in vain) with a rodeo clown.[27] Other than sex, little binds them together, whether in terms of shared interests or allied points of view (though that also seems true of their marriages). Even so, Jack (ever the more expressive) tries to give voice to the prospect of life as a couple:

> Try this one . . . and *I'll* say it just one time. Tell you what, we could a had a good life together, a fuckin' real good life, had us a place of our own. You wouldn't do it, Ennis, so what we got now is Brokeback Mountain. Everything built on that. It's all we got, boy, fuckin' all, so I hope you know that if you don't never know the rest. Count the damn few times we been together in twenty years. Measure the fuckin' short leash you keep me on, then ask me about Mexico and then tell me you'll kill me for needin' somethin' I don't hardly never get.

While the film defines a trajectory tightly welded to the intensity of romance melodrama rather than the Western, it nonetheless fails even in that more

Fig. 17. Ennis Del Mar and Jack Twist caught up in passion, in *Brokeback Mountain* (Focus Features).

secure generic syntax, in pressing so rashly, so self-centeredly for passion that exceeds all social conventions. As Dale points out in films by Douglas Sirk, most obviously *All That Heaven Allows* (1955), certain unyielding social proscriptions define an all but hysterical response, whether against crossing class lines or defying heteronormative standards. Protagonists find it hard to conceive of stepping outside social norms, or otherwise accepting more or less mediated compromises in behavior. That prospect is presented as so inconceivable in Lee's film that both men simply declare they have nothing to do with their behavior, in fear of what outlawed desire might say of them and the conventional social identities they inhabit. As Ennis insists, in his suddenly stuttering resistance to articulating what he otherwise knows: "tryin' to figure out if I was? . . . I know I ain't. I mean, here we both got wives and kids, right? I like doin' it with women, but Jesus H . . . ain't nothin' like this. . . . Never had no thoughts a doin' it with another guy." To which Jack disingenuously responds, "Me neither." The film brilliantly depicts the strictures against passionate male love, but only by posing that love against every and any constraint, whether social, domestic, or psychological.

CONCLUSION: IDENTITIES DENIED

Of the two films, Cronenberg's appears at first far less obviously a Western, lacking as it does so many of the conventionally identifying semantic features. Yet gradually, we respond to the syntactic shape of the whole, not only in its recurrent thematic pressures on family life and civic coherence but as well through plot dynamics that seem a familiar part of a long cinematic tradition. Our very generic knowledge helps us shape an otherwise mysterious narrative into a plot we recognize *as* Western. By contrast, Lee's film more immediately draws us to immediate conclusions through costuming, setting, horses, and singularly understated acting styles, even if it soon becomes clear that this is less a Western than a powerful drama of identity that simply happens to be set *in* the West. As a melodrama, it strenuously denies many of the conventional social and civic values so often endorsed by Westerns in focusing intently on figures unable to resolve their circumstances or do anything other than flee from the families they have chosen. In fact, Ang Lee himself finally admitted the film "has very little to do with the Western genre" (Clarke 2006, 28). Yet ironically, for all the differences between the films, they share (if from alternative perspectives) a persistent concern with the issue of personal identity—of choice and deliberation, of social pressures and the effect of past behavior on present contingencies. Jack Twist's anguished admission to Ennis that "I wish I knew how to quit you" could just as readily serve to express Tom Stall's dismay at the psychological persistence of Joey Cusack as a figure in his life. The ongoing problem raised so persistently in both domestic melodrama and the Western, perhaps more prominently than other genres, concerns this central question of who one really is when pressures rise and circumstances turn adverse.

Yet what crucially separates Tom Stall from Jack Twist and Ennis Del Mar is his thoroughgoing commitment to family relations and community structures, in registering a fierce unwillingness to let go of the life to which he has committed himself, however painful the process of persisting. That is finally less an aesthetic than an ethical judgment, of course, and hardly registers the quality of either film as film. But in generic terms, it helps us understand the way in which cinematic structures and viewer expectations intersect, producing the film we are watching. It should be added that both *Brokeback Mountain* and *A History of Violence* share a central concern with questions of what it means to be a man, a father, and a citizen—questions all variously raised, though addressed in nearly opposite ways. What is perhaps at last most strange, however, is the way in which conventions of the Western and of domestic melodrama continue to drive our readings, even in an era when neither genre is anywhere near the dominant form it once was, but instead more like an increasingly vague memory or receding dream. Well into the twenty-first century, it might seem odd to consider what such generic suasions continue to mean, when so many people are no longer familiar with the films making up those genres. Yet they still dictate our interpretive efforts.

6

DUELING GENRES IN
NO COUNTRY FOR OLD MEN

Clearly, late Westerns trust to viewers' familiarity with the genre's syntax, sometimes hidden in an unfamiliar semantic realm, often contrasting that syntax with alternative film structures (noir, melodrama, crime). What distinguishes the Coen brothers' *No Country for Old Men* is that it not only offers a contrast but ups the stakes with a clash of genre values that finally cannot be resolved. In fact, that very clash initially drew them to the project of adapting Cormac McCarthy's 2005 novel. As Joel admitted, it "was familiar, congenial to us; we're naturally attracted to subverting genre. We liked the fact that the bad guys never really meet the good guys, that McCarthy did not follow through on formula expectations" (Coen 2007). And in this, their efforts integrate points of contention that have emerged in other late Westerns, not only of odd generic intersections but of troubling questions having to do with film adaptation and cultural values. McCarthy, after all, is not only the preeminent Western novelist of his generation but also the most important author who also writes screenplays, which he has done since his career began (not only of original materials but adapting his own early fiction). He lends a special authority to any investigation of late Westerns, especially in a period when formula fiction can sometimes seem derivative. And while the Coen brothers represent the cinematic "epitome of the neo-noir impulse in the twenty-first century" (Dixon 2009, 151), it might be conceded that McCarthy represents something like that status in American fiction.

Perhaps the most intriguing aspect of the Coens' adaptation consists in heightening a tension between Western and noir that seems less apparent in the novel, manifesting how starkly an affirmative vision of the West (its regional optimism, individualist ethos, devotion to civic and family values) no longer prevails, as nostalgia fails to compel contemporary interest. While the film may solicit our desire for the generic affirmations of the Western, it does so only to reveal their utter baselessness—a revelation that ironically, in a belated time, has itself become mildly reassuring. Much like Halsted Welles in his screenplay adaptation of Leonard's story, "3:10 to Yuma," the Coens genuinely aspired to evoke the spirit of McCarthy's novel. Ethan insisted their film was shot from a script so faithful to it that he and his brother Joel simply copied it out as a screenplay: "one of us types into the computer while the other holds the spine of the book open flat" (Patterson 2007). Of course, any cinematic version necessarily strays from its precursor text, but it could well be argued that the Coen's version is less an "adaptation" than, say, Delmer Daves's film since it actually "began as a screenplay and may have sat around in a drawer for some time before McCarthy turned it into a novel" (Ellis 2006, 228). Still, the differences are instructive, as Geoffrey O'Brien admiringly points out: "Only on closer comparison does it become clear how thoroughly the Coens have cut and reshaped the material, not merely conflating or deleting subplots but pervasively reimagining the book and in some respects improving on it" (2007, 31).[1] And that improvement occurs, paradoxically, through their willingness to turn more self-consciously than McCarthy does to generic conventions themselves, adapting his narrative to enhance the novel's informing contradictions.

If *Bad Day at Black Rock* and both versions of *3:10 to Yuma* introduce thematic scenes and camera angles that remind us more of noir films than Westerns, the Coens give an extra turn of the screw, deliberately soliciting us cinematically into a familiar generic space, to which they then dramatically deny entry. As in other late Westerns, viewers are thwarted in assumptions they provisionally make, finding expectations upended by conventional narrative and cinematic patterns. But instead of genres melding together, as often occurs in classic Hollywood cinema, the Coens' film strangely poses genres against one another, drawing on noir techniques to defy what their Western materials seem to solicit. It is as if (to borrow from my earlier figurative invocation) borders emerged as a cinematic gesture dividing one technique from another. Fleeting reminders of wide-open landscape offer a teasing prospect soon abandoned; plush narrative embellishments and wide-angle shots are forsaken for clipped dialogue, spare descriptions, and intense close-ups, locking characters within themselves. And to intensify that effect, the film plays with an unusual series of overhead shots that immure figures in what appears to be a perdurable present. Much as both novelistic and cinematic versions of *No Country for Old Men* initially encourage a conventional Western reading, as we saw with *Brokeback Mountain*, expectations are soon sorely rebuffed. A tradition that had led to the cumulative revisions of Leone, Peckinpah, and Eastwood—each of whom sustained an elegiac mode that Robert Warshow earlier found praiseworthy in the genre's "value of violence"—now has perversely come to rest on a narrative stitched together through little more than outright accident, through pointless brutality and inexplicable savagery.

The beginnings of this trend emerged in 2005 with three successful films (*Three Burials*, *A History of Violence*, and *Brokeback Mountain*) that reshaped our notion of the late Western through inventive generic intersections. But the Coens seem marginally more ambitious in at least one regard: their willingness to move beyond reshaping assumptions to a fuller dismantling of them, undermining one of our most powerful popular cultural visions, and doing so as much via style as by plot. The foundational principles on which the Western has long relied are not simply challenged (which revisionist films had done for decades) but seemingly dismissed out of hand. An intersection of otherwise antithetical generic dynamics had led to a standoff that reveals both a failed hope for the kind of resolution the Western has long provided and the lack of any conviction in settling on an alternative. Unlike other late Westerns that require the viewer's silent assent to generic lineaments less than obvious, *No Country* undermines the very process of adducing a genre identification. As Jay Ellis intriguingly claims, McCarthy's is "a story whose surface merely appears to fit the genre of film noir" (2011, 97). The Coen brothers transform that supposedly mere appearance into a powerful cross tension, though leaving the viewer finally uncertain.

This has twin and opposing effects. On the negative side, it means that landscape is no longer redemptive, or even unremittingly desolate, but altogether irrelevant, and as such drops out of sight. Violence no longer registers as potentially restorative (as it had long seemed in earlier Westerns) or brutally exhilarating (as in more recent revisionist films), but simply run of the mill, gratuitous, excessive, unremitting, and at last likewise disappears from view, occurring off-screen. Finally, an abiding concern with testing versions of masculinity, long central to our interest in the Western's stock figures—the stalwart heroes, amoral villains, drunken professionals, and weak-willed citizenry—has drained away as *No Country* presents instead characters reduced to stunned bewilderment, casual impulse, and sheer irrationality. On the positive side, the aspiration for a vision that might replace what has been lost still lingers, a sensation like that of a phantom limb we still continue to feel. Few characters, it seems, know any longer how to act with moral integrity, but those few do still matter. And while the characterization of "anti-Western" has been invoked before to describe such revisions, they have always had the effect of at least temporarily reviving the genre, bringing its central considerations to life once again. The triumph of Joel and Ethan Coen's adaptation lies in their having grasped how fully McCarthy's novel subverts Western conventions and then revealing via noir techniques how much our desire for generic platitudes may be misdirected, if not unavailing. While the Western refuses to remain dead, as the success of the Coens' own version of *True Grit* (2010) later confirms, *No Country* already reveals how thoroughly the genre keeps finding new ways to revive.

DISAPPEARING LANDSCAPES

Adaptations largely succeed on their own terms, and the Coen brothers (for all their claims of fidelity to McCarthy's novel) are considerably more interested in evoking the Western genre than he, if only to dismantle it. The slippage between their version and McCarthy's is instructive, perhaps more so than any presumed shared identity, in their divergence from the novel right at the start. Where McCarthy begins with a notable absence of any reference to landscape, the Coens intriguingly open their film by concentrating not only on a sense of place but by seducing the viewer with the customary generic suasions of the Western. Following a brief, black-screen title sequence, as dawn gradually burnishes a west-Texas landscape, Sheriff Ed Tom Bell (Tommy Lee Jones) speaks for ninety seconds in contemplative voice-over. That production technique is a feature customarily associated with film noir, rarely occurring in Westerns, and by introducing their film in this acoustic mode conjoined with a landscape sequence identified with the Western, the Coens all but announce their intention to intertwine the two genres.[2]

Sheriff Bell's rumination has been spliced together from italicized openings of three of the novel's thirteen sections, only part of which comes from the actual first entry, with most evoked substantially later: "I was sheriff of this county when I was 25 years old. Hard to believe. Grandfather was a law man. Father too. Me and him was sheriffs at the same time, him up at Plain Ellen, me out here. I think he was pretty proud of that. I know I was." This filial pride in shared vocation, of father and father's father in supposedly less troubled times, has nothing to do with the novel's austere prologue. Still, the Coens place it here as a distinct nostalgic reminder in a sentiment that once again signals the Western. Enforcing that credential, a series of west Texas landscapes materialize like snapshots, first of a morning star hanging over a butte, then of telephone wires in brightening dawn.[3] The third image appears like a cinemagraph of grass rustling, finally seeming to bring the landscape alive, followed by the sun imperceptibly rising over a distant hill, making it clear these are no longer still images but filmed scenes. Wind persists (visually, acoustically) in half the images, at one point spinning a tin windmill, until a panning shot abruptly breaks the rhythm of luminous locales as a deputy quietly walks a man to the back of a police cruiser, places a strange compressed air tank in the front passenger seat, then speeds away. Throughout, light shadows barren hills, starkly desolate and unpeopled, evoking the spare beauty of grassed terrain and barbed-wire fencing in a paean to west Texas that confirms Sheriff Bell's words: the allure of a landscape we want remembered. Like Ang Lee's scenes, or Tommy Lee Jones's in *Three Burials*, the setting represents the West as distinctly iconic American scenery.

The Coen brothers make a deliberate and significant change here, realizing McCarthy ventures none of these visual references. On the contrary, his novel disdains any hint of nostalgic reminiscence conveyed by Sheriff Bell's sour recollection of evil in a world he refuses to engage (the cinematic voice-over cuts off the novel's caustic repudiation, "*I think a man would have to put his soul at hazard. And I wont do that. I think now that maybe I never would*" [2005, 4]). The novel opens, in fact, with the episode that immediately follows the film's landscape shots: an interior scene, with a close-up of the deputy facing the camera on the phone to his sheriff, describing the man he has just arrested. For the Coens, that framing marks a blunt transition from John Ford's mise-en-scène to something more like Samuel Fuller's urban noir vision, of visually confining office space, cinder-block and gray linoleum, all in starkly cold fluorescent lighting. Just as the deputy assures his sheriff that "I've got things under control," the screen explodes in the film's most violent encounter, with Anton Chigurh (Javier Bardem) dropping his handcuffed wrists over the deputy's throat, slowly strangling him. The crucial question raised by this sequence is why the Coens have added generic markers of the Western here (via a tone of nostalgia and an unpeopled landscape) to a novel that initially seems to defy the genre— indeed, in a film that itself will go on to refute any such affiliation.

As dislocating as this opening is, pin-balling against such divergent extremes, it deftly establishes the ways in which the film will continue to disrupt generic presumptions. Rarely are wide-angle vistas lingered over, in contrast with a parade of bleak motel rooms, cramped bathrooms, shabby exteriors, drab automobiles, mostly filmed at night with unsettling close-ups of faces, feet, and odd body parts. And a preponderance of scenes appears from vertically stressed angles, as either extremely high- or low-angle shots. Certainly, the horizontality of the title sequence (all but routine for the Western) is largely abandoned in favor of the constraining signature features of film noir. The Coens, in other words, insert initial landscape references simply to have them abruptly end, as an adaptation of the novel's own milder solicitations of, yet resistance to, the Western genre.

Only once in the entire novel, in fact, does McCarthy call to mind his otherwise remarkable artistry in landscape description with a scene that seems to match the Coens' opening slide show of the Permian Basin. Sheriff Bell gazes "out across the desert. So quiet. Low hum of wind in the wires. High bloodweeds along the road. Wiregrass and sacahuista. Beyond in the stone arroyos the tracks of dragons. The raw rock mountains shadowed in the late sun and to the east the shimmering abscissa of the desert plains under a sky where raincurtains hung dark as soot all along the quadrant" (2005, 45). Delight in the alluring sweep of high west-Texas plains and sky emerges in the characteristic broken rhythms of McCarthy's prose, reminiscent here of large swatches of panoramic illustration in *Blood Meridian* (1985) and *All the Pretty Horses* (1992). Yet just as suddenly, description subsides to brief designations of mere points of a compass, to simple numbers of state roads, to stark names of generic streets and towns. And the Coens capture that sheer indifference to place in their cinematography, with again only one major exception: when Llewelyn Moss (Josh Brolin) first appears hunting pronghorn antelope against a wide-screen pan of untrammeled country. Glancing out over the spare landscape, occasionally through his rifle sight, his gaze becomes the viewer's in a kind of silent admiration.

The camera, however, then concentrates on his face and feet after he misses a risky shot, shifting up and down, back and forth, before making a horizontal pan to a telephoto view of a black dog limping away. Other pans follow as Moss tracks the wounded antelope before stumbling upon abandoned pickups signaling a drug deal gone bad. After he searches for and finds the wounded "last man," the scene ends with Moss retrieving a satchel of cash just as a storm erupts. Despite Joel Coen's later insistence that "landscape becomes a huge, important character" (Coen 2007), that view is the last of any sustained (far less, admiring) contemplation of west-Texas plains.[4] Thereafter, only a few brief glimpses appear: one, after Moss escapes at night from killers at the original site, recovering the next morning near the river; another, the transition to an overhead shot of a Texaco station; a third, the burning of a 1977 Ford as Sheriff Bell and Deputy Wendell watch. In fact, regional apparel reminds us we are in familiar generic terrain far more than panoramas, with high-heeled cowboy boots, buckled belts, and tall hats as the *costume de rigueur*, even Carson Wells (Woody Harrelson) refuses to remove his Stetson inside a Houston office high-rise.[5] In short, the film's semantics suggest variously that this might be a Western, with setting, costume, and characterization all matching the generic model, but only as a means of making viewers wonder the more at the considerable syntactical deflections toward noir.

Landscape is rendered strangely irrelevant in McCarthy's novel again by being all but utterly ignored descriptively, though the Coens' fidelity to this strategy does not really differentiate it from such other late Westerns as *Bad Day at Black Rock* or *A History of Violence*. What does distinguish *No Country* from other films set in west Texas is how fully the border with Mexico is at once delineated yet stripped of any familiar cultural import. Indeed, the Rio Grande is traversed a number of times by Llewelyn Moss, most dramatically when he escapes from Chigurh in Eagle Pass, crossing over to its sister city, Piedras Negras, to receive emergency care in the city hospital. He stashes his stolen cash by throwing it over a border fence—where Wells will later search for it—as if the drug lord Pablo Acosta's cartel profits had found their proper border home. And the novel actually accentuates this accessible border crossing, with Moss earlier leaving Del Rio (having stashed the money in his motel's air conditioning duct) to have dinner across the Rio Grande in Ciudad Acuña. Indeed, McCarthy goes to the trouble of mapping out named towns and numbered highways in his Permian Basin setting: from Eagle Pass to El Paso; from Odessa and Uvalde to Dryden and Lozier Canyon; from Sheffield, Sonorra and Fort Stockton to Balmorhea, Brackettville, and Devil's River; all interconnected by routes 2, 90, 131, and 349 south, including a stop "two miles past the junction of 481 and 57" (2005, 170). Yet for all the precision, which enlivens the novel with Google maps open to guide the reading, none of this is described further or lent any evocative sway. Local names and numbers remain merely that, no different in Texas than Mexico. The Rio Grande, celebrated by Ford, Peckinpah, and Sayles, among others, as a border crossing to be celebrated as an almost mythical divide, becomes in McCarthy simply a river distinction without a difference on either side. Sayles's investment in lines in the dirt has been simply swept aside, or rather over.

The Coens translate this vision by likewise draining any visual significance out of the cultural border that has long seemed a Western trope. Partly this is confirmed by the completeness with which region becomes invisible in a film that takes place largely at night, in crowded interior spaces, via intense close-ups and medium shots. That style is apparent all but immediately in scenes devoted to Moss, who returns in the dark to the Desert Aire Trailer Park where he joins Carla Jean (Kelly Macdonald) on the couch in a tight two-shot watching a television movie. Later, wounded, he patches his shoulder in their tiny trailer bathroom, followed by a severe close-up of his face on a bus as he sends Carla Jean to her mother in Odessa. Thereafter, he appears in additional close-ups: reserving a motel room; selecting items in a clothing store; browsing in a gun shop; then catching a cab to the Eagle Pass motel, once again at night. Interspersed among these moments are extended scenes of hiding the satchel in an air vent using tent poles and Venetian cord, with close-ups of Moss sawing off a shotgun barrel, the camera invariably focused on his hands at work. Chigurh is presented the same way, in medium shots at a Texaco station in menacing dialogue with its owner[6]; later, he looms interrogatively over Moss's stalwart landlady. The combination of interiors and night scenes via frequent close-ups and medium shots seems almost intended to contradict the expansiveness of the opening landscapes, inducing a claustrophobic feeling that at once contributes to and contradicts the Western's semantic tribute to wide-open space (in this regard, we are reminded of Geoffrey O'Brien's description of claustrophobia as actually, if counterintuitively, a constituent of the traditional Western).

This aversion to landscape in preference for confinement (either with characters physically restricted or cinematically represented as such through camera framing itself) enacts the emotional curbs that nearly everyone feels, cut off from choices and opportunities, unable to break free. The clichéd gesture of the Western has invariably been to proffer the option of riding off, remaining footloose and free (at least as a masculine privilege), and that alternative has been updated in this modern setting with automobiles, which normally represent a transecting of space, offering a panoramic pleasure in wide-open vistas. Yet in a film that begins with Chigurh being arrested and placed in a police car (we never learn why he is stopped[7]) and that ends with an unexpected car crash (we never learn why a street sign is ignored), the iconic association of automobiles with landscape is slyly twisted. In both novel and film, vehicles themselves turn ironically into static spectatorial sites, notably of mayhem and violence, beginning with Chigurh's escape in a stolen police cruiser, pulling over a sedan to murder an innocent driver. Moss then stumbles upon five trucks clustered at a drug shoot-out and later that night is chased by gunmen in a speeding Dodge Ramcharger. When he escapes from the Eagle Pass hotel, the Coens add a scene to McCarthy's novel by having him wave down a pickup truck, all at foot-level, offering bland assurances ("Don't worry, I ain't gonna hurt ya") just before the driver is unexpectedly blasted from behind by Chigurh. Wounded himself, Chigurh goes the next morning to torch a sedan sitting in front of a pharmacy, merely to create a convenient distraction. And later, in a stalled stolen truck, he is aided by a jump-starting Samaritan chicken farmer, whose unseen murder is gruesomely confirmed by Chigurh's casual hosing feathers out of the man's stolen truck bed. When Moss is murdered (in another scene never shown), Sheriff Bell grimly watches a pickup careen around a corner as Hispanic killers jump into the open bed to escape.

Sedans, taxis, semis, muscle trucks, station wagons, pickups of varying vintage: all become instruments of impromptu violence but serve only fleetingly in their usual function as vehicles of transport. In a film (and novel) where figures are continually compelled to traverse a landscape, rarely do we observe them move from place to place, which lends a curiously mysterious, spectral aspect to character. "As we can see with the first line that opens nearly all of the novel's sequences," Stephen Tatum observes, "Chigurh never journeys, which is to say departs, travels, and then arrives somewhere. He—like the other characters in the novel—is always *arriving* somewhere, the temporal duration of the journey compressed or entirely elided in McCarthy's screenplay-like narration. . . . Chigurh magically appears and disappears" (2011, 89). Yet one could easily say the same of Moss and Sheriff Bell, neither of whom is actually seen journeying any more than Chigurh. In the novel, vehicles "back out" or "pull up," signaling movement about to occur or having just been completed, but movement never itself described. We are given a vague sense of direction without temporal motion, as Sheriff Bell "and Wendell pulled onto the paved shoulder in front of the unit and parked and got out" (McCarthy 2005, 42); or as Bell "drove out in Torbert's four wheel drive truck" (McCarthy 2005, 95); or "It was almost a three hour drive to Odessa and dark when he got there" (McCarthy 2005, 125). The Coens effectively capture these narrative lacunae interspersed throughout by McCarthy in avoiding the feeling of being in motion, of having wind in one's hair and lingering over vistas (a feeling frequently celebrated in their other films, and in any case, part of the semantics of the Western). No one looks to see where they are, or where they might be going, or what the landscape displays—with the notable exception of Chigurh eyeing his electronic receiver, hunting among cheap motels for the transponder and stolen money, slowly perusing hidden possibilities on the basis of sonic frequency, not visual fields. Instead of looking outward, toward the horizon, surveying the terrain (in an automotive variant of horses traversing the cinematic frame of the Western), the film regularly focuses on being closed in, as characters duck into or slide out of vehicles, or simply stare sightlessly off, sitting motionless behind the wheel. The dynamic movement that so often characterizes the genre is utterly absent, in favor once again of a deliberately static frame that seems to incarcerate characters.

INSCRUTABLE CLOSE-UPS

That persistent feeling of being thwarted, imprisoned in a deadlocked moment, closed off from opportunity, registers a noir vision of the past's hold on the present. And if the film embodies that vision in its cinematic flight from space—in a focus on cramped interiors rather than wide-open spaces and in a concomitant shunning of vehicular freedom—Roger Deakins's cinematography compounds that impression with unusual camera angles that more self-consciously close down broad perspectives, first visually but also psychologically. McCarthy's novel achieves this effect through a brutally pared-down style, in which stichomythic dialogue occurs with little indirect discourse accompanying it, offering meager insight into characters' feelings about what is being said either by others or by themselves. And the narrator is appropriately tight lipped, offering minimal or nonexistent physical descriptions of figures and events, often in detached paratactic constructions that reinforce a scene's disconnectedness. Deakins registers this disconnection among McCarthy's characters cinematically by tightening the camera frame on actors' faces so intensely as to sequester figures within themselves—once again, bordered off from others—much as Phedon Papamichael had done in *3:10 to Yuma*, to similar effect. Visually, this noir style compounds the narrative's isolating crunch (never, for instance, having the three central figures meet, segregating them physically *from* one another), focusing so intently on bodies constrained within the camera frame that the determinants of character themselves come under pressure.[8] Among the more dramatic moments in the film occurs precisely through our desire for a confrontation that is denied, in the scene of Bell nearly discovering Chigurh after Moss has been killed. As Jay Ellis has detected, "Only by watching the scene on DVD at extreme slow motion can one see that as Bell pulls up to the motel in the film, *two* deadbolt locks have been shot out by Chigurh. Through editing, the Coens have their audience struggling with what seems an imminent encounter between the last remaining hero and the evil Chigurh" (2011, 109).[9] In fact, the image of Chigurh's reflected face in the brass of the lock barrel seems a physical impossibility. More generally, however, the repeated emphasis on the three main characters' severe isolation from one another makes us wonder why they do what they do. Their motivations remain mysterious (Moss's unnecessary risk taking; Chigurh's regular invocation of a deranged nihilism; Sheriff Bell's melancholy policing), each acting independently for reasons hardly apparent.

Billy Wilder had adroitly anticipated this technique in *Double Indemnity* (1944), presenting the faces of Fred MacMurray, Barbara Stanwyck, and Edward G. Robinson regularly in close-up, frequently separating the characters as well (via flashback and voice-over)—a style grotesquely exaggerated to telling effect in Orson Welles's *The Lady from Shanghai* (1948). Yet more than simply isolating characters within themselves, *No Country* more generally undercuts a generally affirmative, Western ideology by repeatedly registering the irrevocable hold of a shadowed past, once again much as film noir regularly does. The very title of Jacques Tourneur's *Out of the Past* (1947) reflects the inability of a reformed Jeff Bailey (Robert Mitchum) to escape the relentless, vengeful gangster, Whit Sterling (Kirk Douglas). And John Huston's *The Maltese Falcon* (1941) had likewise traced a violent plot inescapably aligned with the fateful legacy of the titular statue. In each of these noir films, the very constraints of the past are enforced by the framing of the camera itself, which seems to close in on characters, to set them behind visual borders that sequester and divide, to heighten the temporal coercions of their lives through spatial suppressions displayed cinematically.

Take the scene of Moss reserving a motel room, having put Carla Jean on a bus to her mother's. The owner offers a rate card while she fixedly intones, "You pick the option that goes with the applicable rate." The irony of her unwittingly judicious words is to remind us of Moss's complete lack of prudence, having already picked an option that comes with an excessive "rate."[10] Yet what seems more significant here is that the scene (expanded from McCarthy's novel) consists of extreme close-ups—of the owner, of Moss, of the rate card itself—that echo Chigurh's encounter at the Texaco station, as if they were taking cues from each other. And the frequency of single-head shots increases as the scene progresses, with faces seemingly constrained by the camera frame itself. Sometimes, the focus is tighter, initiated in the deputy's opening arrest of Chigurh as he places the stun gun in his cruiser, then replicated in the low-angle shot of Chigurh's feet and compressed air tank as he strides up to Moss's double-wide to blow out the cylinder lock. Deakins's camera moves from boots to hand in an intense close-up repeated multiple times in the film, including Chigurh's feet as he slowly strides to a motel room to kill three Hispanics, with only socks, silencer, and tank visible. Later, his socked feet stride into a Dallas high-rise where he shotguns a corrupt businessman—an image soon echoed in a low-angle close-up of Moss limping along the Rio Grande, approaching three college boys to purchase a coat. Cinematography itself seems, through the oddity of its perspectives, to establish the curiously detached, strangely unknowable psychologies we encounter.

At other times, the camera centers tightly on faces: Chigurh sits on Moss's trailer couch, watching TV precisely as Moss did the night before and as Bell will do in a few hours. Here the Coens offer a mildly baffling identification of Bell with Chigurh that is only barely suggested in the novel (McCarthy 2005, 80, 94). What does this conflation suggest, or is it simply one more exhibition of the mystery of character? Later, Deakins focuses on the back of Chigurh's head when he's on the phone to Carla Jean's mother, repeated on two other eerie occasions: having just killed his Hispanic opposite numbers at the motel room, as he ponders where the money is stashed; and having just shot his businessman employer in the Houston high-rise, as we stare from behind at his "Dorothy Hamill wedge-cut" (Stewart 2008). The effect is to make him not more under-

Fig. 18. The low view of a bolt gun and heels on the way to mayhem and murder in *No Country for Old Men* (Miramax Films).

standable, but less, seeing him turned away, resisting our inquiring gaze. Both earlier and later, moreover, Deakins focuses on nothing suggesting rumination or introspection—insignificant cotton balls and tail lights, gas tanks and wounded legs, close-ups of conversations in hotels and hospital beds—right up to the point where Chigurh drives away after killing Carla Jean, only to be unexpectedly hit by another car, with a side close-up of his eyes on the rear-view mirror increasing the shock of the crash.

The cumulative weight of these cinematic choices is to foreclose psychology, to make character seem somehow inscrutable or otherwise unavailable, as if (again) beyond some invisible border where we are precluded from going. Signaling this premise is the Coens' idiosyncratic citing of a 1953 black-and-white film, Charles Warren's *Flight to Tangier*, which Carla Jean is watching on television when Moss first returns home. Corinne Calvet, driving a car with Jack Palance, is presented in a close two-shot concluding an exchange with the ominous warning, "My place is wrong." Nothing more of the film is presented, a scene lasting mere seconds, but it registers once again a distinct cinematic style (facial close-up, shadowed interior, automobile) along with a portentous admonition that any place is unsuitable, granting neither shelter nor security, simply "wrong." That judgment seems an echo of McCarthy's title, referring to Yeats's reminder that "an aged man is but a paltry thing," though his novel more generally speculates in passing whether "no country for old men" is also no country for anyone else. No place here exists that is immune from suffering or danger, even if leaving west Texas seems itself inconceivable (the obvious solution to Moss's dilemma, after all, would simply have been to take the money and fly away, though that is a prospect never considered). In short, "my place is wrong," inserted arbitrarily, echoes as silent reminder through the film, marking at once the need to escape, to find another place, coupled with the constant, ineluctable frustrations of that desire.

The resonances of that spoken line are hardly the only echo of Warren's film, which eerily seems to have anticipated not only the Coen brothers' adaptation but to some extent McCarthy's novel as well. Granted, genres intersect and alter over time, and the influence of noir has been pervasive over the Western's history. Still, the very structure of *No Country* mirrors that of *Flight to Tangier*, which is also filled with characters in cars, who *do* succeed in traversing a Moroccan landscape that looks remarkably like the Permean Basin. Journeying through Tangier and south in search of stolen money, the three main characters flee past checkpoints and escape pursuing criminals, while hiding and sleeping in their vehicles. Chigurh's dramatic search for stolen loot with a beeping receiver forms an updated version of Warren's cinematic search for a missing three million dollars. More compellingly, the earlier film aligns three disparate characters who are far from what they seem, concealing themselves and their pasts almost melodramatically from each other—and from us. Appearing greedy when they are not, selfish when actually self-sacrificing, they enact a plot similar to McCarthy's but whose psychological presences are the converse. The film seems to have led the Coens to realize how much the body at once expresses and withholds, obscuring character just as the body is visually exposed to ever greater (if unrevealing) scrutiny.

That "obscuring" takes place sonically as well, in the strangely uncharacteristic silence (certainly for the Coen brothers) of the sound track. An
all-but-complete absence of non-diegetic music characterizes their two-hour
film, corroborating initially what we already knew: how little landscape (or
other settings) is meant to resonate either psychologically or emotionally,
matching McCarthy's own verbal silences.[11] More generally, the silenced
orchestral acoustics so familiar to most films here accentuates the lack of
knowable psychology, confirming characters as mysterious, with motives
and emotions that remain enigmatic. Westerns conventionally present
characters so clearly as to seem all but allegorical, making us rarely wonder about motivation or psychology in narratives pitched toward historical
crises that variously resolve issues of justice and law.[12] By contrast, noir
figures are the opposite in their persistently mulling over what has gone
wrong (often in extended voice-over), reflecting all but obsessively on
others' inscrutable behavior (most commonly, femmes fatales), or one's
own disastrous missteps. *Double Indemnity* forms a perfect match for
these generic fixations, embodied in Stanwyck's brilliantly implacable
unreadability. And Jane Greer's chameleonlike inexpressiveness in *Out of
the Past* regularly masks an encyclopedia of selfish feelings and ambitions.
Placing everything on the surface of faces is the domain of the Western,
whereas noir seems defiantly to suppress conscious revelation. Dan Flory
paradoxically observes, perhaps aware of such generic tendencies: "One of
the more remarkable features of McCarthy's novel is the number of times
he describes characters thinking about and contemplating their lives" (2011,
118). Yet as he adds, far from being reassured by such self-consciousness
on the part of each of the main characters, we are placed in "an anxious,
perplexed, and nostalgic state of contemplation" (2011, 121), largely because
their efforts do little to make them less inscrutable.[13] Sheriff Ed Tom Bell
is persistently bewildered by the decline of civic standards, reminding us
of Carson Wells's description in the novel of him as "a redneck sheriff in
a hick town in a hick country. In a hick state" (McCarthy 2005, 157); Anton
Chigurh embodies a bafflingly principled malevolence, as he patiently,

sociopathically, expounds his philosophy to befuddled victims; Llewelyn Moss seems merely capricious, alternating between rash opportunism and equally rash charitable gestures. Yet if each of these three seem entangled by untoward events, it is hardly clear why they act as they do or what drives them psychologically. That lack of psychological coherence, or at least of transparency, seems to have become a feature common to late Westerns, and the reasons may simply be that standards of masculine identity themselves have become unmoored in a more permissive, less gender-strict era.

Part of this obfuscation of character, curiously enough, seems conveyed by the novel's unusual devotion to otherwise minor details, with the very irrelevance of certain objects calling attention to the absence of unified temperaments or personalities. The narrative turns away from unrevealing faces and bodies out of what seems like frustration, focusing instead on furniture and random commodities. The Coens aptly adapt this narrative pattern in the visual curiosity about different brands of cowboy boots; or Moss's careful assembling of a tool out of tent poles, cord, wire hangers, and duct tape; or his hiding the money satchel in an air conditioning system; or his shopping for clothes and guns; or Chigurh's cleaning, anesthetizing, then repairing a leg wound. As Jay Ellis observes, "Usually, when loving detail is lavished on something possessed by the hero of genre fiction, it will save his neck. Here, the details prove meaningless" (2011, 235). Yet details are never insignificant in fiction or in film, and we might better understand both McCarthy's and the Coens' lavishing of "loving detail" in terms of Roland Barthes "*effet réal*": the theory that "useless details" are an inevitable part of a "referential illusion" (1986, 142), and in doing little to convey specific meanings actually establish a general "category of 'the real' (and not its contingent contents)" (1986, 148). In film, more pointedly, what Umberto Eco described as this "technique of the aimless glance" (1970, 166) seems part of a taut tension between narrative and description, contributing to scenes in which action can be delayed yet heightened, without psychology entering into question.[14] In the process, characters are established as genuine yet inscrutable, vivid yet somehow unfathomable. *No Country*'s series of lingering, sometimes probing shots of articles and commodities seems of a piece with its images of separate physiognomies, reducing all to the status of objects that remain at last unrevealing.

The effort to make character *un*revealing might seem strange at first glance, certainly within parameters of the late Western, where Jack Twist and Ennis Del Mar, or Tom Stahl, or Sam Deeds each have their psychologies gradually exposed—indeed, where the films in which they appear make that effort central and distinctive. Yet Joel Coen has described his film's opening as a literal attempt to conceal, to engage the viewer by "controlling the disclosure of the principle of characters through an extended sequence.... So you don't see Javier's face until that overhead shot where he's strangling the deputy.... We were going, let's deliberately keep these characters, let's shoot it all from behind, let's keep them rim-lit, and not exactly see them until they stop and the light changes. That was sort of a way of sort of bringing you into the story" (Baumbach 2011).[15] Once "into the story," however, that "principle of characters" is clearly sustained, informing much of the rest of the film. The Coens' insight into McCarthy's antipsychological bias, in fact, may help explain why they omit the novel's most direct engagement with the issue of character, which makes explicit what is already clear cinematically. Moss has picked up a hitchhiker traveling to California to begin a new life and soon protests against her free-spirited belief that she can escape the past, as if it were a matter of picking up stakes in a Western and starting over on some new frontier:

> The point is there aint no point.... It's not about knowin where you are. It's about thinkin you got there without takin anything with you. Your notions about startin over. Or anybody's. You don't start over. That's what it's about. Ever step you take is forever. You cant make it go away. None of it. You understand what I'm sayin? ... You think when you wake up in the mornin yesterday don't count. But yesterday is all that does count. What else is there? Your life is made out of the

days it's made out of. Nothin else. You might think you could run away and change your name and I don't know what all. Start over. And then one mornin you wake up and look at the ceilin and guess who's layin there? (McCarthy 2005, 227–28)

Here, Moss suggests a perspective that appears more beholden to dark noir assumptions than to Westerns in the sheer unchangeable intractability of our lives, that character is blindly cumulative, built up ineradicably over time, explicable as a series of customary gestures performed, a pattern become inescapable: "Your life is made out of the days it's made out of. Nothin else." The statement sounds relatively uncharacteristic of Westerns, even late Westerns, which eye the prospect of self-transformation with grudging confidence, sometimes faith. Yet Moss's contention could easily describe the leading characters in *Out of the Past* or *Double Indemnity* or Fritz Lang's *Scarlet Street* (1945), all inextricably bound to their histories, all trying desperately to flee from yesterday, all unable despite a fervent resolve to "live like other people" (as Keechie [Cathy O'Donnell] pleads in *They Live by Night*). For all Moss's Emersonian earnestness about the passive intransigency of our lives, what proves curiously paradoxical in both novel and film once again is how little actions reveal of psychology.[16] More important than his conviction that we cannot alter ourselves because we are bound to our pasts is the realization that we cannot know why we are *as* we are in the world envisioned by McCarthy and the Coen brothers. Looking at oneself, however intently, discloses all too little.

ANGLING UP

No Country self-consciously stresses this effort at idle gazing, taking a page from the philosophy Moss expresses in the novel—"you wake up and look at the ceilin and guess who's layin there?"—and translating it into recurrent overhead and low-angle shots that supplant the Western's more characteristic horizontal pan. Here is where the film brings together theme and cinematography, melding a relatively dark vision of character with an oblique perspective on bodies. All successful films achieve that integrated union, but it is worth attending to Deakins's efforts beyond his focus on faces since his signature style is to gaze up at them, then down, immuring characters in thought, hinting at displaced mental removes from the present that are as futile *as* that present, as "wrong" imaginatively as any actual place in the novel.[17] That camera style was anticipated with a different effect by Charles Lawton Jr., whose high-angle crane shots in the first *3:10 to Yuma* granted the viewer an apparent sense of command. Yet Deakins interestingly seems to combine Lawton's and Papamichael's cinematic choices, not only in denying the viewer any sure access to characters' psychology by moving the camera closer, but also in elevating and lowering the lens, underscoring from a supposedly more informed perspective how little can be done, or known. "The Coens offer rhythmically the extreme high over-head angle," Joan Mellen observes, and by doing so they "distance themselves from events that no one has hope of mediating" (2008, 28). She goes on to contend more pointedly that "the high angle creates an abiding sense that the film itself is frightened of Chigurh" (2008, 28). That observation certainly explains the violent opening of Chigurh strangling the deputy, dragging him to the linoleum floor, as both men strain face-upward for a full half minute, establishing immediately a stark contrast with the opening sequence of horizontal landscape images. Then Chigurh washes his bloody wrists in the bathroom, viewed from a camera directly overhead, pointed down on the porcelain sink and its mirror image; seconds later, the camera focuses down to Chigurh's pointed boots as he picks up his bolt gun. This first full scene of the film unequivocally announces that this is the vertiginous angle from which the camera will continue to focus.

Accurate as Mellen's visual reading of Chigurh is, she ignores how often the film enforces an identical perspective on Moss and Sheriff Bell, with the same noir effect of estranging the viewer, making us pause at the suddenly unstable workings of character, denying us any fuller knowledge. Deakins nicely captures that strain, which McCarthy renders through psychological

Fig. 19. Mirrored overhead shot of Anton Chigurh's bloody wrists, doubling the pleasure and pain in *No Country for Old Men* (Miramax Films).

allusion, as when Bell informs Carla Jean that Moss is "in trouble" and then pauses as "he sipped his coffee. The face that lapped and shifted in the dark liquid in the cup seemed an omen of things to come. Things losing shape. Taking you with them" (McCarthy 2005, 127). That vivid moment of shape-shifting face coalescing as an "omen" in the swirl of black coffee is illustrated variously through cinematic images and angles. And Deakins confirms this unsettling process early on in high-angle shots of Moss as well, trailing a wounded antelope, looking down at blood spoor, followed by a reverse shot back up at him (a sequence matched by Chigurh later gazing down at bloody footprints of Moss himself after their Eagle Hotel shootout). The self-enclosing perspectives here, especially made from the vertical, reinforce our sense of stricture, of subjectivity being mildly oppressed.

On the first night, as Moss returns to his double-wide with the drug money, the camera focuses down on him crawling under the trailer to hide his H&K machine pistol. The next night, the scene is reinforced dramatically as he recovers the pistol despite being wounded, with Carla Jean now peering down in a high shot as he glares back up at her in response.

Earlier, he had awakened in the night, staring up at the camera, which slowly zooms in to capture him swayed in a fateful moment of sympathy, deciding to fetch water back to a wounded Hispanic ("All right"). That pivotal scene is later repeated almost exactly when he wakes in his Eagle Pass hotel room, gazing pensively upward, as the camera again zooms gradually down to register his face suddenly grasp that a transponder must be in the satchel ("There just ain't no way"). Overhead shots proliferate throughout, pressing us into a strangely disorienting mental state that corresponds to current cinematic practice across the board but seems more intense (certainly, the shots contrast vividly with Stuart Dryburgh's morphing pans in *Lone Star*). Consider, again, when Moss goes to buy boots, then retreats to the store's bathroom, with a view directed down to the narrow space as he changes bloody socks, spraying his injured feet with disinfectant. Later, likewise, Chigurh retreats to his motel to nurse a badly wounded leg, relaxing in a bath, rinsing his thigh, all shot from either overhead or extreme upward-looking perspectives. Even Sheriff Bell is filmed eating at a café, first looking up at Deputy Wendell explaining a lab report, then at Wendell in a reverse shot looking down acutely at Bell, followed by an aerial shot of Moss strolling into a gun store. Carson Wells hunts along the Rio Grande at Eagle Pass, searching the border in an effort to locate Moss's hidden satchel in a sequence that opens dramatically from grass-level upward through a chain-link fence against the sky, finally focusing on Wells's face. And then, "He took out his camera and snapped a picture of the sky, the river, the world" (McCarthy 2005, 168), casting about cinematically in a fashion that ironically Deakins himself seems to adopt. Throughout, establishing shots are frequently high- or low-angle: of the Texaco Station on the plains; of the clothing store where Moss stops; of Chigurh's bolt gun, or of Chigurh and Moss staring up at air conditioning vents.

At a minimum, Deakins's cinematic gestures are mildly disruptive, keeping the viewer visually off balance as they link the three main characters via common, repeated associations of angles, perspectives, and body parts. More importantly, such cinematography reinforces our sense of human character as unknowable, somehow slanted. In this, the Coens dramatically adapt that tendency of McCarthy's novel rarely to indulge in subjective prospects, if only because each character seems imprisoned in his own understated narrative construct. We are who we are, attests the telegraphic prose, with pasts that can only be regretted not changed, with presents we can but rarely control, pointing toward futures we can never predict. That is the burden of Moss's assertion to the hitchhiker, encapsulating what otherwise appears as the premise of both novel and film. The Western may protest against the idea that one is bound by a web of unsolicited consequences, of fractious events and hapless circumstance, but once again noir assiduously stresses an alternate world view. That explains the bleak vulnerability of Chris Cross (Edward G. Robinson) in *Scarlet Street*; and nothing Mildred Pierce (Joan Crawford) can do will alter the pathological destructiveness of her daughter Veda in Michael Curtiz's 1945 film; nor can Bowie Bowers (Farley Granger) turn over a new leaf in *They Live by Night*, saddled as he is by the threat of being returned to prison.

That strain of fatalism, which McCarthy's novel articulates through Moss, is verbalized in Sheriff Bell's judgment that "*whatever you do in your life it will get back to you*" (McCarthy 2005, 281). And this intractability is echoed in turn by Chigurh before he kills Carla Jean: "When I came into your life your life was over. It had a beginning, a middle, and an end. This is the end. You can say that things could have turned out differently. That they could have been some other way. But what does that mean? They are not some other way. They are this way. You're asking that I second say the world. Do you see?" (McCarthy 2005, 260). The persistence of this premise among all three figures—that nothing about our personal wishes, misgivings, or dispositions has any effect on events or can alter our view of what has ensued—effectively diminishes the relevance of individual psychology, could it be known. And in translating that vision to the screen, Deakins gets us to view characters in terms of trajectories, intersections, obliquities rather than as recognizable personalities, familiarly understood. Ironically, characters are returned to us as stock figures in a nihilist Western, with Chigurh simply the villain, Sheriff Bell the confused old man, and Moss the brash young interloper. Character, in short, has been reduced to familiar stereotype.

Yet while that judgment is largely true, it does not preclude certain contradictory moments, including Moss's own persuasive expression of how little one can be persuaded. Another rare occasion in which a character ruminates over this intractability occurs when Sheriff Bell expresses regret that he "cut and run" during a battle in World War II for which he won a Bronze Star: "If I was supposed to die over there doin what I'd give my word to do then that's what I should of done . . . and I didn't. And some part of me has never quit wishin I could go back. And I cant. I didn't know you could steal your own life. And I didn't know that it would bring you no more benefit than about anything else you might steal. I think I done the best with it I knew how but it still wasnt mine. It never has been" (McCarthy 2005, 278). That sense of remorse, however mistaken, seems to lend Bell a certain moral conviction. Yet the notion that "you could steal your own life," or derail it by acting at odds with character, ironically corresponds to the novel's actual vision of personality as simply an accumulation of fortuitous events. Bell's remorse is unearned, both novel and film seem to say, since the conventional Western ideal he here expresses is invalidated by noir elements in the world he inhabits. Just as the novel undercuts psychological depth through its reliance on clipped descriptions and its avoidance of emotional elaborations, so the film achieves a similar effect through an array of partial perspectives, bewildering close-ups, disarming high shots, and at last a shrinking away from landscape itself in favor of dark, enclosed spaces.

CONCLUSION: WESTERN UNDONE

In both novel and film, *No Country for Old Men* resists the generic suasions they seem to invite, in refusing the Western's broad turn to landscape, its Turneresque notion of frontier progress, its generic promise of Ameri-

canizing self-transformation, in preference for a bleak concession to the
corrosive forces that make any civilizing gesture seem finally futile. Borders
of any sort are more or less inconsequential, whether cultural distinctions
marked by history and a river or ethical contrasts supposedly delineated
by excess and restraint. As Uncle Ellis (Barry Corbin) reminds Sheriff Bell
near the end in what sounds like an unexpected retort to Bell's bleak fear of
stealing his own life: "Well all the time you spend trying to get back what's
been took from you, the more's goin' out the door, and after a while you
just need to get a tourniquet on it" (McCarthy 2005, 267). Significantly,
that scene echoes a charged encounter in *High Noon* between Sheriff
Will Kane (Gary Cooper) and ex-lawman Martin Howe (Lon Chaney Jr.),
as Will pleads with his predecessor: "You've been a friend all my life, you
got me this job. You made 'em send for me. Ever since I was a kid I—I
wanted to be like you Mart. You've been a lawman all your life." To which
Martin scornfully retorts: "Yeah, all my life, it's a great life! You risk your
skin catching killers and the juries turn 'em lose so they can come back
and shoot at you again. If you're honest, you're poor all your life and then
in the end you wind up dying all alone on some dirty street. For what?
For nothing. For a tin star."[18] More than half a century separates these
two harangues that share a cynical vision of the informing premise of
Westerns: somehow, via either law or extralegal measures, violence can
be controlled and eliminated as an element of civic exchange. And Ellis
disavows any attempt at redress in the deeply disheartening belief that
things would only further fall apart: "Anyway, you never know what worse
luck your bad luck has saved you from."

The vision finally seems too bleak, as each film pulls back from its
implications to confirm a marginally more positive (and affirmatively
Western) ending. Uncle Ellis may give voice to pessimism in a setting
that apparently confirms his dismay, and yet Sheriff Bell refuses (unlike
Will Kane) quite to accept its necessary logic. Despite forces of havoc and
destruction, despite acknowledging that his efforts may be foredoomed,
Bell holds to the possibility of renewed community, of change, reprisal,

and restitution, and also of understanding. His admission of cowardly behavior in the war is met by Ellis's comforting "You didn't have no choice," to which Bell responds on the contrary, declaring his beleaguered belief in fidelity, honor, commitment: all old-fashioned virtues he associates with his father. Granted, Bell's vision is tinged with nostalgia for the world of the Western that everywhere in this film seems denied by cancerous contingencies and a noir atmosphere. But it nonetheless stands as a tenacious desire, however unavailing, to reverse the deteriorating civic conditions that have led to the present state of affairs, exemplifying the battle drawn between noir and the Western that persists in the film.[19]

Of course, Sheriff Bell's hope is declared only to be soundly rejected by the facts, supplanted by further scenes in the novel of Bell's inquiry into Carla Jean's murder, the reluctance of witnesses, the violent intransigence of untoward events. And against the film's notion of character as somehow external, arbitrary, unknowable—manifested guilelessly in the circumstances that have brought one to this point in life—Bell's more traditional understanding seems futile, part of a nostalgic lost cause, a sentimental gesture in a narrative that offers little reason to agree. Still, the gesture *is* made and in its generic futility alerts us to how to understand the conclusion of both novel and film. For at the end, Sheriff Bell maintains the desire to cherish *"some sort of promise in his heart"* (McCarthy 2005, 308). Against all the cumulative forces of senseless mayhem and dire failure, he attests to another possibility that emerges in the dream he has of his father, a dream mildly disconnected from nearly all that has happened. The moment comes as a surprise in its apparently dislocated placement until we realize that this desire for a connection to fathers has been part of the film's dynamic all along, beginning with Bell's initial voice-over. There, the silent hope represented by a Western landscape was confirmed in his ruminations (thoughts expressed much later in the novel), as he introduces the issue of issue—of paternal guidance, of filial pride, of civic self-improvement.

As a late Western, the film needs to remind us of its syntax even if, as here, it seems to be persuading itself *into* a Western generic mode. Each of these possibilities of issue has been persistently undermined throughout via noir techniques that have exposed such hopes as barren. Still, Bell finally realizes he has not talked enough of his father, and at that point conveys his dream:

> It was cold and there was snow on the ground and he rode past me and kept on goin. Never said nothin. He just rode on past and he had this blanket wrapped around him and he had his head down and when he rode past I seen he was carryin fire in a horn the way people used to do and I could see the horn from the light inside of it. About the color of the moon. And in the dream I knew that he was goin on ahead and that he was fixin to make a fire somewhere out there in all that dark and all that cold and I knew that whenever I got there he would be there. And then I woke up. (McCarthy 2005, 309)[20]

The dream, which becomes the basis of McCarthy's next novel, *The Road* (2006), invokes the possibility of generational continuity, expressing a desire for filial transmission of culture as the civilizing "fire in a horn" carried by his father riding west—an enactment Sheriff Ed Tom Bell must reenact in his own turn. Yet the surprising swerve at the end of the film (if not the novel), of Bell having "woke up" from his dream, reminds us of the split between Western desire and noir reality, of the persistent hope for cultural transmission that is part of the fabric of American myth and the just as persistent reminder of what exists day by violent day in contemporary America.

At the end of their film as at the beginning, the Coens investigate generic contrasts, reminding us of the way genres dictate understanding, with some genres more powerfully persuasive than the facts quite allow. Refusing to visualize Bell's italicized ruminations from the novel, the brothers offer a revision to McCarthy that is as significant generically as their opening landscape images of west Texas. Bell's dream narrative, revealed by McCarthy as intoned sub-vocally to himself, is transformed by the Coens into a domestic scene between Bell and his wife, Loretta, framed once again in tight facial close-ups. In that, the film ends resisting the Western dream's visual promise just as it gestures toward a faintly expressed (Western) family hope of communication, transmission, conciliation. We realize the allure of belief in a stalwart, civilizing character, much as the Hollywood Western has nearly always claimed. But we also confront the tension between that nostalgic allure of character ("*I knew that he was goin on ahead*") and the stark realization of its impossibility ("*And then I woke up.*")—a tension defined in the image of the dream father himself, head down, wrapped in a blanket, vividly there but unseen, and unknown (at least to us).

McCarthy's masterful accomplishment is to have invoked once again, however fleetingly and belatedly, the Western's most pressing and enduring question: what it means to act with honor in a time too late, a country too harsh, a cultural environment that seems no longer recognizable, where "all neglect / Monuments of unaging intellect." The sign of his brilliance is in refusing to capitulate to that question's allure, recognizing it as an *ignus fatuus*, a false glimmer of possibility, with Sheriff Bell himself a victim of our culture's dominant generic way of thinking. And the Coens' adaptation likewise succeeds precisely by sustaining that failed vision, in both its power and its inadequacy. We end as the lights come up realizing again (having read the novel) how little we understand individual characters, and yet how we are nonetheless swayed by a vision of character that exists nowhere in the world we have seen. Noir techniques have been invoked to lay to rest what many assume is the disingenuously sustaining vision of the Western, yet its continuing generic appeal defies those equally generic efforts. Once again, a late Western relies on viewers to construct a vision of hope even in a world that seems so decisively placed beyond its generic power.

7

SUBVERTING LATE WESTERNS
IN *THE COUNSELOR*

If late Westerns form an exhilarating extension of the genre, inventively reshaping it via a series of cross-generic influences (noir, action-adventure), the swerve taken by Ridley Scott's *The Counselor* (2013) may well mark a border for how far audiences are willing to engage such revamped configurations. In fact, critics with few exceptions roundly rejected the film on first appearance, and it baffled audiences enough to seriously batter box-office receipts (though it has recently begun to build an underground reputation as worth the price of admission).[1] Its repudiation seems hard to fathom against the acclaim for other late Westerns, since it encompasses many of the same features we have seen informing them, including the semantics of its locale on the Ciudad Juarez–El Paso border and the pressures of narcocorrido trafficking. More to the point, syntaxes of both Westerns and noir converge in the film, articulated self-consciously by characters in open ruminations about identity and obligation, as well as the role of the past; about domestic relations involving a couple newly in love; about regret, revenge, and restitution as responses to events gone awry; and notably, about violence, though hardly in a context of Robert Warshow's proclaimed "value" as either restorative or regenerative.

Yet if these themes are focused so as to initially remind us of generic pressures, Scott's film ends by renouncing familiar resolutions, exposing them as woefully inadequate. What may have seemed worth pondering about questions of cultural, gendered, or ethical identity, say, in *Three Burials* or *Lone Star* or *No Country*—each of which addresses a similar conflict between good intentions and bad luck—is emphatically repudiated by *The Counselor*. Still, the engagement with that conflict signals the film's desire to reconsider assumptions in other late Westerns as well as those fundamental to genre configuration itself. The very look of the film reminds us of formal techniques characteristic of those other films: the broad panoramas of west Texas, the fragmented narratives, the frequent close-ups of people and objects. Yet despite such similarities, *The Counselor* resists being identified generically, defying the viewer to accept it as either Western or actively "neo-noir" (at least, so far as sheer style is concerned). The fact that Cormac McCarthy wrote the screenplay—himself an obvious noir Western writer—only underlines how fully expectations are being reversed.

That makes it hard to know how to take the film, except as a self-conscious rejection of Hollywood genres no longer capable of intersecting and crossbreeding, and in the process refusing to engage the audience generically. Scenes may seem inchoate and disconnected, as with many contemporary films, but Dariusz Wolski's cinematography resists generic templates that identify the plot as either Western, noir, or something otherwise mixed. And that may help in part to explain its initial reception, which seems to owe less to inordinate violence or incoherent plot than its brash refusal to accept the syntactic terms of a genre film. Instead of disavowing its louche cinematic pleasures (as *A History of Violence* and *No Country* do), it remains staunchly skeptical about moral distinctions at all, questioning how violence might ever have social "value" other than simply being functional, as a vicious form of release, feeding viewers' undisguised appetites. Posing that issue as an indirect address to viewers, the middleman Westray (Brad Pitt) explains to the anonymous Counselor (Michael Fassbender) the logic of snuff films: "the consumer of the product is essential to its production. You cannot watch without being an accessory to a murder." So stark a judgment suggests something of this film's inculpation of us for relishing its animal savagery, indulging in its sun-scorched scenes of icily heartless barbarism—hardly a reassuring tone to take with an audience looking to be entertained.

More than just a ruthless understanding of violence makes the film unpalatable, however: particularly the unsettling presentation of figures who seem less like those with whom we might identify than as ambulatory zombies or hollowed-out aliens.[2] Scott challenges notions of identity familiar from Western and noir films by shaping a severely reduced impression of character itself in the reiterated presumption that problematic actions, often inadvertent ones, constitute the persons we invariably are. That premise recurs in various late Westerns clearly preoccupied with issues of identity (prominently, *Three Burials*, *Brokeback Mountain*, and *A History of Violence*), which may help explain McCarthy's interest, since his fiction returns almost obsessively to the question of character. Consequences can often seem unfair, but the film gives no quarter to those sympathetic with good intentions, since actions always expose us to a world beyond our control. Whatever motives happen to be, it is the way things turn out that invariably defines us (a question McCarthy had already addressed in *No Country for Old Men*). In fact, McCarthy's screenplay itself attests more fully than the film to this disquieting conception of character, exploring in dialogue—sometimes at length—the disjunction between a view of oneself assumed prospectively on the one hand, and on the other a perspective taken after the fact. Scott deftly translates that vision cinematically, offering frequent close-ups drawn from the vocabulary of late Westerns that seem deliberately, all but self-consciously, to fail to bring us nearer to insight, omitting dialogue so as to further derail our sympathies and in general thwarting typical presumptions of psychological coherence.

As a means of understanding more fully McCarthy and Scott's critique of the late Western, the following explores these two intertwined issues: our guilt at indulging voyeuristically in the pleasures of violence and our bewilderment in watching characters fail to understand themselves, experiencing consequences they refuse to accept as their own. Guilt and bewilderment are not unconnected, since hesitating to admit our secret pleasure at rapacious behavior on-screen (of characters doing what we can only imagine and doing it with glee) seems little different from the characters' confusion at being held accountable for actions they never intended. Like them, we resist accepting that they are defined exclusively by what they do, though the film denies its audience a comforting glimpse of them as deliberative agents capable of taking control of their fates and altering their histories. Instead, a beleaguered Westray who admits his vulnerability ("In a word? Women") still ends up betrayed by one. The motorcycling drug mule, Green Hornet (Richard Cabral), flashily heralds his flaw as excessive speed, which just as predictably becomes the means of his self-destruction. The flamboyantly coifed and groomed drug kingpin Reiner (Javier Bardem) yearns for his partner Malkina (Cameron Diaz) and yet fails to heed the heartlessness of a woman who is hardly eye candy, or acknowledge the hazards of associating with a Mexican drug cartel. Most prominently, the Counselor is warned repeatedly about the narrative's key financial deal with nothing we learn explaining his persistent desire to risk so much.[3]

The film turns on this pivotal problem of action divorced from deliberation, so often conceived as a permeable boundary but here projected as a fixed border. That understanding of action takes a while to project onscreen, though McCarthy's provocative breaks in the script reveal how fully expected sequence has been transmuted into a disruptive cinematic experience. And what McCarthy expresses through conversation is transformed by Scott via close-ups and editing. That contrast between McCarthy's sometimes elaborate dialogue and the visual minimalism of Scott's cinematography helps create tensions that sustain the film's radical challenge to our conventional notions of identity. For *The Counselor* resists becoming a genre film not by simply mixing generic features but by defying them, exposing Western and noir ingredients as (in each case) either self-fulfilling or incoherent. Labeling the film with a vague designation of "thriller," in fact, acknowledges the lack of any recognizable generic constraint and instead simply describes the mood induced in a viewer. In the failure of intentions to lead to deliberative acts, or of characters to seize a sense of self from their own behavior, *The Counselor* offers something like an indictment of genre itself as more generally lending false hope for either consistency or clarity.[4] What we are left with is the exhilaration of characters surprised by their lives, unprepared for their futures, in a drama that frequently resembles late Westerns but that refuses to follow rules we have come to expect from them.

RAPACIOUS VISIONARY

The Counselor may be the film's titular hero, but the figure who most fully embodies its philosophy is Malkina, who as a woman is already rare in the pantheon of Western or late-Western protagonists. Silver nailed and sybaritic, she nicely conforms to the role of femme fatale so central to noir even as she acts on principles rarely found in that genre, summed up near the conclusion when she recalls her cheetahs in action: "The hunter has grace, beauty, and purity of heart to be found nowhere else. You can make no distinction between what they are and what they do. And what they do is kill. We, of course, are another matter. It is our faintness of heart that has driven us to the edge of ruin." Malkina's admiration confirms the sheer futility of regret since what we do and who we are remain ever one (according to her). Actions simply *are* intentions (with a nod toward Freudian slips), revealing incontestably what our true desires must originally have been. And though belated self-consciousness may lead us to think that we differ from what we have done, or that appetite pitched against circumstance unsettles some inner gyroscope of ethical guidance, the contrary is actually the case. For Malkina, any subjective attempt at self-determination is simply a will-o'-the-wisp that no more defines us independently of what in fact occurs than does serendipity. All it achieves is to leave us in confusion about ourselves.

In self-conscious defiance of both late Westerns and noir, Malkina advances a philosophy based on what happens to happen always dictating the judgments we ought to make about ourselves. Suitably, her admiration for cheetahs (aligned with how she discerns her life) leads her to transform herself visually as well. Her two-tone hair, black eye-liner, cat-paw tattoos, and animal-print clothes, all herald a feral nature ruthlessly sexual, dangerously predatory, entirely without misgivings. Cameron Diaz maintains throughout a dead-eyed stare that radiates the absence of emotional entanglement, comporting herself in vivid contrast to the film's misplaced tilting toward the value of remorse. She cooly admits never knowing her parents, both of whom were thrust from a helicopter when she was three; but the larger point is that such a narrative does little to explain her. Malkina's personality corresponds exactly to her behavior, uninflected by psychological nuance or inner recriminations. As Reiner admits to the Counselor, "she'd done everything before," though as he also confesses, his affection for her is "like being in love with . . . Easeful death?"—a surprising invocation of Keats that acknowledges her inscrutable (sometimes fatal) pleasures.

Notably, this frees Malkina from constraints burdening characters in noir and late Westerns, for as much as she may seem deadened, and certainly more inhuman, she responds completely, ever rapaciously to experience, without the strain of expectations about how she should act. When Reiner initially claims that she enjoys the mesa in Arizona "because it reminds you of somewhere else," she immediately retorts, "That's not why I like it. I like it for itself." Defying a usual notion of selfhood as standing outside oneself, contrasting present with past to enforce one's identity, she spurns emotions of unease, shame, disappointment, embarrassment, annoyance, or guilt as so much noise, irrelevant to the way we are. Notably, she corrects Reiner who wants to distinguish between experience and recollection: "I don't think I miss things. I think to miss something is to hope it will come back . . . but it's not coming back. I've always known that since I was a girl." The otherwise normal desire to improve one's lot or to seek revenge, to protect one's family or murder one's husband—all standard motives in both Westerns and noir—has for her no special sway over events or identity, and the scene ends by capturing the notion that something is "not coming back" in a sunset that fades too quickly, in a swirl so fleeting it seems the film has been deliberately sped up. As she observes, completely without emotion: "There it goes." Phenomenal experience is evanescent, rarely

Fig. 20. Malkina, witness to life as nasty, brutish, and short in *The Counselor* (20th Century Fox).

the result of circumspection, even if Malkina is clever enough to control effects and move others at whim. Even when events turn sideways, even as her drug deal falls apart, she realizes that things happen *as* effects, reducing motive and retrospection to little more than the random play of events as they happen to occur.

Oddly, the inconsequent scene of visiting a priest's confessional booth confirms her defiant refusal to impose morality on behavior. Her impulse to confess without being Catholic, simply to experience the process in a closed booth, perceptibly annoys the priest (Édgar Ramírez), though it is intellectually consistent. Malkina just wants to revel in another disturbing encounter, doing little more than "rattling your cage," as she says earlier when she teases Laura (Penélope Cruz) in the process of defying conventional feminine norms. Here, it is the masculine power of the church that she wants to "rattle," flouting the time-honored logic of a necessary additional component to the sacrament of confession, of needing to redeem the presumed feeling of penitence by a visible act of penance. Absolution is meaningless to Malkina, since internal subjectivity just is, not something to be shaped into appropriate perspectives and postures aligned with external behavior. She is what she does, helping to explain why she survives as the sole character not distracted by a notion of intention somehow divided from event.

Malkina represents, in short, not simply the recurrent theme of the film but a larger Hobbesian view familiar in many of McCarthy's novels: life as nasty, brutish, and short.[5] Shackles of culture bind us, she realizes, by binding the random episodes of a personal history into a misleading impression of oneself as a person. Repeatedly, this audaciously Promethean motif threads through McCarthy's fiction in scenes at once scarifying yet resistant to psychologizing. Whether experienced firsthand as a character or at a second remove as reader and viewer, the impulse to explain ferocious appetites in terms of social standards invariably misleads, or so McCarthy here at least seems to hold.[6] Part of the tenor of his writing suggests that brutality represented symbolically as narrative recreation is more eviscerating, and invigorating, than characters experiencing the event itself firsthand.[7] Malkina does in fact register the unstable beauty attached to such moments, but she stands nearly alone as a fictional figure, cherishing scenes as something like a viewer outside the frame.

In that regard, she becomes the film's emblematic figure, not simply in giving expression to a brazen aesthetic philosophy but more generally in embodying it as a woman with appetites, evoking Tacitus in his claim that "nothing human is alien to me." Her playful admission to Reiner that she loved life in Barbados—which she recalls as "a steamy pit of sexual abandon. . . . Well, it used to be. I left"—confirms those insatiable cravings. And that fervor is corroborated in Reiner's recollection of her "fucking my car," writhing on his windshield in a scene that reveals her as thoroughly self-sufficient, having no need for others except as reflectors of her own swashbuckling subjectivity. That garish voraciousness is apparent to all, with her early admission to Reiner that she's "starving" appropriately echoed in the film's closing word confirming that she's "famished." Marked as her passions are, other characters share a similar hunger for more, like viewers themselves compelled into a covert alliance with Reiner in their inability to turn away. Desire always exceeds satisfaction and therefore invariably leads to regret, at least for those less hardened than she. Both her excessive proclivities and her refusal ever to regret their denial constitute a mentality we have not seen in familiar genres, and they represent a dilemma now worth exploring.

CAUTIONS, COSTS, AND CLOSE-UPS

Never looking back in either disappointment or satisfaction, Malvina is likewise quick-footed and hesitant about the future, realizing that planning is one thing, expectation another—the former, essential for anyone hoping to thrive; the latter, meaningless given how little our efforts can sidestep contingencies. Though this perspective seems to inform the film's basic premise, she is hardly alone in appreciating it. Just after the early scene of sunset in Arizona, the Counselor consults an Amsterdam jeweler (Bruno Ganz) about an engagement ring, initiating a conversation that extends the implications of Malkina's admission to Reiner about lacking the feeling of regret, but alluding as well to future outcomes rather than the past. Speaking of diamonds, the dealer explains that their attraction has less to do with purity than a perceived "imperfection," expatiating on the larger theme of forestalled expectation that threads through the film: "The truth is that anything you can say about a diamond is in the nature of a flaw. The perfect diamond would be composed simply of light." Nicely inverting normal evaluative standards, his claim establishes perfection as ever elusive, and instead of being cynical about defects that lure us on, urges calm acceptance. That is why "every diamond is cautionary," reminding us of our recurrent if futile desire for lives to be other than what they are. We need to learn instead "that we will not be diminished by the brevity of our lives. That we will not thereby be made less." In the imperfection that comprises their beauty, diamonds admonish us toward a kind of Quietism that accepts a life as it is, with no undue striving or regret.

If this seems a peculiar strain for a thriller (or any genre) to espouse, its implications are made more explicit in dialogue cut from McCarthy's screenplay. The dealer's description of diamond cutting, for instance, deftly evokes the pervasive theme of intention's inconsequence: "Once the first facet is cut there can be no going back. What was meant to be a union remains forever untrue and we see a troubling truth in that the forms of our undertakings are complete at their beginnings. For good or for ill" (McCarthy 2013, 17). Clearly, this all but determinist insight governs the film, anticipated by the Counselor's colleagues and later offered in a sustained rumination by the senior cartel associate, Jefe (Rubén Blades). Yet the reason for dropping this dialogue is that its point about irrevocable action seems more forcefully dramatized by the very absence of such pronouncements. Other conversations are likewise omitted for similar reasons. Reiner reports a joke played by his friend Peterson on a Brazilian cousin, encouraging him to approach a woman despite not speaking English, telling him that asking her to dance is pronounced "I. want. to. eat. your. pussy" (McCarthy 2013, 76). When the woman, recognizing Peterson's ploy, decides to oblige the cousin, Peterson himself is encouraged to try the line on another woman, only to have her husband break his jaw. Again, the sequence exemplifies strains weaving through *The Counselor* of impulse leading to action, of untoward consequence ensuing from a decision lightly made. And again, the sequence defies the syntaxes of Westerns and noir, which each depend on deliberation and a set of conventional social codes. The film's strength, however, lies in dropping dialogue from McCarthy's screenplay that makes its premise explicit, allowing viewers to respond more directly to the suasive power of irreversible events rather than being expressly informed by an allegorical narrative inserted as conversation. Throughout the film, the immutable border between errant gesture and abiding aftereffect remains, making a description of diamond cutting as cautionary example unneeded, as already evident in plot twists and turns.

Gruesomely, the film presses these implications, accompanied by ever more self-conscious injunctions against any choice at all, squeezing dry the implications of its antigeneric premise in frequent admonishments about the strict lines one must not cross. Repeatedly, the Counselor is urged to decline Reiner's proffered drug deal, including by Reiner himself: "If you pursue this road, that you've embarked upon, you will eventually come to moral decisions that will take you completely by surprise." That warning, already anticipated by the diamond dealer's counsel that there is no turning back from decisions, is immediately followed by Reiner's detailed description of a bolito (cousin to the air-bolt gun in *No Country for Old Men*), a weapon that stands as emblem for relentless irreversibility: "there's no easy way to turn the thing off. Or reason to. It just keeps running until the noose closes completely and then it self-destructs." The machine is an exemplary engine of fate, inexorable against protective measures, with Reiner's early description forming a Chekhovian gesture of implacability that perfectly anticipates Westray's grisly death near the end.

The warning hardly needs reinforcing, though Westray stipulates the cartel as people for whom neither contingency nor accident suffice as excuse (as if they embodied in this recalcitrant vision the film's own psychological skepticism). When the Counselor admits to being "a little taken aback at the cautionary nature of this conversation," Westray can only concur: "Good word, 'cautionary.'" That should be portentous enough, but he then goes on to describe the retributive beheadings ordinarily arranged by Mexican drug lords, explaining that "It's not like there's some smoldering rage at the bottom of it," before pointedly confirming the person they have in their sights is: "You, counselor. You." By this point, the stakes involved are crystal clear, with viewers meant to discern more keenly than the Counselor the weight of such admonitions. Strangely, these very reiterations of what will happen seem to derail plot itself, closing down the alternative possibilities that normally ensure our interest, no matter the genre. Instead, however, we are reduced to one track, fixed and obvious, with the effect of defying the genre dynamics that maintain our continuing involvement.

What makes the warnings seem excessive is that the Counselor has not done anything yet nor been even casually involved in risky behavior or otherwise slipped up. And compounding the strange sense of foreboding about actions still to be undertaken is that Westray feels removed from the conditions he describes, supposing himself somehow immune from implacable forces. That lack of self-knowledge emerges in his unduly sanguine claim that "I can vanish, in a heart beat, with my money. Can you? Truth is, counselor, I can walk away from all of this. . . . I can live in a monastery. Scrub the steps. Clean the pots. Try some gardening." But for all the ostentation on display, Westray actually has no more sense for his own exposure than the Counselor, expressing the very self-confidence he is warning against. Unable to alter his behavior, Westray is immured in the same, seemingly fated grid as the Counselor, as is Reiner, whom Westray describes as "beyond advising. Reiner thinks nothing bad can happen. And he's in love." What yokes the three together is this shared inability to realize how fully contingency governs a world where inner resources are never adequate to the dangers looming beyond clear borders of possibility. The three may seem aware, may appear to gird themselves against vicissitudes and exigencies, but their prudence in fact can never suffice in contexts where accident always occurs. Unlike any of the other figures so prominent in late Westerns, many of whom feel inadequate or otherwise out-matched, these embody a dire premise of outright human insufficiency against all that may ensue. And Mexico comes to stand, perhaps especially in terms evoked by narcocorrido lyrics, for a border that needs to be walled off since it can no longer be negotiated (as if the violence that had mystified Sheriff Ed Tom Bell in *No Country* were now embodied as an utterly implacable force). Unlike Ford, Peckinpah, and Sayles, McCarthy and Scott share little of a sentimental view of Mexico, unwilling to grant distinctive humanist values to a culture south of the border simply for being south.

Reiterated variously, the film's informing premise emerges in people who, for all their blithe self-confidence, are imprisoned by events. That might seem like a version of feelings frequently manifest in late Westerns and noir—where characters find either social forces that are apparently overpowering or events from a past that seem impossible to escape. But

The Counselor presses the point further in denying any way out, excluding the alternative options that always emerge in familiar genres. Characters are defined from the outside in by contexts over which they have no control, blinding them to their impotence in the face of events they have set in motion themselves, if inadvertently. Starting in the precredit sequence of the Counselor and Laura in bed, the film establishes the idea of sexual desire erasing conscious thought in a scene that ends with her playful admission that "you've ruined me," ironically prefiguring the film's grim conclusion. The pleasures of their dalliance, again like ours in watching, cannot anticipate the costs that will ensue. And costs are the film's central concern: of what we pay for what we enjoy, of the risks parceled out for behavior for which we will always be called to account. That may be a strong consideration in noir, almost central to the genre in its recurrent focus on the inescapable effects of the past, but it is never so thoroughly stressed to the exclusion of the very possibility of freeing oneself. *The Counselor* adumbrates a closed alternative vision right from the opening in the first of many transformations where the film improves on the screenplay: instead of beginning with McCarthy's bedroom scene, Scott adds a ten-second view of the Green Hornet racing his motorcycle from Juarez to El Paso, signaling at the outset the drug-running plot that will cross the Counselor's life.

Odd as the precredit love scene appears in launching a narcocorrido-inspired narrative, it establishes what turns out to be the film's disorienting reliance on close-ups, targeting faces, body parts, familiar activities, curtains and sheets.[8] Of course, that cinematic practice is part of a broader contemporary style in both Hollywood and independent films, addressed above in discussions of Phedan Papamichael's and Roger Deakins's camera work. As with them, cinematographer Dariusz Wolski adopts the mode as stylistic enforcement of his narrative's concern with circumscribed borders that cannot be crossed, if at the most minimal visual level. Interspersing the credits themselves are tightly focused shots of cocaine packets newly prepared, oil drum tops heavily pounded down, trucks noisily backing up, a drug courier sleeping. The abrupt transition to Amsterdam is filmed much the same way, following the establishing shot of the city: first, a view through a jeweler's loupe of a diamond; then, alternating close-ups of Bruno Ganz's wrinkled brow and Fassbinder's impassive blue eyes. Wolski regularly slides into this characteristic mode, focusing on faces in all their revelatory detail in a vain effort to read the psychology beneath. The Counselor, the diamond dealer, Reiner, and Malkina are each introduced in tight close-up shots, and when the Counselor finally presents a diamond ring to Laura, we watch their magnified faces intently, as we do thereafter when he chats in his car over the speaker phone about money problems or later casually greets Westray in a bar. The face of the inmate Ruth (Rosie Perez) is framed by bars at the Texas State Penitentiary for Women and scrutinized in close-up as she smokes, just as her son, the Green Hornet, is likewise viewed, feeding his dog. Throughout, everyone is projected as if only inches away, talking about themselves or their past and present troubles, until at last the Counselor is shown conversing via phone with Jefe as the camera slowly pulls in to an increasingly tight composition, Jefe weary if sympathetic, the Counselor gradually becoming hysterical.

This consistent cinematic framing is not particularly odd or surprising, certainly given its mildly defamiliarizing repetition in *Three Burials* and *No Country*. But it seems that Wolski wants to intensify the pattern to stress—through an ongoing series of closely viewed faces in conversation with each other—how fully individuals need to talk about themselves, to tell their stories in hopes of being understood. Deakins, by contrast, enforced the Coen brothers' vision to simply reveal a certain inscrutability, though characters regularly do persuade each other. Wolski's similar framed one-shots of faces go further, reinforcing the impression that spoken accounts have mere minimal effect, leaving people as isolated as before with no recourse for their walled-in conditions. Laura expresses interest in hearing about the Counselor's former sexual experiences, then declines, and later tells Malkina of her dream of her, but is uncertain why she tells her, or what she wants. Reiner tells the Counselor the detailed story of Malkina

Fig. 21. Diamonds, jewelers' loupes, irrelevant details, and increasingly close views in *The Counselor* (20th Century Fox).

Fig. 22. So close as to have only bearded cheeks visible, as the Jefe advices telephone client in *The Counselor* (20th Century Fox).

masturbating on his Ferrari then realizes he should have refrained, as both wonder "what it is that you're trying to tell me." Still, neither has any idea what it might mean to "'Forget it.' . . . 'How do you propose that I do that?'" The sentiment lingers that telling others of ourselves ought to reveal something *of* ourselves, yet the film never reassures us that this might possibly be true, quite the contrary.

In the bizarre scene where Malkina attempts to simulate a church confession, she seems to exemplify this notion of conversation, of opening oneself to another, of being at least partially understood. Yet for her it is just a game, driving the priest from the confessional with her brazen admissions, even though her accented plea—"All you have to do is listen"—does speak to an impulse shared by nearly everyone else. Alone in the film, the priest resists such unearned disclosures, perhaps in part because he is beyond psychologizing, already aware of what the film strives to prove in collapsing intention and action. As interesting cinematically is when he storms out from the confessional booth, with the camera pulling back from its habitual framing close-up as Malkina's shouted "Where are you going?" accompanies him out of the shot, apparently out of the film itself. Here, he defines himself as wholly different from us as viewers, refusing to hear or see any more, walking away from the suasions of a deeply anarchic inclination.

Predictably, the film aligns itself against the priest's confessional role, resisting any such deflection to the past, denying the very notion of narrative recursiveness. Each scene registers an all but chronological sequence in its relentless motion forward and reveals itself as a rejection of any rearward glance at all, whether in hopeful nostalgia for better times (as in the Western) or regret over the irrepressible burden of past transgressions (as in noir). The late Western sometimes brought these intersecting narrative patterns together (as in *Lone Star* and *Three Burials*), and *The Counselor* does occasionally suggest this might occur. But instead, it offers a series of interconnecting narratives that advance along an inflexibly forward-moving temporal line, acknowledging that the past might dictate the present but permitting only the present to matter.

Once again, either regret or nostalgia is each beside the point, counter to prevalent themes in the late Western, for as Jefe resolutely counsels, "grief is worthless." Nothing can be achieved by revisiting the past, which always remains inexorably past, explaining why only one flashback occurs in the entire film—the scene of the Green Hornet speeding on his motorcycle *after* Ruth has told the Counselor that he has been arrested. This helps clarify why Wolski regularly pulls so closely in, cutting people off from their bodies, offering fragmented views of their faces alone, if only because the effort to express themselves never quite succeeds. The concern with intentions, motivations, psychology, or drives is always defeated by a vain focus on faces that remain inexorably inexpressive. The cinematography itself, that is, offers a lesson on how to understand the argument being presented by characters. Take the rather unexceptional scene of the Counselor uncorking a bottle of wine in a normal medium shot as he talks on the phone to Laura. Only his side of the exchange is shown, as the camera moves slowly closer to him describing his desire to take off her panties, before he realizes he is having phone sex. That very dollying in for a close view suggests a greater intimacy, a fuller knowledge, than the scene itself can provide. Laura is unseen, unheard, in this one-sided conversation; the Counselor is merely titillated, left staring vaguely off into space; the whole ends without resolution or knowledge, only unassuaged lust.

FRAGMENTATION AND QUIETISM

In part, this sustained enigma of intention and psychology is reinforced by Scott's shrewd casting, though *The Counselor* is hardly different from countless noir and Western films where impassivity is cherished as a paramount feature of characterization. The significant difference lies not in the practiced impassivity of its actors, but in the self-consciously invented, studiously honed detachment of characters themselves, whom we are repeatedly urged to see close up. While Cameron Diaz performs her role with a glossy sheen and dead-fish eyes, it is Malkina who also seems to be performing, deliberately offering a routinely blank expression that culminates in a dazzlingly fake smile to the Blonde (Natalie Dormer) she has hired to seduce Westray. Just as notable is Michael Fassbender's vacant stare, though again his character chooses to convey an unflappable demeanor as a means of guarding himself—a demeanor that only alters late in the film when control wrenchingly vanishes, and he sheds a tear, then becomes distraught. Javier Bardem plays against type (certainly the type earlier defined by Chigurh) as a flashily dressed entrepreneur with spiky hair and colorful dashikis that seem of a piece with his ostentatious comportment. Still, the garishness of his performance seems only intended to keep others at a firm psychological remove, as does Brad Pitt's amused, twinkly-eyed middleman Westray.

Clearly, Wolski's camera cannot break through these self-imposed facades of character that are created *by* the characters self-consciously, despite moving ever closer to faces that resist divulging their psychologies, lending an irony to close-cropped "talking heads" revealing stories that are finally discredited because they are so often self-exculpatory. As Westray observes, the Mexican cartel "doesn't believe in coincidences," which is to say it does not believe in accounts that do not match its own reductive reading of human behavior. And the irony of this cinematic style is compounded by the brutal fate suffered by so many: being decapitated, actually enacting the figurative beheading performed by Wolski's framing technique (consider the hideous annihilations of the Green Hornet, of Laura, of Westray, of the woman in Westray's snuff film or analogously, of the fatal head shots that kill Reiner, the disguised cartel policeman, and the bystander on the road).

In the Western and noir films *The Counselor* seems tacitly to address, psychology tends to be knowable, available, readable on the surface if only because relatively simple and straightforward. Noir regularly reduces characters to lust, revenge, greed, and other cardinal sins; Westerns regularly gender characters according to masculine and feminine stereotypes, converting bodily performance into a sign of temperament and disposition. Yet augmenting Scott's film in its disquieting dismissal of psychology—dissolving any distinction between what characters (or cheetahs) "are and what they do"—is its intense narrative fragmentation, which once again borrows from contemporary cinema but does so far more intensely than we have hitherto seen. Shifting among disparate locations, personalities, and events, it shows little regard for sequence, with the disorienting transition from El Paso condominium to Arizona high plains to Amsterdam canals to Ciudad Juárez trucking station, all of which are meant less to confuse the viewer than to infuse a sense of arbitrariness in both action and consequence. McCarthy's script nicely exaggerates this fragmentation by offering disparate scenes in quick succession, which are absent any dialogue at all. Scott modified what he must have construed as a disorienting mélange without lessening the sense of discontinuousness, of individual stories that seem somehow unrelated. And in the process, he reshuffled the order of scenes, slowing their transposition—though less to straighten out a presumed narrative logic than to engage a mildly more sympathetic cinematic rhythm.

McCarthy's premise still stands: that the sequence of scenes only be chronological, which distorts our sense of the emotional or psychological web holding it all together, leaving us still unclear by half an hour into the film about what is going on or what a putative deal involves among the Counselor, Reiner, and Mexican drug suppliers. That narrative instability continues throughout in a presumptive challenge to all genre films that value coherence, continuity, successiveness, predictability. The question of why Malkina should visit a priest has already been addressed, but why must the Counselor head to Amsterdam only a day after returning to Laura—as she plaintively inquires (certainly not simply to buy her a ring)? Why the scene of delivering cocaine to a Chicago repacking center or the revelation of the fetid corpse jammed into an oil drum (certainly not to further establish the drug cartel's obscene ruthlessness)? Why the scenes of African cheetahs hunting jackrabbits on Arizona high plains (certainly less bizarre testimonials to hunter and prey could be imagined)? Scott tempers McCarthy's discordant, fragmented sequences but only enough to tantalize instead of bewilder, as a persistent strain attesting to our need to encounter a world best described in *Blood Meridian* as "no longer bled of its strangeness" (245). Recovering that experience of novelty, of experience savored anew, can only be achieved by disrupting domesticating structures of consciousness, suspending preconfigured narrative sequences. And of course, that process unsettles generic assumptions most of all, revealing in their absence the comforting function of genre itself.

Contributing to this evocative uncertainty are plot threads that likewise raise more questions than they resolve, a number of them deliberately added to the finished film to tease us in grasping a logic of cause and effect where none actually exists. How does Malkina, for instance, learn the Green Hornet possesses an electronic control for the drug truck, explaining why she then hires Jaime the Wire-Man (Sam Spruell) to retrieve it? How does the drug cartel track Laura via her cell phone (Malkina is the only person other than the Counselor who has her number, and she hardly seems likely to have given it away)? Perhaps we have been prepared for such disorientation in the central plot link itself, with the suspicion that the Counselor killed a high-ranking cartel member, the Green Hornet, simply because the Counselor had "paid a speeding ticket for him." Proximity alone becomes fatally consequential, especially since logic can hardly explain why a lawyer would kill his presumed client simply to get the tracer lock on a drug shipment truck. Given the web of such associations, Ruth assumes her lawyer, the Counselor, is guilty. And the illogical misgivings spread, extending deadly effects to those only casually involved in a film that binds together coincidence, unexplained patterns, and an arbitrary matrix of relations. Bystanders suffer for simply being in the wrong place at an inappropriate time: an innocent woman lends her phone to the Counselor out of misplaced civility, to her ghastly regret; a passerby happens to observe a deadly truck heist and instead of abruptly backing up, performs a slow K-turn that costs him both precious minutes and his life; a woman agrees to prostitute herself with Westray only to discover the stakes have risen from sex to murder and that, as Malkina declares, "You already are" involved in his imminent death; and Laura, simply because she is unaware of her fiancé's business arrangements, finds herself at risk, then abducted and decapitated.

In the end, answers to questions of means or motive matter little if at all, which comes as some surprise in a film that so regularly presses those very questions. But again, the film's premise is more broadly to explore the underlying premise of genres themselves, and to tilt against them. *The Counselor* invokes generic thriller and noir materials for scant reason other than to make us aware of them *as* noir—a kind of postmodern pastiche that excites the viewer simply by recognizing them. Consider the extraneous nature of much of the film's dialogue, giving us more information than we need about topics inessential to the plot. The diamond dealer goes into inordinate detail about carets, facets, and grades—an expertise then matched by a sharp-eyed Malkina when she inspects Laura's gaudy ring ("Probably an F or a G. Nothing visible so it's at least a vs-2. Do you want to know what it's worth?"). Similarly, Westray responds to the Counselor's surprise at the "cautionary nature of this conversation" by citing Scots Law ("it defines an instrument in which one person stands as surety for another"), offering a law-school response to a street-corner conversation. Admittedly, this forms part of McCarthy's signature style, but it also mirrors the consideration so often paid in noir to techniques incidental to plot. Consider the attention lavished on other special skills, as when a cartel truck driver expertly carves a plug to stop sewage flow from the bullet-ridden vehicle he has just stolen, or when Jaime the Wire-Man deftly measures a showroom motorcycle in anticipation of carefully setting up his wire-and-lights trap for the Green Hornet.

These otherwise inessential scenes—consisting of either unduly erudite conversations or elaborate technical performances—do nothing so much as draw attention to specialized if meaningless details and thereby (once again) away from larger psychological matters. That ploy tends to constitute what I elsewhere have described as the "furniture" of noir in Dashiell Hammett and Raymond Chandler, diverting our eyes from the supposedly central plot mechanics that are finally generic, nothing more.[9] Exteriors reveal little of disposition or psychology, and Scott translates this premise via an electric cinematic pace that sometimes resembles a slick Michael Mann film, or the style of his own *Hannibal* (2001). Wolski's camera once more closes in, but now on objects for their purely diversionary texture and appeal, whether diamonds, oil drums, or semitrailer rigs. And while those close-ups are occasionally interspersed with brief distant vistas, more often they remain uninterrupted; the binoculars and jewelers' loupes that pop up throughout are simply meant to signal attention to irrelevant details with inordinate consequences that also characterize the dialogue. *No Country* anticipated this pattern in obscuring character through diversionary details, but McCarthy and Scott offer a wider array of digressive scenes, including details not simply unrevealing of personality but seemingly unrelated to the narrative sequence itself or in fostering its suspense. Pitching in this way toward tightly framed close-ups, the film registers its larger thematic concentration on the effect of circumstances as if minute details could somehow catalog a realization of our own helplessness in the unceasing if modest fear of what will invariably ensue.

Confirming that ineluctable visual field is the strangely suggestive, mildly repetitive music composed by Daniel Pemberton (whose forte had been video games and advertising, as well as television compositions). Offering an incessantly forward-moving, incremental sonic pressure, his score has the effect of subliminally encouraging the audience nondiegetically to believe in a fated narrowing down. The sound track breaks time into cumulative units that represent not variation but the ceaseless lockstep structure of a minimalist piece by Steve Reich or Philip Glass, sometimes suggesting a form of phase music constituted by echoes and doublings, sonically inducing us into a sense of immobility. Again, the fragmentation of sequences, the lack of continuity, the strangely irrelevant exchanges, the conspiratorial mode of the whole, all are part of McCarthy's and Scott's joint impulse to produce a thriller on the basis of scrambled materials that deliberately do not pull together. That cinematic rationale disorients even as it offers a determinist, almost fatalistic aura evoking a view of human behavior unlike anything normally familiar to us. We start with a film that calls on recognizable genre conventions, only to discover its confusions about identity and character are such as to undermine expectations for genre at all—indeed, to subvert expectations for the way in which behavior itself should be understood.

If *The Counselor* offers a narrative that defies our persistent expectation for change, in the process it also defies both late Westerns and noir, undoing what they do so well if only to show that flouting genre stratagems has its appeal (or not, given the film's poor sales and low reputation[10]). Yet adding to this disconcerting air of inevitability, of events paradoxically resisting the assumption that they can be modified, is the growing realization by characters themselves that they are largely inscrutable to each other. That revelation is first dramatically highlighted as the Counselor dines al fresco with Laura and a former client interrupts. Annoyed at some past negotiation gone wrong, Tony (Toby Kebbell) finally announces to Laura that the Counselor's "thin skin makes it OK in his eyes to make you lie under the bus." Apart from what we can surmise here about the Counselor's unsavory practice, the scene more pointedly suggests how little Laura knows of him and why such ignorance later contributes to her fate. Lacking familiarity with one another, basing our knowledge on things that happen to happen, forms an exceedingly fragile basis on which to build alliances, much less marriage; and for all its conversational self-reflections, *The Counselor* does not make that fragility any more palatable. But McCarthy does make it at least understandable in the film's culminating scene: a philosophically charged conversation between the title character and Jefe, who explains at length why he can do nothing to help and why the Counselor is likewise impotent to avoid a fate already in process. Finally, issues central to the plot begin to become clear.

First, however, it is worth knowing that one of the more intriguing changes made from screenplay to film involves Jefe, who has lost his own son to abductors two years earlier, just as the Counselor has recently lost Laura. Yet in dropping this admission, the film once again would seem to acknowledge that any imputed sympathy has nothing to do with Jefe's response, nor is his wisdom more valuable for having been somehow earned through suffering. The philosophical theme has been clear if unstated throughout, not to be diminished by so sentimental an addition: the need for taking a stark view of one's situation; the realization that supposed mistakes we make in life cannot be reversed; the doubt that one can designate substitute prospects or choose alternative paths rather than weather the adverse events we have somehow unknowingly authored. Jefe invokes the celebrated 1912 poem by Antonio Machado—"Campos de Castilla," written after his young wife's unexpected terminal diagnosis with tuberculosis—and recites the lines, *"Caminante, no hay camino. Se hace camino al andar"* ("wanderer, there is no road, the road is made by walking"). As Jefe elaborates "You are the world you have created," which comes close to representing the film's philosophy, as already expressed by Malkina. But unlike her, Jefe realizes the appropriate stance one needs to take and calmly admonishes the Counselor in tones that suggest a reliance on patience and perseverance, that all one can do is learn to endure: "The world in which you seek to undo the mistakes that you make is different from the world where the mistakes were made. You're now at the crossing. And you want to choose, but there is no choosing there. There's only accepting. The choosing was done a long time ago. . . . Are you there Counselor?" That question itself already marks an estrangement as the Counselor continues to plead and protest the Jefe's explanation of the inefficacy of such efforts. Ending the conversation in order to take a nap, Jefe seems at once cold and correct as the film's continuing logic suggests that his response can be read neither way (neither as unsympathetic nor appropriate), but only according to the possible consequences that ensue.

After hanging up, the Counselor is left to reflect on this metaphysical fatalism. Like us, he cannot acquiesce to the idea that regret is somehow a waste of energy; he refuses to bow before "the understanding that life is not going to take you back. . . . And when you cease to exist, this world that you have created will also cease to exist." Of course, this kind of nihilism, if that's what it is, explicitly spurns both the dark vision of noir and the more generally affirming tilt of the Western. Jefe's understanding prevails, explaining a logic sustained by the entire film: how little profit accrues to bewailing circumstances since those very circumstances make us what we are, "the world is in fact oneself." In that regard, the film fulfills the script's demand to confront a dehumanizing realm without self-pity, and yet to discredit an unearned humanism as well. We are left impressed by the transformation of McCarthy's considered dialogue into Scott's visually minimalist polish. Yet the whole culminates in the inherent paradox of Jefe's admonition, warning against any regret for choices already made by encouraging the Counselor to actively choose not to feel regret, as if one could effect a cessation of sorrow by an effort of will that Jefe himself proposes as unavailable. He summarizes contradictions lying at the heart of the film—embraced in both its gruesome action and its fragmented cinematic technique—that despite its reiterated conviction, the desire for understanding either oneself or another cannot be inferred from episodes as they occur or actions as they are performed. For all the generic reminders of a late Western offered by the film, it finally succeeds as a defiance of genre, spurning our residual desire for the cohesion we nostalgically recall from a long, shape-shifting Western tradition.

CONCLUSION: IMPLICATING VIEWERS

The Counselor daringly endeavors to undermine twin notions of character and morality held dear by viewers: that we can make active choices about the life we want to live; and that we can more generally choose the kind of person we hope to be. Perhaps this helps explain the film's failure to engage a larger audience. After all, viewers resist a challenge to their cultural belief in self-command, especially in a film combining aspects of popular genres: the crime film, the Western, the neo-noir thriller. Repeatedly, we are led to believe—by what occurs to characters as well as by what they express—that nothing can alter events once set in motion. As well, the very form of the film is self-reflexive, commenting through its violence as well as its camera angles and cinematic sequencing on the viewer's own love of violence. If enough has already been said about the first point, it may nonetheless be worth addressing those moments where we are made aware of our own lack of agency, with the lesson the Counselor fails to learn from Jefe becoming one that we as viewers have yet to accept for ourselves. After Reiner explains the bolito's operation, the Counselor (at least in the screenplay, though not the film) asks why no one actually sees the garroter escape after dropping the device over a victim's head: "Oh. Well, given a choice between watching someone walk away down the street and watching someone being slowly decapitated by a device apparently engineered and patented in the halls of hell you are going to watch the latter. That's just the way it is. You may think you should avert your gaze. But you wont" (McCarthy 2013, 38–39). That assurance describes not only the behavior of actual witnesses but our own investment as "witnesses" of a film that has already made the lesson obvious, which may explain why the dialogue was dropped (once again) as unnecessary.

Moreover, the description intimates that the coherence we desire in our lives is an illusion, whether on-screen for characters or sitting as we do in the audience. The dissociative aspect of the film's episodes undoes any more integrated or progressive plot we might hope to imagine for characters. And the lesson seems to be that much the same is true for our own fragmented lives, which are lived according to possible plots that keep breaking down in the event. Given how actions in the film abide by a course of their own, with intentions stymied by circumstances, it makes sense for us to be more circumspect about our own behavior. Yet in fact, the lesson itself is nugatory since caution (like either regret or revenge) has little sway in the world represented on screen. Nor can one point to Malkina's survival, possibly her success at the end, as a defiance of such logic since no guarantees attach to her more than to anyone else. She distinguishes herself purely by avoiding sentimental bromides *about* herself without buying into the comforting notion that she can be protected in a world where events so easily undo themselves at any moment.[11] The film ends as it began, refusing to be accommodated within neat genre conventions (even opposing them, if supposedly for our enjoyment). All we come to realize is that the confusion we feel at characters whose behavior seems disconnected, who suffer consequences wholly unintended, is embodied in the cinematography and fragmented sequence of the film itself, which stymies just as it draws us in. The triumph of *The Counselor* is, among other things, not only to have translated Cormac McCarthy's long-standing dour philosophy into a Ridley Scott cinematic vision at once restrained and extreme, but also to form a narrative out of generic materials that do not add up to a genre product at all. And that, again, may ironically form part of the problem of its reception, defying an audience that still wants its genres, late Westerns and all.

EPILOGUE

Habits of Imagination

A major premise threading through the preceding chapters has been a relatively simple one: preconceptions, stereotypes, and received ideas actively shape the judgments we make in art, as in life. And genre conventions are little different; they dictate the tentative expectations that spring up whenever we encounter the title of a painting, the poster for an upcoming movie, the splashy cover for a popular novel. Generally, those expectations become less tentative the further we advance (actually seeing the painting or film, reading the novel's opening chapters). And with simpler compositions, we soon feel comfortably assured about what it is that confronts us, though as the configurations become more complex, such certainty is more and more deferred. After all, genre expectations may be triggered immediately, but they can also mislead if only because they are never really fixed except in the most derivative members of a genre. Acknowledging that deceptive craftedness, however, is not the same as admitting we need to remain in utter uncertainty—a state of mind that is, in any event, never possible. Granted, our expectations are continually being reshaped by generic reshapings themselves, which alter our convictions about slippery categories we regularly fall into thinking have somehow remained the same. Knowing things do change even in responding as if they had not is part of the paradoxical, playful experience of indulging in genre itself.

The chapter discussions above illustrate the ways in which individual films—most often at their best—succeed in misleading us, teasing us via their cross-fertilizing of genres, sometimes disguising those efforts to evoke greater viewing pleasure. My initial assumption (which explains the argument for "late Westerns") is that this process occurs for all genres in their later stages, though closer assessment of those very genres reveals how much they must always have functioned this way, purely as logical necessity. The assumption that genres emerged fully formed and fixed, as if from the head of Zeus, simply disregards how messy (and necessarily inventive) the process of popular entertainment always proves. The only "pure" examples of a genre are those selected long after the fact, when that genre has already shifted and become notably "impure" by the necessary transmogrifications that have kept it alive and well appreciated. Moreover, and more often than not, absolutely "pure" examples achieve that reputation of generic exemplarity by being less interesting than the impure outliers that help reshape the genre in new ways, usually by drawing on other contemporary generic influences to spice up their narratives.

The reason for the rubric "late Westerns" is simply to clarify the historical era when they appeared. Perhaps "neo-Westerns" or "contemporary Westerns" might be better, giving less a false sense of some common thread binding these films into a cohesive group. But that rationale also serves to explain why "postwestern" is misleading in suggesting a distinct and different status for recent versions of a genre, marking those films off as supposedly representing something completely new and unexplored in the genre before. In fact, what seems most salient about the films above is precisely their link to earlier examples of genre busting and melding. The question that persists is how these perceived versions of a genre (whenever they emerged, in the 1930s or '60s or yesterday) distinguish themselves in an environment where films that appeal to an audience have to be, by the nature of the beast, amalgamated and hybridized. Later versions of a genre may (indeed, must) differ from earlier ones, but those differences have less to do with any supposed syntactical structure dividing earlier "pure" instances from "impure" ones than it does with viewers' own shifts in sensibility and viewing habits. After all, once a genre's syntax fundamentally changes, rather than shifting askew or becoming crossbred, the genre itself no longer exists, having become transfigured into something else entirely. Westerns can become "late" and "later," and regularly do, but they cannot become "post" without turning into something else: romances or detective films or space odysseys.

Still, as generic markers coalesce with those from other genres (action-adventure, or noir, or mystery and melodrama), it becomes harder to discern what constitutes a thoroughly distinct and identifiable genre. And as unquestioned codes of honor disappear, or contentious issues of family dynamics dissipate, or unsettled disputes between justice and the law come to seem beside the point, or anxieties about masculinity and its appropriate expression finally settle, then so will the Western. Crime films may resemble the Western in their preoccupation with honor (acting nobly *outside* the law) or with appropriate family obligations (contemplating what is owed to blood relatives as well as to one's confreres), but they reflect a different semantic and syntactical vehicle than the Western. Noir fixates on the inexorable hold of the past, but rarely is that preoccupation tinged with warm nostalgia, and invariably it emerges from a private perspective, not from any sense of civic mindedness. Mystery arises from the revelation of dark secrets withheld, of actions unexplained, of figures dimly understood, but all needing to be known and recovered. In each case, we are presented with versions of possibilities that might well drive a Western, mixing with its energies, but by themselves these possibilities define a set of issues quite distinct.

The point is that we can never reside in a postgenre realm, since expectations have always been shaped by the genres we have inherited, which are often reshaped in turn by inventive screenwriters and well-informed directors alert to cinematic trends. Even as successful films necessarily trope their predecessors, altering plot strategies, revamping narrative styles, recasting tensions among characters pressured by the conflicting demands of contemporary life, they nonetheless maintain a hold on our attention through familiar generic syntaxes that only gradually become recognizable. If we are rarely, in films or in life, completely certain about the narrative judgments we regularly make, genres are no different in their unwillingness to offer interpretive security. Midway through a scene, a characterization, a line of dialogue, we often shift from one possibility to another, altering certainty, devising an interpretation that allows us to make better sense of what has occurred, and what soon will.[1] In short, films ignite generic signals that are registered with delight as we confront sometimes unfamiliar materials and structures in hesitant unease, at the border of comprehension where conflicting expectations await. And that means (once again) that the semantics of the Western hardly suffice to define the genre's persistence (or its decline). It takes more than simply being set in the West, beyond the one-hundredth meridian where rainfall diminishes drastically, where young mountains and younger rural communities thrive, to make a film successfully a Western. And that has always been true.

Still, the selection of late Westerns chosen for this book may well raise questions (Why not more? What links these particular films together? What about the other important titles that were given short shrift?); but few should question whether these films on their own continue to warrant attention. Clearly they do, as much for their commanding visual and cinematic allure as for their narrative and thematic innovations. In fact, their range as well as their individual accomplishment may best be grasped in a fleeting glance backward to the sustained achievement of their cinematographers. William C. Mellor created a stifling sense of claustrophobia in *Bad Day at Black Rock* through his tight focus on inner rooms and mirrored reflections, suggesting something of a zombielike citizenry in blocking that depended on men sitting or standing in lines. Charles Lawton Jr. combined crane shots and close-ups in Daves's *3:10 to Yuma* to generate a mildly expansive yet constrained vision, encompassing a range of emotional possibilities from anxious insufficiency to sanguine self-confidence. Stuart Dryburgh decided instead to enforce borders between cultures and races, genders and temporalities, inventively stitching scenes together in *Lone Star* via a series of varied cuts, including most dramatically a half dozen morphing pans that linked the uncertain present with a closed-off past.

Chris Menges is one of the few cinematographers to quote directly from the generic past (rather than from plot memories) in *The Three Burials of Melquiades Estrada*, citing not only specific iconographic scenes from Ford and Hawks but also the larger, sweeping landscape and masculine endeavors that made the genre attractive for so long, which has largely been ignored by other late Westerns. Rodrigo Prieto follows that lead in *Brokeback Mountain*, likewise celebrating the glory of western mountains and male physiognomies in a vain effort (given the narrative syntax) to convince us the film is primarily a Western. By contrast, Peter Suschitzky offers a series of tracking shots in *A History of Violence* that declares at the outset (in another quote from notable Westerns) its generic bona fides, while the wide-angle lens he used thereafter creates a further disquieting undercurrent that comes to seem generic. Roger Deakins offers a creative revision to Lawton's high-angle camera work, moving in more closely, shooting *No Country for Old Men* from high and low perspectives, again to disorient and to defamiliarize our sense of what the characters actually are. Sharing in this intense focus on faces, Phedon Papamichael borrows instead from other generic practitioners in adapting Mangold's *3:10 to Yuma* for contemporary cine- matic tastes, jump cutting sequences to achieve a compellingly frenzied emotional effect. Dariusz Wolski extended this cinematic style in *The Counselor*, with irrelevant objects warranting as much attention as faces, as if to suggest how little the talking heads of the film are having any actual suasive effect on one another. For all the variety of these films as diverse narratives of a supposedly singular Western experience, they seem immediately recognizable cinematically, as part of a common generic strain and yet displaying distinctive visual styles that have as much to do with their immediate historical era as with their generic identification. They engage new generations of viewers distinctively, idiosyncratically, of course, but also by relying on familiar strains and techniques that have characterized genre exemplars ranging back over the Western's century-old past.

Of course, the preceding analyses have been intended not to show formulaic similarities but rather significant and engaging differences among films that hardly fit a cookie-cutter template. That is as true of earlier Westerns in almost any given period, which alter generic expectations to make viewing more exciting, more compelling, more adequate to contemporary fashions. In each of these, the question of borders remains as important as it always has, but it does so, predictably, in disparate forms and discrepant narrative extensions. And though family dissension matters likewise as a central subject, it is invariably dealt with according to current, less-cohesive social assumptions. The other transitions that define late Westerns might well seem to reveal a larger cultural turn, as a national genre becomes ever darker, relying on noir increasingly to express itself, less confident about national ambitions, or individualist autonomy, or civic accommodation among other supposedly shared values.

Perhaps the more prominent issue has less to do with the past of the late Western than with its coming days, in the inveterate query, Where will it go from here? For a genre long presumed to be on its last legs but that nonetheless keeps reviving, the successive responses to this familiar question rarely succeed in getting it right. A safe prediction is that Hollywood will turn back to the future, seizing on successful films that have already proved their (cash-paying) audience appeal in order to try once again, with sometimes awkward remakes and thin adaptations. Still, in the effort to achieve an edge the industry always risks too little, and it is to be feared that these versions will tend to become ever more tired and self-referential. Recently, the evidence is in with Gore Verbinski's *The Lone Ranger* (2013), Antoine Fuqua's *The Magnificent Seven* (2016), even (by some lights) the Coen brothers' *True Grit*. And reinforcing this cynical industry move ("if it worked once, then") is the financially expedient gesture toward the tired belief that the Western's semantics are still attractive—plots situated in Texas and the Rocky Mountain states in the period 1840–1890 with horse-riding outlaws and small-town citizenries involved in standoffs and shootdowns. Such films include Kristian Levering's *Salvation* (2014), Tommy Lee Jones's *The Homesman*, S. Craig Zahler's *Bone Tomahawk* (2015), Lawrence Roeck's *Diablo* (2015), Quentin Tarantino's *The Hateful Eight*, Frank Coraci's *The Ridiculous Six* (2015), Jon Cassar's *Forsaken* (2015), Kieran Darcy-Smith's *The Duel* (2016), Gavin O'Connor's *Jane Got a Gun* (2016), and David Mackenzie's *Hell or High Water*. The continued production and consumption of these undisguised Westerns cut from traditional cloth in whatever generic hybridization confirms that the genre is not dying out at least quite yet, however antiquated it may seem from an early, twenty-first-century perspective.

But what has also become increasingly clear is that films bearing no resemblance to Westerns semantically—ones that occur in distinctly modern urban settings and are driven by issues and crises very different from the genre's cloistered past standards—will also emerge to tantalize viewers with their inventively transformed syntactic structures. Films, that is, like *The Counselor* and *A History of Violence* demand to be read *as* Westerns, at least partially or largely so, along with many others that appear initially more like noir thrillers, or crime films, or melodramas and comedy variants. Their syntax will invite such a viewing, indeed play upon it, and the excitement we feel will be generated by our recognition of certain codes that have been altered and reshaped, compelling us into interpretations based on our familiarity with supposedly classic prototypes. The lesson to be learned from such analysis of late Westerns is no different than in other late genres, which also offer structures that entertain us with deflections and suspensions of our generic expectations.

Older genres recur not as the same but as different, revivifying themselves through their reformulation of genre givens. Supposedly "new" films surprise us, sometimes explosively, sometimes quietly, at their best always reformulating familiar plots and cinematic treatments. The genre I grew up with as part of my childhood in the 1950s, when the Western was at its presumed height commercially, cinematically, televisually (and some would argue critically), is no longer the same, and thankfully so. But its appeal still remains, strangely and finally inexplicably, as a vehicle supremely equipped to address our continuing cultural conflicts as an aesthetic form that seems commensurately capable of delighting us in everchanging, shape-shifting, border-crossing configurations. May they long continue.

NOTES

Introduction

1. For evidence of the exaggerated reports of the genre's death over the course of the twentieth century, see my conclusion to *Westerns: Making the Man in Fiction and Film*, which begins: "Almost the moment the Western emerged, critics hastened to pronounce the last rites, as if a melancholy nostalgia that would come to permeate the genre was already part of its reception" (1996, 257).

2. In Wittgenstein's formulation, "We see a complicated network of similarities overlapping and criss-crossing: sometimes overall similarities, sometimes similarities of detail. I can think of no better expression to characterize these similarities than 'family resemblances'; for the various resemblances between members of a family: build, features, colour of eyes, gait, temperament, etc. etc. overlap and criss-cross in the same way.—And I shall say: 'games' form a family" (1998, 32).

3. To anticipate what should become progressively clear, genres are constituted of examples that always differ from one another in some respect and yet that are understood to share certain distinctive features. That "family resemblance" is invariably contested and also necessarily shifts over time as new examples (likewise different) become identified with a genre (and often, more than one). Hence, my discussion of improvisation, of hybridization, of retrospective coherence, and so on, is meant always to be in service to the idea that genres are fluid, unstable, altering over time.

4. Andrew Patrick Nelson has best depicted this supposed "golden age" of genre identification, and its perpetual mislabeling (2015, 20).

5. In disputing the category of the "post Western," Matthew Carter correctly "argues against the implications of this term, suggesting that the Western

metamorphoses according to the exigencies of a given time and the visions of individual artists, but refuses any defined pattern of continuous development" (cited in Cant 2012, 92). In this regard, Neil Campbell ignores how much of what he argues is distinctively "post Western" has always existed in the Western genre. He claims Wim Wenders, for instance, "jolts the viewer into new frames of reference," and then adds: "Post-Westerns contain traces of this uncanny effect as they traverse a generic tradition, a mythic history, and a national narrative with suspicion, unsettling the very scripts of settlement embedded in classic Westerns. Thus they *repeat strangely* what was familiar, returning through tropes, landscapes, and themes as if compelled to look back over and revise old ground precisely in order to unground and disturb the territory, kick over the dust, and pick through the remains of narratives" (2013, 257). One need look no further than John Ford to realize how even single directors embody this impulse.

6. As T. S. Eliot asserted a century ago,

> What happens when a new work of art is created is something that happens simultaneously to all the works of art that preceded it. The existing monuments form an ideal order among themselves, which is modified by the introduction of the new (the really new) work of art among them. The existing order is complete before the new work arrives; for order to persist after the supervention of novelty, the *whole* existing order must be, if ever so slightly altered; and so the relations, proportions, values of each work of art toward the whole are readjusted; and this is conformity between the old and the new. (1919, 4)

7. Steve Neale contends: "Whether 'new revisionist' or 'neo-traditional' are useful as terms, what I want to underline here is the plurality of the emerging new cycle and its films" (1999, 32). And he cites others who in 1998 and 1999 first observed this emergence: "John Cawelti suggests the term 'post-Western' in *The Six-Gun Mystique Sequel*. . . ; Lynette Tan the term 'post-revisionist western' in her unpublished PhD thesis . . . ; and Rick Worland and Edward Countryman the term 'new Western.' . . . The problem with all of these terms is that they tend to unify what I regard as a two-pronged plural phenomenon" (2002, 43n38). Jesús Ángel González agrees on the "indefiniteness" (2015, 52) of what is included in the label

"postwestern," observing that few writers "agree on its features or on the films or books that could be included in the category" (2015, 51). For an interesting if predictably contradictory claim, see Deborah Allison's review of earlier title sequences that themselves defined the genre.

8. Jameson first identified these "seemingly incompatible tendencies at work" in contemporary genre criticism (1981, 107), though he clearly had a different conception in mind in contrasting the two vis-a-vis the text as "what it *means*" and "how it *works*" (1981, 108). Altman's reconception, introduced in 1987, used as an example "the western, endowed from the dime-novel days with a picturesque semantics of adventure and violence, only in the thirties develops the characteristic syntax whereby a divided hero is opposed both to the savage and to the civilized. . . . Once a genre has established a syntactic base, it may develop by semantic shifts . . . as in the western's shift, as described by Wright, from a 'classical' to a 'professional' syntax" (1987, 117). Since then, Altman has elaborated this contrast of syntax and semantics in *Film/Genre*.

9. Altman clearly argues against Neale and others who have tended to see genres as distinct, categorical, defined by the "industry" (1984, 9). As one contrasting study by David Meuel observes, "In the 21st century alone, the impact of the early noir western continues strong in films ranging from Mangold's remake of *3:10 to Yuma* (2007), to Anderson's *There Will Be Blood* (2007), to Dominik's *The Assassination of Jesse James by the Coward Robert Ford* (2007), to the Coen Brothers' remake of *True Grit* (2010)" (2015, 17). Altman's skeptical vision has been supported by many others, including Deleyto (2012, 218), Harries (2002, 281), Simmon (2003, 207), even Neale (2002, 27).

More specifically, Altman notably claimed in 1998: "The constant sliding of generic terms from adjective to noun offers important insight into film genres and their development. Before the western became a separate genre and a household word virtually around the world, there were such things as western chase films, western scenics, western melodramas, western romances, western adventure films, and even western comedies, western dramas, and western epics. That is, each of these already existing genres could be and was produced with settings, plots, characters, and props corresponding to current notions of the West" (1998, 4). He adds,

"But does the problem involve nothing more than stressing one group of films at the expense of others? Russell Merritt suggests that something else is at stake. Under the intriguing title 'Melodrama: Postmortem for a Phantom Genre,' he points out that film critics have regularly written about melodrama as if the term were 'self-evidently clear and coherent.' For Merritt, however, melodrama is a slippery and evolving category. Citing examples from the first two decades of this century, Ben Singer provides still greater historical specificity in support of a similar argument. He points out that although most recent critics have treated melodrama as an introspective, psychological, women's genre, in the early years of cinema melodrama was specifically associated with action, adventure, and working-class men. Carefully attending to the critical practice of the silent period, Merritt and Singer successfully question current usage of the term melodrama" (1990, 26).

10. As Deleyto observes, "Altman's Derrida-inspired defense of the constitutive impurity not only of Hollywood films but also of its genres satisfactorily solves traditional problems of 'genre belonging'—whether *Oklahoma!* (Fred Zinnemann, 1955) is a western or a musical, whether *Mildred Pierce* (Michael Curtiz, 1945) is melodrama or film noir—while also emphasizing the industrial and internal nature of genre evolution" (2012, 224). Or as he later asserts: "Since genres are not fixed categories and constantly mutate into new forms, what critics call transgression or subversion is often nothing more than part of the evolution inherent to all film genres. There can only be transgression against a fixed norm. If the norm is flexible and it is part of its nature to constantly change, change is not particularly transgressive" (2012, 229).

One instance of an unnecessarily rigid claim for genre purity is Neil Campbell's assertion that the Coen brothers' *The Big Lebowski* (1998) is a post Western, rather than a modern film that playfully incorporates various generic codes and syntaxes, as a strangely engaging crossbreed (2011, 414). For an alternative view of this cross-fertilization, consider Robert Cumbow's observation: "*A Fistful of Dollars* remains a special case of film history, being a sometimes shot-for-shot remake of Akira Kurosawa's *Yojimbo* (1961). Of course the story's roots go deeper than that: *Yojimbo* is reputedly based upon the Budd Boetticher-Randolph Scott film *Buchanan Rides Alone* (1958), based on Jonas Ward's novel. . . . The structure, theme, and amoral-comic tone are reminiscent of Dashiell Hammett's *Red Harvest* (1929)" (1987, 2).

11. Or as Altman claims, "The repetitive nature of genre films tends to diminish the importance of each film's ending, along with the cause-and-effect sequence that leads to that conclusion. Instead, genre films depend on the *cumulative* effect of the film's often repeated situations, themes and icons" (1999, 25).

12. Linda Williams adds to this historical insight by treating genre as the return of the repressed:

> A particular syntax, as Altman points out, is never a neutral pattern of meaning. Meaning is made possible only because other meanings have been repressed—and this repressed side will often return in self-reflexive and self-destructive bursts during late moments of a genre's history. . . . The idea that a given syntax represses elements of its own meaning is suggestive in light of the traditional stag film's repression of the female subject. It seems possible to argue that the new narrative syntax showing female protagonists seeking pleasure has facilitated the return of this repressive component. Similarly suggestive is Altman's idea that a genre can undergo "semantic shifts" which take on entirely new subject matters—such as the introduction of "folk motifs" into the forties musical in response to the wartime need for nationalistic fables. In other words, although a new semantic element may be triggered by historical phenomena, it cannot enter a genre except through accommodation to already existing syntaxes—to use the musical example again, by means of backstage narratives of troop shows. (1989, 183)

13. Earlier, Carol Clover nicely contends that the redneck forms a version of the redskin, "a kind of universal blame figure" (1992, 135). And other features attest to a tacit merging of Western and horror genres: "Like the world of the movie Apache, the world of the horror movie's redneck is a world of tribal law, prim hygiene, tyrannical patriarchs (or matriarchs), cannibalism, incest, genetic failure, inbreeding, enslaved women, drunkenness, poverty, and cognomina in place of Christian names" (1992, 136).

14. In that sense, Neil Campbell overstates in claiming that recently "the western has in fact shown a remarkable 'impurity,' over-spilling its boundaries,

becoming mobile and 'rhizomatic,'" since evidence does not suggest it is any more impure now or earlier, than any other genre (2011, 410). Nor do "post-westerns assert an archeological probing into foundations forgotten, repressed, or built over" any more than earlier Westerns did (2011, 412), since the genre (like all genres) was never stable but always already investigating rifts.

15. As Scott Simmon has declared: "What's indisputable is that *My Darling Clementine* employs 'emptiness' about as deeply as any Western—both in creating meaning from seemingly blank visuals *and* in historical evasions" (2003, 197). But Simmon nicely goes on to argue about the style of the film itself, as Clementine brings brightness to the film a half hour in, after its strikingly darkened opening: "The escape from film noir—that, put simply, is the first story that *My Darling Clementine* tells. This visual tale was told often in the movies in the first years after World War II: The family and community restore themselves from a maze of threats expressed through film-noir styles" (2003, 198–99). Simmon nicely compares this opening to Capra's *It's a Wonderful Life* (1946), appearing the same year, with its own strikingly similar noirish opening sequence.

16. On the other hand, including Courtney Hunt's *Frozen River* (2008) as a Western at all, post or otherwise, ignores both the semantic and syntactic qualities that actually do inhere in the rather loose genre. Jesús Ángel González is representative of such claims: "As a post-Western, the film explores the idea of the *border* as a substitute for the Turnerian *frontier*. The border is a 'contact zone,' as established by Mary Louise Pratt, or 'space of colonial encounter' where 'disparate cultures meet, clash and grapple with each other." (2015, 58).

17. Kowalewski continues, in strikingly incisive terms:

Slotkin's indifference to how these scenes are actually depicted and to what verbal features distinguish them from or connect them with the rest of a text, makes him representative of a sizable portion of contemporary criticism. There is relatively scant attention paid today to how something is said in fiction. I refer here not just to some connoisseurship of *le mot juste* but to a more basic attentiveness to aural or auditory forms of imagining, a sensitivity to the idioms and rhythms of an author's voice rather than to merely what that voice represents. Critical energy is now more immediately engaged by and devoted to some image or aspect of represented life than by the verbal choices those images exemplify and the consequences attendant upon those choices. ("A criticism that loves imagery," Helen Vendler reminds us, "is likely to slight both phrasing and syntax.") The effort to gain leverage on a text, to lift images from books and then subsume or "implicate" them within ideological categories (say, of race, gender, class, or ethnicity) seems ultimately less rewarding to me than an attention to the more subtle and revealing movements of mind by which a writer entertains and then resists and reimagines his own images and ideas. American fiction still seldom gets a hearing in contemporary criticism, though it sometimes seems to be on trial. (1993, 18)

18. Philip French cites Howard Mumford Jones's list of "five 'significant components in the delineation of the Western landscape in paint and words': astonishment, plenitude, vastness, incongruity and melancholy. All these are present in varying degrees whenever a camera is turned upon the American landscape" (1997, 105).

19. According to Warshow,

There is little cruelty in Western movies, and little sentimentality; our eyes are not focused on the sufferings of the defeated but on the deportment of the hero. Really it is not violence at all which is the "point" of the Western movie, but a certain image of man, a style, which expresses itself most clearly in violence. Watch a child with his toy guns and you will see: what most interests him is not (as we so much fear) the fantasy of hurting others, but to work out how a man might look when he shoots or is shot. A hero is one who looks like a hero. ([1954] 1962,153)

20. Stephen Gaunson analyzes the film "as a measured and unnerving tragedy between two psychologically unsettled characters, trapped in an insular and claustrophobic chamber. Images of the landscape, regularly shot through old-fashioned wavy glass windows, create a confused Edenic landscape that denies the character (and audience) any sense of space or depth of focus" (2013, 63).

21. Similar passing suggestions have been made for other major films. Douglas Brode states that George Lucas's *Star Wars* (1981) "reinvent[ed] the Western

by repositioning its essence not on the old frontier but in an entirely other galaxy" (2012, 5), and that it had "far more in common with epic Westerns than science fiction" (2012, 10). See also Carl Abbott, who in general terms identifies "overlaps" between these genres (2006, vii), mostly in terms of setting, frontier imagery, and plot adaptations (2006, 19). Martina Allen makes a more intriguing observation of Martin Scorsese's *Taxi Driver* (1976) "in terms of the Western . . . show[ing] that the collective belief in the adequacy of a projection *can make it real*" (2016, 210). See also Amy Taubin, who briefly reads Martin Scorsese's *Taxi Driver* as a re-envisioning of John Ford's *The Searchers* (1956) (2012, 25–26). Roger Berkowitz and Drucilla Cornell argue that Clint Eastwood's *Mystic River* (2003) differs from most revenge dramas, exemplified by Ford's film (2005, 320).

22. Even the occasional rural exceptions, like Nicholas Ray's *They Live by Night* (1949), Tay Garnett's *The Postman Always Rings Twice* (1946), or Joseph H. Lewis's *Gun Crazy* (1950), ignore landscape in their focus on interiors, automobiles, and night scenes. Michael Shepler is one of the few to assess generic crossovers. In a claim that allows for crossover even as it establishes the different terms, Imogen Sara Smith states: "At first glance, the western and the film noir seem too dissimilar to produce a hybrid: wide-open spaces versus claustrophobic cities, color versus black-and-white, epic grandeur versus knotty, inward-looking plots, easy moral clarity versus anxious ambivalence, a robust and hopeful portrait of America versus a sour and skeptical one. But westerns have always encompassed more complexity than the simplistic 'oaters'" (2008, 179).

23. As Paul Schrader observes: "The over-riding *noir* theme [is] a passion for the past and present, but also a fear of the future" ([1972] 1996, 58).

24. Some critics follow Raymond Borde and Etienne Chaumenton in their contention that "*Film noir* is not a genre. . . . It is not defined, as are the western and gangster movies, by conventions of setting and conflict, but rather by the more subtle qualities of tone and mood" ([1955] 1996, 53). But many others, perhaps most, treat film noir as a genre (see Dimendberg, I. S. Smith).

25. The very title of Edward Dimendberg's recent study, *Film Noir and the Spaces of Modernity*, suggests this pervasive theme, or as he states: "The loss of public space, the homogenization of everyday life, the intensification of surveillance, and the eradication of older neighborhoods by urban renewal

and redevelopment projects are seldom absent from these films (2004, 7). Imogen Sara Smith concurs, in a study whose subtitle (*Film Noir Beyond the City*) suggests otherwise, though she demurs from critics who claim that in noir "the common denominator must always be the city" (2011, 3).

1. Ghostly Evocations

1. Rob Nixon has rightly observed that Spencer Tracy's age coupled with his cautious demeanor intrigues us, "playing against expectations": "We don't know until very far into the movie exactly what he's doing in Black Rock. Until then, he's just a stranger in search of a Japanese farmer who has reputedly run away, and Macreedy becomes increasingly aware of the web of deception enveloping the town and the grave danger he's in. Precisely because he is so tight-lipped, polite, and dignified . . . when Macreedy does erupt into violence, it is startling and unsettling. And we pull for him to win, even though we don't know precisely what he wants, because the townspeople are such a hateful bunch" (Nixon, n.d.).

2. The scene seems devised to support Leo Marx's influential study, *The Machine in the Garden: Technology and the Pastoral Idea in America* (1964), which traces a persistent theme in American art for more than two centuries: technology invading a natural landscape. Kaufman had intended this new scene to consist of dramatic shots of the train crossing the landscape, though stunt pilot Paul Mantz realized a helicopter would have been "sucked into the train's slipstream" (2008, 79). He recommended instead shooting the train going backwards: "the helicopter hovered above the locomotive. The copter pulled up and off. The train galloped backward. When the film was reversed we had precisely what the screenplay dictated" (2008, 79).

3. The initiating influence in this realm is Arthur Honegger's "Pacific 231" (1923), a noise-music piece about a train that builds momentum as the tempo of the music slows.

4. "One has to wonder," Rob Nixon conjectures, "if Sturges didn't slightly regret agreeing to the studio's decision to add a musical score and aerial train footage at the opening. . . . As released, the film's opening is the only overstated and theatrical aspect in an otherwise extremely lean and muscular film" (Nixon, n.d.).

The paradox of this opening sequence is best captured by Deborah Allison's survey of "title sequences in the Western genre," which were "at the forefront" of a movement among all genres beginning in the late 1940s of presenting titles through moving images rather than still pictures. Drawing on Edward Buscombe's notion of archetypal Western title sequences, she expands his reading of these signature moments, with the mandatory "confident opening on a huge, flat landscape, followed by (as with all proper Westerns) a shot under the titles of a man riding toward the camera" (2008, 109). She adds, "Whatever the case, the landscape almost invariably displays the characteristic John G. Cawelti has isolated: 'its openness, its aridity and general inhospitality to human life, its extremes of light and climate and, paradoxically, its grandeur and beauty'" (2008, 110). Of course, Sturges does have a "huge landscape . . . [and] a man riding toward the camera," as well as the other constituent elements she adds, but they hardly contribute to a sense of "grandeur and beauty."

5. Howard Breslin's original story had already established this feature: "The glaring sunshine has baked everything, thoroughly, into one color—sepia. Even the dust that swirls up as the Streamliner passes is the same thinned-out, tired brown" ([1954] 1989, 17).

6. "Needless" as this description by screenwriter Millard Kaufman may be, its wording is highly metaphorical and strangely poetic, defying the film's visuals through its divergent language. Of course, script and film converge in terms of what the language more generally points to, but here is an instance of language also doing something else, quite vibrantly, as Anne Sobel has remarked in private correspondence.

7. Curiously, with little evidence, Linda Costanzo Cahir asserts: "Shot in Cinemascope, *Bad Day at Black Rock* builds tension in unconventional ways: in the vast, sweeping open space of panoramic view (rather than in closed, constricted space traditionally used to heighten suspense) and in the full light of day" (2006, 221).

8. Part of what Wenders may also have had in mind concerns the film's dialogue, which often converts visual motifs to verbal conceits. At the hotel, Hector cruelly claims, "It looks like you need a hand," which Macreedy ignores after a long stare, though this moment is made more intentionally violent in the script by a parenthetic "(slowly, his eyes glued to Macreedy's

stiff arm)" that precedes Hector's comment. Later in the hotel lobby, Hector manhandles a slot machine, otherwise familiarly known as a "one-armed bandit" (again, a crude if silent inside joke).

9. Underlining this ghostliness of the town in its lack of activity, only four vehicles appear: Reno Smith's wood-paneled Ford station wagon; Doc Velie's "old-fashioned hearse, with plate glass sides and elaborate lead candelabra" (McGuire); Liz's army-surplus jeep; and Trimble's rusted 1936 Packard sedan. The dearth of automobiles also suggests the town's enervation, indeed its immobility.

10. According to Glenn Lovell: "Before the fight between Macreedy and Coley at Sam's Sanitary Bar & Grill, four men seated at the bar . . . agree that they want nothing to do with whatever is in store for the stranger. A boy called T. J. (Mickey Little) also had a few lines outside the garage." But though Sturges shot both sequences, he fell back on "His mantra: 'No people. Cast only'" (2008, 100–101). As Lovell adds, quoting Sturges: "A poor assistant put some lady in the background hanging out her wash. I said, 'Get rid of her.' Then he had somebody drive by. 'Get rid of him.' Nobody is ever seen arriving or leaving town, except a clump of cops at the very end" (cited in Lovell, 2008, 101).

11. John Streamas has argued for the film's racial theme: "Absence is every-where in Sturges' film, more important than even the death that causes it. Sturges seems to say that, even in a remote and desolate place such as Black Rock, to render a people absent is the surest way to write them out of history" (2003, 104). Yet Kaufman seems closer to the mark in this regard: "I wrote the thing in three weeks because I thought it would never be made. Not because of its political content, which I thought was negligible, but simply because it had this history of fights and giving bad luck a workout" (2008, 99). In 1964, he was "invited to Japan to receive an award for treating the Japanese with uncommon dignity. 'The whole thing was absurd because there were no Japanese in the movie. But I knew what they meant.'" (cited in Lovell 2008, 113).

12. The plot has other strange moments, as Kaufman knew: "Macreedy man-ages to coax the vehicle back to town. Why? Why doesn't he drive it as far away from Black Rock as his gas tank allows? Because I couldn't figure out how else to build a third act" (2008, 82). Moreover, major scenes of the

film seem oriented towards the conflict between water and fire: Komoko being killed because he drilled for water and then is burned out of his home before being shot; and Smith being lit up by a Molotoff cocktail at the end.

13. John Streamas anticipates this observation in noting of Komoko: "Certainly his absence becomes, when Macreedy arrives in Black Rock, an almost palpable object in every scene, a ghost standing over the shoulder of Smith. Appropriately, Sturges creates several ghostly images of his living characters, as their diaphanous reflections in the hotel's front window are passed through by characters in the street" (2003, 107).

14. As Fritz Lang (playing himself) retorts in Godard's *Contempt* (1963), to a character who expresses admiration for CinemaScope, "Oh, it wasn't meant for human beings. Just for snakes—and funerals." Guy Ducker has pointed out, however, two contrasting advantages to CinemaScope (an aspect ratio of 2.35:1): "It's difficult to dispute that Cinemascope is great for wide open landscapes—it's become the adoptive aspect ratio of the Wild West, one of the first things we think about when we bring to mind the spaghetti westerns of Sergio Leone. It betokens 'epic'. Ironically 'Scope is also great at the other extreme: it's the aspect ratio of psychological thrillers. There's something about it that draws the camera close and takes us into the character's head. Not by chance is it the shape that best fits a big close up on a pair of eyes" (2013, n.p.).

15. John Streamas confirms this:

> Perhaps the only flaw in the film's tight plot is a historical oversight. If Komoko's son Joe had been in the army before Pearl Harbor, he would probably have been dismissed; Dillon Myer, head of the civilian agency that managed the camps, writes in his memoir that the War Department declared that nisei "were not acceptable in the army." If he had not been in the military before Pearl Harbor, Joe Komoko would have been sent to a camp. Either way, he would have known enough about his father's fate to tell Macreedy later in the war. And residents of Black Rock would probably have known of his existence. (2003, 107n47)

16. Rob Nixon declares that "The film had an influence on future movies about lone figures in hostile settings drawing on their considerable—and surprising—combat skills to defeat their enemies, including Kurosawa's

Yojimbo (1961) and the American film *Billy Jack* (1971). Director John Sturges, in turn, was influenced by Kurosawa, remaking the Japanese director's *Seven Samurai* (1954) as the Western *The Magnificent Seven* (1960)." He adds: "According to the records of the screening room projector at the White House, *Bad Day at Black Rock* has become one of the most frequently shown films there" (Nixon, n.d.).

17. John Streamas maintains: "In the closing images, power inheres not in Macreedy or in a medal that is likely to be shelved and forgotten but in the Streamliner as it leaves town" (2003, 109).

18. Rob Nixon makes an interesting claim for its modern value:

> Perhaps a contemporary filmmaker could bring *Bad Day at Black Rock* into today's world with very little changes. Considering recent trends, it's not hard to imagine that if it were, the citizens of Black Rock would be turned into zombies. Filmmakers and their audiences have long been attracted to stories centered on an outsider reluctantly drawn into a difficult and dangerous conflict whose positive outcome is the advancement of civilization into wild and lawless territory. Tracy's character is very much in this tradition, and the almost surrealistically minimalist telling of this story, the mounting odds against him amid frightening isolation, and the actions necessary to survive it, is obviously an influence on many of today's horror films. That the outcome of this version of the reluctant hero motif remains uncertain once the outsider has done his job and moved on only makes it even more contemporary. (Nixon, n.d.)

2. Catching the 3:10 to Yuma

1. Among the more prominent theoreticians of the problems of adaptation, Thomas Leitch has notably commented that "Adaptations are texts whose status depends on the audience's acceptance of a deliberate invitation to read them as adaptations" (2012, 95).

2. Bazin said he "would find not a novel out of which a play and a film had been 'made,' but rather a single work reflected through three art forms, an artistic pyramid with three sides, all equal in the eyes of the critic. The 'work' would then be only an ideal point at the top of this figure, which itself is an ideal construct. The chronological precedence of one

part over another would not be an aesthetic criterion any more than the chronological precedence of one twin over the other is a genealogical one" (1997, 50). And Leitch would seem to extend this understanding in finding the effective modes of adaptation from one media to another, "whereby a promising earlier text is rendered more suitable for filming by one or more of a wide variety of strategies" (2007, 98). In short, Leitch protests the arguments of fidelity yet keeps returning to it, while MacCabe fosters a suitably skeptical view of what "truth to the spirit" might actually mean in a different medium. For Leitch's more recent consideration of the issues involved in adaptation, see "Adaptation and Intertextuality." Walter Benjamin has claimed, "The task of the translator consists in finding that intended effect [*Intention*] upon the language into which he is translating which produces in it the echo of the original. This is a feature of translation which basically differentiates it from the poet's work, because the effort of the latter is never directed at the language as such, at its totality, but solely and immediately at specific linguistic contextual aspects. Unlike a work of literature, translation does not find itself in the center of the language forest but on the outside facing the wooded ridge" (1969, 76).

3. George Bluestone's initial concern was to "assess the key additions, deletions, and alterations revealed in the film and center on certain significant implications which seemed to follow from the remnants of, and deviations from, the novel" (1957, x). That lead has been reiterated more recently by, among others, Linda Costanzo Cahir: "Fidelity, accuracy, and truth are all important measuring devices that should not be neglected in evaluating a film translated from a literary or dramatic source" (2006, 5). In "Adaptation as an Undecidable," Rochelle Hurst offers an insightful examination of the continuing standoff beyond advocates of fidelity and proponents of adaptation studies. And see also Simone Murray, *The Adaptation Industry*.

4. Berliner has thus summed up an entire decade of brilliant films: "Films of the 1970s often aim for moments of narrative incoherence. I use the word 'incoherence' here, and everywhere in this book . . . in the literal sense to mean a lack of connectedness or integration among different elements. The incoherences in seventies cinema are like those of a drawer full of knickknacks" (2010, 25). He adds, "Conceptual incongruity . . . denotes a lack of connectedness among the ideas generated by a film" (2010, 27).

5. The adaptation of "3:10 to Yuma" forms an interesting contrast with *Valdez Is Coming*. In 1961 Leonard had written a twelve-page short story, "Only Good Ones," then transformed it in 1970 into the novel *Valdez Is Coming* (converted into Edwin Sherin's film a year later starring Burt Lancaster). Instead of embellishing and expanding his short story, Leonard simply inserted it as the novel's opening chapter and then spun out a sequel in subsequent chapters, following Valdez's career. "'Look what I got away with,' Elmore says. 'In the final scene of *Valdez* there is no shootout, not even in the film version. Writing this one I found that I could loosen up, concentrate on bringing the characters to life with recognizable traits, and ignore some of the conventions found in most Western stories'" (cited by Sutter, xiv). By contrast, Leonard's novel *Hombre* (1961) was transformed into Martin Ritt's film *Hombre* (1967), which follows the novel closely, in contrast to the transformations imposed upon "3:10 to Yuma."

6. Still, it takes a delicate interpretive lens to assess the larger trajectory of such screened dramas, though on changed visions of gender construction in the two films, see Carol MacCurdy, "Masculinity in *3:10 to Yuma*." This form of analysis, as popularized by Richard Slotkin, tends to resort to tautological claims of popular culture mirroring the values an era presumably shares. As he states: "Whether the battle is fought on the Little Big Horn, in the streets of Chicago, or in the Philippine jungle, the *war* is the same" (1992, 121). And in his reading, all 1960s films become a commentary on Vietnam. Yet to return to paternal relations in 1950s films, one would need to include many films that already offer depictions of strained relations between parents and adolescents, starting with Nicholas Ray's *Rebel without a Cause* (1955). By contrast, consider Todd Berliner's claim: "Indeed, analyzing ideology and culture does not much account for the attraction of one film over another. I have seen no compelling evidence that a film's ideology and social relevance influence its popularity or acclaim over decades" (2010, 17). For an account of contradictions in popular culture, see Mitchell (*Westerns*).

7. Fran Pheasant-Kelly has observed of this scene:

Shadows are deployed particularly effectively to convey the hanging of Alex Potter from the central stair chandelier in the Contention Hotel. While this approach may have been to satisfy censors at that time, it nonetheless heightens the dramatic and ominous effect of the interplay between light and dark. As Butterfield re-enters the bridal suite to inform Evans of Potter's death, the tight framing of the two men pulls out to include Wade, the positioning of the three men again carefully orchestrated to create a leading diagonal from the left lower corner of the frame. The image is replete with shadows of each man cast against the adjacent man, perhaps suggesting that one can influence the other, but also promoting a sense of claustrophobia. Together with dramatic extra-diegetic music, the confines of the room heighten the film's noir sensibilities. Equally, the use of close-ups, extreme close-ups, and extreme camera angles, together with the intermittently exaggerated sound of the ticking clock, accentuate the intense atmosphere that each man seems to feel as the time approaches ten past three. Such intensity is signaled by Evans' behavior in the form of angry outbursts, these being mediated through extreme low- and high-angled camera positions and more rapid editing. (2016, 159)

8. David Thomson complained of Ford's "inability to be nasty," but as Kent Jones (who cites this remark) claims, "that is pretty much the point" (n.d., 9). See also Danks on Ford's "glinting and smartly darting eyes" (2016, 107).

9. Daves's film is discernibly patterned after *High Noon*, with clocks ticking, a brooding, non-diegetic theme song, black-and-white photography, all centered on a theme of civic insufficiency nowhere stressed in Leonard's original story. But in a comparison less obvious, the film also reminds us of *Shane* in the appearance of Van Heflin again as tired husband lacking sexual passion in contrast to the genial charisma of the loner, Alan Ladd. Michael Walker observes, "It's as if the narrative springs in part from a conscious reworking of *Shane*: here Van Heflin will assume the mantle of 'Western hero' that was denied him in the earlier movie" (1996, 143).

10. According to Simon Petch, the film fails in its conclusion: "Dan's explanation to Alice why he has to see the job through is not convincing. . . . Dan Evans, like the vanishing Contention conscripts, seems to think he is in *High Noon*. His true reasons are more personal than he can know" (2007/2008, 64). MacCurdy agrees (2009, 282).

11. Leonard now considers this the best adaptation of his work (cited by K. Jones, n.d., 4), which constitutes considerable praise given the many adaptations of his fiction to film.

12. Fran Pheasant-Kelly offers perhaps the best account of the reception history of both films, noting that there has been little detailed discussion of style: "This is surprising given that cinematographer Charles Lawton's interpretation is often described as atmospheric, striking or skillful. Specifically, such stylization involves a propensity for extreme camera angles, rising crane shots, shadows, and doubling effects, aspects that often endow the film with a noir sensibility. At the same time, if, under Daves' direction, Lawton's rendering of the landscape addresses the harsh reality of sustained drought and consequent impoverishment that this causes, it also contrives sublime and poetic images" (2016, 151).

13. Fran Pheasant-Kelly, again, nicely observes: "Its characteristic visual features include the deployment of leading diagonals, and generally balanced and often symmetrical composition; the consistent use of naturalistic side- and high-contrast lighting; extremes of tonality and contrast; shadows and doubling effects; extreme camera perspectives and rising crane shots; consistent deep focus; and interactions between cinematography and *mise-en-scène* that effect a dynamism and energy across the frame and invest the landscape with narrative and historical significance" (2016, 152).

14. Adrian Danks has deftly argued:

> this emphasis upon time is most consistently developed and built into the narrative of the film. A key tension of the drama revolves around whether Dan Evans (Van Heflin) will be able to escort Wade to Yuma prison on the scheduled train conveniently announced in the title. Despite this telescoping of time and event, much of the film is made up of scenes where characters snatch a few moments of respite or rest, or experience time in a radically altered fashion (Emmy: "Down here everybody sleeps between one and two"). Plainly, time distends and elongates for those who are hoping the train will reach Contention City before the arrival of Wade's gang. But for Wade, time seems of little consequence as he weighs up the possibilities of the events he commands and their always-possible reversibility. (2016, 109)

As Danks adds, of the sexual encounter that follows between Ben Wade and Emmy: "The somewhat cryptic dialogue between the pair that concludes this encounter further reinforces this sense of the characters being out of time (or occupying a different conception of it). After their tryst, Emmy exclaims to Ben, 'Funny, some men you can see every day for ten years and never notice; some men you see once and they're with you the rest of your life' (2016, 110).

15. As part of her reading of the supposedly homoerotic aspect of the 2007 film, Carol MacCurdy declares that "the 1957 Charlie Prince does not doggedly follow Ben; he is just the gang member assigned to Contention in case Ben shows up there. The 2007 film dramatically transforms the character, showing Charlie's unconcealed love for Ben, his devotion to Ben's celebrity status, and his willingness to take loyalty to a frightening level. As devoted son and passionate lover of Ben Wade, Charlie Prince is willing to die to preserve Ben's masculine omnipotence" (2009, 287).

16. Falconer maintains that "enough of the 1957 screenplay is retained to earn its writer, Halsted Welles, a joint credit in 2007." Yet he points out the confusion that thereby results in a number of plot details:

> Given the shifts in emphasis and tone between the two movies, it seems strange that so much material is reused. Much of what remains feels incongruous and contradictory. The lingering references to the drought seem particularly out of place. It is given passing mention early in the film, but only as one of the several reasons why Dan Evans is in debt. It is given no special emphasis. The Arizona that we see does not look as though it has gone without rain for very long: the sky is often grey, the ground is not particularly dry, and there is even some snow. And yet, references to the drought are persistent enough that the newer film eventually has to remind us that it is not Dan's major motivation. (2009, 69)

17. Still, Berliner has difficulty explaining two versions of *Get Carter*: "In the 2000 remake, Sylvester Stallone portrays an equally tough and determined Carter, but Stallone's Carter has a more conventional morality. . . . A more typical Hollywood production than the original film, the remake supplants moments of moral ambiguity with story events that more fully resolve the film's moral incongruities" (2010, 45). The question to ask, however, is *why* this shift occurred in the thirty years between the versions. It is also unclear what supports his claim for a higher number of "incoherent" (2010, 50) films in the 1970s than other decades. Yet consider his concluding

observation: "Some readers may still find it strange to think of incoherence in a film as an aesthetic virtue since people often describe bad movies as incoherent. Indeed, many great movies have something in common with bad movies: They are often disorganized, disjointed, or inconsistent. Their lapses in unity and story logic, however, generally fall just beyond the range of spectators' conscious detection. Bad movies often strike us as being full of holes" (2010, 218).

18. As Fran Pheasant-Kelly insists in her praise of Daves:

> Much of this energy arises out of Daves' proclivity for the rising crane shot, a tendency that pervades all of his films, although, according to Walker, "it was on this movie that Daves began to use the crane shot more overtly." Daves uses a Chapman crane and, in conversation with Derek Todd, commented that "To my mind there's nothing more arresting than a crane's eye view of the characters in relation to their background and events in their lives. . . . By combining the eye of the camera with the crane you give the audience the unique experience of relating human relationships with the infinity of space that surrounds each human being." (2016, 154)

19. Indeed, Mangold identified what he takes to be a pitfall particularly hazardous for Western genre films that might ironically be taken to characterize his own adaptation:

> Something happens to a director when he makes a Western; he begins basing a movie on other movies and quoting other movies. We don't do that when we make modern films; we make movies from our gut. But somehow we enter this landscape of the West and we all turn into these postmodern whores who start quoting things and regurgitating things we learned in film school, to the point where I don't think the film has a life. . . . There's a kind of over-fascination of the iconography of the West until what you're making is not a Western but a simulacra of a Western, with all of the iconography but none of the life. (Levy 2007, n.p.)

Notably, Mangold was so enamored of Sturges's original that he "used the film as a 'plot template' while directing *Cop Land*. But his reverence for the pic was what worried Mangold most. 'I felt a danger as a director that

I would be caught up in the fantasy of making a Western,' Mangold says. 'You can end up making a movie about movies, instead of a movie about characters'" (Barker 2007, A15).

20. Mangold has clearly misread Daves's film and Van Heflin's performance, in claiming: "The difference between the original version of *3:10 to Yuma* and this one was that I tried hard to make sure that you see Dan Evans as someone who is not just a coward—which is how he's played in the original, as the innately hesitant or nervous man—but a man who has been wounded. When he stood up, he was knocked down. At some point, when you keep standing up and getting knocked down, you start to hesitate standing up. We understand that man as opposed to saying, 'He's frightened'" (Barker 2007, A15). See also Falconer 2009, 66.

21. As Mangold exclaims in response to this question:

> Yes! I hate record bins. Why is Professor Longhair in "New Orleans"? He fucking rocks! Why is Johnny Cash in "Country"? Why is Al Jarreau in "Rock"? I'm like, "Nothing fucking makes sense." It's all based on these corporate labels from a time long gone. It only serves to alienate work. I know if I were Emmylou Harris I would be desperately trying to make an album that was put in the "Rock" section instead of "Country" because nobody's walking by that "Country" section. She's one of the great voices in American music of the last seventy years. Maybe that's why I'm always trying to avoid a label. There's a tragedy in the way people get pushed to the side if they do one thing over and over again. (Esther 2007, 30)

3. Border-Crossing

1. Among more notable examples of films decades earlier set on or across the Mexican border are John Sturges's *The Magnificent Seven* (1960), Richard Brooks's *The Professionals* (1966), Peckinpah's *The Wild Bunch* and *Pat Garrett and Billy the Kid* (1973), *A Fistful of Dollars*, and Tony Richardson's *The Border* (1982).

2. Jack Ryan rightly observes that Sayles deliberately undercuts conventions familiar to the Western: the opening landscape scene is colorless and washed out; "the rifle range has been tamed and abandoned"; Cliff and

Mikey are costumed "like guys from New Jersey"; and the lawman Sam Deeds has no gun (2010, 231).

3. Sayles continued, "a border is where you draw the line and say, 'This is where I end and somebody else begins.' In a metaphorical sense, it can be any of the symbols we erect against each other—sex, class, race, age" (Carson 1999, 210). Later, he added:

> I was very aware of borders and the way they can be geographical or manmade. Within the movie there are lines between people that they choose to honor or not to honor. It may be this enforced border between Mexico and the United States, it may be one between class, race, ethnicity, or even military rank. There's an important scene where Joe Morton's character, an army colonel, says, "I want to know what you think," and the private says, "Really?" She has to say that because privates do not get to say what they think to colonels and you have to have a special dispensation. On the other hand, once you cross that border, you may find out things you don't want to know" (Carson 1999, 211).

4. As David Shumway points out, "Scholars have often recognized *Lone Star* as making some of the same points as cultural studies itself about the 'liminality' of borders and the hybridity of cultures" (2012, 99).

5. Sayles has explained: "That scene with Bunny serves two purposes. One is metaphoric: This is a woman who has not escaped the past. It's clear that the weight of her family and their money doomed the marriage. The two of them came into it carrying this shit on their backs that made it impossible. He was still in love with another woman and he was still dealing with his father who wasn't there and was eventually dead. She was still dealing with her father who was very much there, and who gave both of them very little room to breathe" (cited by G. Smith 1998, 224). For a reading of Bunny, see Todd Davis and Kenneth Womack (1998, 478–79).

6. Critics invoke different terms to describe this transitional technique, from "pan shot" (Barr 2003, 371) to "elliptical dissolve" (Campbell 2011, 203) to "glides" (Ryan 2010, 230), though I will use the term "morphing pan." More generally, Neil Campbell nicely observes, "It's a film full of ghosts captured by Sayles's use of the elliptical dissolves that invite the viewer back and forth, as if eroding the frontiers of past and present and reminding

us of the consequences of time, memory, and history working themselves out in the actions and lives of the present" (2011, 203).

7. This is only one of a number of echoes of Ford's 1962 film, including the long-delayed question of who killed the villain, and how that killing affects the status of the hero.

8. Wendy Somerson has aptly claimed:

> Lone Star reinforces the boundary between male and female characters by constructing a realm of interracial brotherhood in which men of different races and nationalities can grapple with historical political issues, but from which women are generally excluded. Women of color are often positioned to help white men straddle the border of national, racial, and cultural differences through romantic relationships, whereas white women are completely left out of this domain. Although the film portrays at least three interracial relationships, they all involve white men and women of color: in this vision, white women seem incapable of crossing any national, racial, or cultural boundaries. (2004, 230–31)

9. Kim Magowan observes: "While Sam and Pilar constitute the movie's central example of an interracial couple, sexual border-crossing occurs repeatedly in Lone Star, in several permutations. Instances of interracial coupling include the two army officers, white Cliff Potts and his African-American girlfriend Priscilla; Cliff's officer friend, Mikey Hogan, and his Japanese ex-wife; and Buddy Deeds and Mercedes Cruz. Miscegenation is an integral part of the Frontera community, generating much of its population. For instance, Otis's ancestor is John Horse, who is both African American and Native American" (2003, 25).

10. Critics often note the supposed influence of Faulkner's Absalom, Absalom! (1936) as the locus for such a narrative, but incest is also central to many modernist American novels, including Fitzgerald's Tender Is the Night (1934), Ellison's Invisible Man (1952), Roth's American Pastoral (1997), and (statutorily) Nabokov's Lolita (1955) and Morrison's Beloved (1987).

11. Significantly, Sayles deliberately made Wesley Birdsong a Kickapoo in part because his tribal affiliation defined his borderline personality: "Those are people who have been everywhere, including both sides of the border. It's a very split tribe right now, with about four different outposts" (Carson 1999, 217).

12. George Handley contends: "The lines dividing contemporary communities in the film are blurred at first simply with the use of montage. Instead of implying merely the contrast between seemingly unrelated stories, Sayles's montage begins to hint at interconnectedness, especially because Sayles introduces characters from one context into another. . . . The dramatic irony these shadow presences create in each scene render the independence of each narrative unstable. We begin to see that 'all stories inevitably impinge upon one another'" (2004, 169).

13. Actually, the film playing at the drive-in is an anachronism, appearing a year after the supposed drive-in scene; but it nicely hints at Pilar's mixed parentage of Hispanic Mexican and Anglo: Eddie Romero's *Black Mama, White Mama* (1973).

14. Sayles has said that music in the film was intended to bridge the borders between cultures:

> Because I wanted to deal with three different cultures in two or three different time periods in *Lone Star*, we decided that these are people who listen to music and it would often be a bridge. For instance, when Delmore Payne first walks into his father's bar, you're hearing Ivory Joe Turner singing "Since I Met You Baby." When Sam and Pilar dance, you're hearing "Desde de Conosco"—which is "Since I Met You Baby" [in Spanish]. This great black piano crooner had a hit with "When I Lost My Baby I Almost Lost My Mind" on the black charts, but really that was kind of chump change. Then a country-western guy covered it and made a fortune. Then Turner covered his *own* song with a sound-alike song ("Since I Met You Baby") that crossed over to the white charts. Then Freddie Fender had the first really big rock 'n' roll hit in Latin America with "Desde de Conosco." You don't have to know the history to feel it underneath. Music and sports are very often where cultures meet first, where they blend. (Carson 1999, 205–6)

Neil Campbell adds:

> Just as the multilayered soundtrack shifts seamlessly between Tejano music, mariachi, rock and roll, R and B, and country and western as a measure of the cultural mix of the border, so the film explores the implications of a world with no boundaries in which there is an imbricated

piling up into a sophisticated cultural collage where "place is a palimpsest." Sayles once commented that "there's some interesting incest on the soundtrack," demonstrating his determination to interlink form and content throughout the film, both visually, as we have seen with the panning shots, and aurally in the use of parallel musical tracks. (2011, 220)

15. See Campbell (2011, 211), R. Gordon (2006, 218), Handley (2004, 169), Magowan (2003, 27), Shumway (2012, 93). Sayles has observed of his seamless transitions: "It is kind of an obvious conclusion because there's not even the separation of a dissolve, which is a soft cut. The purpose of a cut or a dissolve is to say this is a border, and the things on opposite sides of the border are meant to be different in some way, and I wanted to erase that border and show that these people are still reacting to things in the past" (Carson 1999, 213–14).

Jack Ryan argues that "it is the powerful, unedited glides into the past that mark the visual style of *Lone Star*" (2010, 233). He also observes of the morphing pan for Chucho Montoya that there is a need for two different lighting keys: Chucho in the tire yard, and the wide-angle shot of Eladio Cruz on the bridge. Sayles's production crew had to erect a small version of the tire yard near the bridge. Combined, these two filmmaking units created a visually tantalizing transition into the past. Eladio's clothes and the make of his truck tell us that we have crossed four decades. Yet the shift in screen time is borderless, transporting the audience into the past in a cinematic, fluid, organic fashion. An edit cuts, or breaks, the film strip. *Lone Star*, which is about the psychological power of history, the inability to break away from the stories that affect each character and the entire community, uses the editing process thematically. On the visual level Sayles attempted to avoid breaks of any kind, particularly when moving into or out of the past. (2010, 229–30)

16. Sayles himself claimed that the problem of legends was at the heart of the film:

One of the things that inspired me to make *Lone Star* was seeing how our legends, the things that we believe about ourselves, can be useful and they can be destructive. It was made during a lot of the wars in the former Yugoslavia. People were fighting each other over legends, basically, over "Oh, you people, back in the 13th century, did this to us, and we owned this land in the 15th century." Well, these were things that there was some history in them, but mostly they were popular legends. The popular legend of the Alamo is one that needed to be looked into, what was really going on there. (Goodman 2011)

17. Davis and Womack stress these scenes in Genette's terms as "summaries" of the past, offering "explicit ellipses" (1998, 474–75).

18. As Alan P. Barr has observed of all these gliding transitions: "These pans reinforce the film's thematic treatment of borders—in much the same way that the frequency with which the dialog actually incorporates such phrases as 'lines of demarcation,' 'borders,' 'borderline,' and the pointed if ironically named constabulary, the Border Patrol, support it" (2003, 371).

19. Brian Gingrich has observed that there is no absolute confirmation of Hollis's assertion and Otis's concurrence that Hollis himself shot Charley Wade. Only the film's pressure of narrative closure establishes this as the "true" reading, and though the alternative may not be altogether plausible, they could in fact be covering up for Buddy as the true murderer, much as Sam had initially suspected. That very possibility makes us aware of the suasive borders of narrative itself, which Sayles has everywhere emphasized (Brian Gingrich, pers. correspondence).

20. As Rebecca Gordon has argued, addressing the way Sayles's morphing pans suggest a fragmentation of knowledge:

> Formally, *Lone Star* revisits *Citizen Kane*: other people tell a story about what a man was like, from their own perspectives. However, in *Lone Star*, more often than not, one story that begins with one teller and from one perspective—a medium shot pushed into a medium close-up by tracking, a pan, or a flashback—will end with another person finishing the story. Or a pan rather than a cut will merge the "present" into the "past," proof that Buddy's story is still very much alive for some people. As the pan shots suggest, however, that story is circumscribed within tight circles or areas of knowledge that one teller cannot escape, or will not, because there are things Sam does not and should not know. (2006, 218)

21. Sayles admitted: "You have a last line in the picture, 'Forget the Alamo,' which I once considered having be the title of the movie. There is an extent

to which romantic love is antisocial. Not marriage, which is very social, that's when you make it public" (G. Smith 1998, 219).

22. In fact, Sayles himself seems slightly confused about his own film. When asked "Why did you call the film *Lone Star*?," he responded in a straightforwardly affirmative fashion about Sam's transformation from rigid lawman to accommodating social citizen: "It's kind of like *High Noon*—the man against the town, that's how he sees himself. By the end, what you hope is that he doesn't see himself that way anymore. He's starting to reintegrate himself in society. . . . Very literally, Texas was the Lone Star State before they were part of the Union, after they had kicked the Mexicans out" (G. Smith 1998, 232). Yet the film's ending would seem to contradict this, in Sam and Pilar's turn from a social contract, walking away from Frontera.

23. Again, Kim Magowan observes:

> The movie concludes with a long-shot of the lovers facing the movie screen—a highly self-referential way for a film to end. Emma Pérez proposes that "the blank screen in front of [Sam and Pilar] represents newness," but, as its dilapidated condition should signal, the screen has a more ambiguous function. The drive-in movie setting is an emotionally intense site for these two lovers, as it marks paradoxically the scene for their most explicit connection—this is where they met as teenagers to have sex—and also their separation. It is here that Buddy, years earlier, invaded their space, pulling his son out of the car and Pilar's arms, and sending his (illegitimate, unacknowledged) daughter home. (2014, 26)

Neil Campbell offers an affirmative reading of the film—"we can humanize and open that identity" of America (2011, 222)—and claims that Sayles supposedly offers "a recognition of increasingly interlinked, interdependent communities" (2011, 223). For him, incest at the end "suggests an allegorical hybrid American identity, a mixing of bloods, not in war, violence, and disagreement but in hope and renewed possibility as an ironic, revisionist Edenic couple heading a symbolic new family." This, however, seems a dubious claim for a couple who cannot bear children and who, according to Sayles, will have to move away. Janet Walker seems closer to an accurate reading in asserting: "Sam's patrilinear researches in *Lone Star* backfire all around. That Buddy is not after all Wade's killer renders

Sam's longtime animosity misguided. That the townspeople admire Buddy all the more because of their mistaken belief that he *is* Wade's killer is simply more of the same old elitist disregard for truth that has galled Sam all along. That Buddy had to have Mercedes before Sam could have Pilar must be the last straw. The trauma of succession in *Lone Star* lies in its impossibility. Sam can't have Pilar because Buddy had her mother. Or can he?" (2001, 247).

24. Sayles admitted in an interview, speaking of Chet Payne: "At the end Chet says, 'My father says you have to start from scratch and pull yourself up from there,' which isn't true. Nobody does that. Everybody starts with some kind of handicap or advantage, and that's their personal history. And it's also their group history. I was interested in the way those two interact: both the personal, and the social and group history. But also, 'Is there escape from that?'" (G. Smith 1998, 217–18).

4. Alternative Facts

1. As Jones himself remarks in the voice-over commentary, Melquiades is shot "for nothing."

2. Matthew Carter offers a reading of the film that rightly stresses the first half's "arbitrariness as a textual construct" (2014, 168).

3. As I have argued elsewhere about the film:

Ford, in short, insists upon both the "fact" *and* the "legend," viewing them as mutually sustaining interpretive gestures rather than one as a misreading of the other. So fully has the legend of Ransom Stoddard's victory become a social fact that the film's central flashback appears to be less a neutral representation of things as they once were than the wish-fulfillment reconstruction on the part of a later generation. Tag Gallagher's remark of the film, that "everything speaks of age," thus tells only half the story, as confirmed in Ford's presentation of his mature actors, John Wayne, James Stewart, and Sara Miles, each decades older (and allowed to look it) than the youthful characters they play in the flashback. Token gestures, makeup and coiffure, do far more than merely draw attention to the oddness of aging actors playing twenty-year-olds. Such gestures quietly generate an eerie sense that what we see before us are introspective elderly figures, continuing to play out myth, perform it in the present, prompted to this theater of memory by their very attempt to recall the past.

Everything in the film speaks not simply of age, then, but of age's reconstruction of its own youth—of the past's continuing grip on the present, which reshapes that past to present needs. Thus if Westerns are always stage settings for the enactment of solutions to cultural problems, then here we literally detect the stage mechanism revealed within the work (as if Ford were exposing the dynamic common to all Westerns). For this trick to work, we cannot witness events "as they occurred" (with Wayne, Stewart, and Miles filmed as if actually young, or with younger actors cast in the flashback). Rather, we must be made to see distinctly older figures imagining themselves *as* young, trying dimly to put a past to rest that has not yet been resolved and doing so according to strategies that Westerns have invoked from the beginning. The foregrounding of conventions achieved by Crane stylistically through pressure on narrative clichés, then, Ford accomplishes with a play of shifted temporal perspectives." (Mitchell 1996, 23–24)

4. Arriaga had already established his signature style of fragmented narrative in earlier scripts for *Amores Perros* (2000) and *21 Grams* (2004). Clearly, that disruptive technique creates intriguing interpretive conditions, functioning differently in each of his films (including *Babel*, released a year after *Three Burials*). Without drawing comparisons to them, my argument rests on the particular deconstructive ways in which his use of Western materials compels the viewer into a specific interpretive frame, with isolated materials themselves creating expectations for the genre that then provides the film's meaning.

5. Matthew Carter has also commented on the "chronologically disjointed scenes" in an analysis I only saw after completing this chapter:

Here the mythic simplicity is replaced by a series of complex, often repetitive flashbacks of the circumstances leading up to his [Norton's] part in Mel's death. These are relayed in disorientating fashion with staccato bursts of varying lengths, which invade the contemporary action of the narrative at seemingly random points. For instance, in one scene we see Norton responding to the sound of rifle fire. He is aiming at something off-screen, but there is no accompanying reverse-shot to illuminate what (if anything) is contained within his point-of-view. Another such moment revealed earlier in the narrative sees a panicked Norton burying Mel's body in a scratch-dug hole. (Of course, this is chronologically illogical as it is revealed before the revelation of his shooting of Mel.) Another such moment is framed between shots of Norton gazing after Lou Ann as she heads into a shopping mall, the colour of her red miniskirt apparently enough to trigger his memory: a very brief hand-held shot reveals Norton looking at his shaking, blood-stained hands as he kneels over Mel's body. A cut forward in time to a close-up shot showing Norton's pained expression, his eyes watering, not only frames the flashback, it also reveals his trauma regarding the dreadful psychological consequences of taking another man's life. (2014, 171)

6. Matthew Carter again has anticipated my claim, though he assumes we are meant to simply adopt the film as a Western *because* of its scenery: "It is, of course, the borderlands that provide the geography in which Pete can live out his mythic role as the hero. Its constitution of deserts, mountains and canyons likens itself to the historical epic and immediately begs comparison with the aesthetic qualities of Westerns past, the Monument Valley terrain of Ford or the apocalyptic deserts of Leone and Sam Peckinpah; perhaps also with the southwestern novels of Cormac McCarthy" (2014, 175).

7. Matthew Carter observes that the self-reflexive quality of the film is emphasized at reflective moments, for example

where Pete and Mel are herding cattle together. Cinematographer Chris Menges' camera encompasses the epic landscape of the Texas southwest in slow, broad sweeps; heat-hazed long shots "fix" these attractive images "as memories of experienced places and spaces," while composer Marco Beltrami's gentle music plays over the soundtrack, giving the whole scene a romanticised, timeless air. . . . We then cut to a contemporary shot of Pete sitting, brooding in his lodging, at once indicating that this has been his subjective memory of Mel and not objective reality. This is soon followed by another such flashback when, in an endearing act of friendship, Mel gives Pete his best horse. (2014, 170–71)

8. As I have elsewhere observed, there is a strong "link between landscape and death . . . in the Western as a process of bodies being returned to

their source, forced back into the landscape from which they emerged. This motif helps explain the ubiquity of cemeteries in the fictional West, as settings for the numerous funerals and burials that punctuate its narratives" (1996, 173–74).

9. Film noir is the only other genre to locate Mexico as a utopian site. Joseph H. Lewis's *Gun Crazy* (1950) has Bart Tare (John Dall) exclaim, "You know what we're gonna do when we get to Mexico? Buy ourselves a nice ranch and settle down. Maybe even raise those kids we talked about once." Likewise, see Nicholas Ray's *They Live by Night* (1949), Jacques Tourneur's *Out of the Past* (1947), and Orson Welles's *Touch of Evil* (1958). For fuller analysis, see Imogen Sara Smith, chapter 5, "Mirage of Safety: Noir on the Mexican Border," 135–58 in *In Lonely Places: Film Noir beyond the City*.

10. Douglas Pye too confidently claims that "neither the family nor Jiménez actually exists" but then observes quite accurately: "*Three Burials* contains a form of suppressive narrative in which the revelation, late in the movie, of something we had no cause to suspect, completely changes a central character's relationship to his world—and simultaneously changes the spectator's" (2010, 2). As he later adds, "The film gives us no insight into Melquiades' motivation for making up his story and no explanation of how he came to be in the photograph with the woman and her children" (2010, 4).

5. Defying Expectations

1. Cronenberg clearly "thought of the western" in devising his film (Beaty 2008, 37). The most comprehensive critic of the film in multigeneric terms is Bart Beaty, who claims: "In the same way that it is not a comic book film, not a serial killer film, not a bully film, not a small family drama, it is about the intersection of all of these generic conventions at once." But as he adds: "it is clear that the film owes as much to the noir tradition as to any genre, save, perhaps, the western" (2008, 54). Beaty also says, "On the DVD commentary, Cronenberg suggests that *A History of Violence* is 'a modern Western,' and further that 'I suppose the mall now stands in for the saloon, or perhaps the general store, that you would find in a Western movie'" (2008, 61–62).

According to Beaty:

Few film genres speak as plainly and directly to American mythologies as the western, which is, perhaps, why Cronenberg repeatedly evokes the genre in his commentary, despite the lack of obvious western trappings in the film. For instance, in discussing Howard Shore's score for the film, he says that the music "has some hints of great American music from American western movies—John Ford, Howard Hawks." The citation of Hawks and Ford as stylistic influences is particularly telling about the film's intention to be read as a western, not as much in genre trappings as in tone. Indeed, as Robert B. Ray has highlighted, the western, more than many genres, is particularly flexible and available to trans-genre experimentation. The lack of formal narrative expectations and the reliance on visual idioms in the construction of the western highlight the way that it is easily evoked as a sensibility, an ideology, or a disposition towards notions of American individualism, family, and nation. The mere presence of a horse beside the Stall barn seems enough to confirm Cronenberg's sense that *A History of Violence* is, at least in part, a highly revisionist western or, to use Ray's term, a "disguised western." (2008, 82–83)

2. Beaty reads the opening sequence as potentially "merely Sarah's dream" (2008, 44).

3. Kent Jones perceptively notes the cinematic citation of the Western: "The Americana is indeed laid on thick in the film's opening half-hour. There are crane shots of sprawling vistas and vast corn fields straight out of Delmer Daves at his crane-happiest" (2007, 96).

4. Mark Browning comments:

The presence onscreen twice of a large town clock is symbolic. It appears to emphasize the passage of time but, on both occasions, the time displayed is the same: 1:15. Paradoxically, the narrative takes place within an extended frozen moment. It concerns the past but principally how this co-exists with the present *at the same time and within the same person*— Viggo Mortensen's character. We have no flashback structure, . . . very little direct reference to what has happened twenty years before and in the final section of the film, Tom Stall now transformed into Joey Cusack, confronts his brother via a sudden shift of setting from Indiana to Philadelphia, not by a chronological shift. The past doesn't meet the present—the two have always coexisted. (2007, 37).

Adam Ochonicky adds: "Considered from this perspective, the overlapping Tom Stall and Joey Cusack personas reflect back upon the museum-like Midwestern setting, which is characterized by temporal simultaneity; past American culture somehow occupies the same space as the present within the region. The ultimate desire of the nostalgic subject—to restore or relive an idealized version of the past—is made available by the very regional landscape itself" (2015, 131).

5. Cronenberg has spoken more generally of his characters' transformations, claiming: "But because of our necessity to impose our own structure of perception on things we look on ourselves as being relatively stable. But, in fact, when I look at a person I see this maelstrom of organic, chemical and electron chaos; volatility and instability, shimmering; and the ability to change and transform and transmute" (B. Gordon 2006, n.p.). And though speaking of *Dead Ringers* (1988), his comments a year later clearly could be taken to anticipate his conception of Tom Stall in *A History of Violence*:

> I think it's my interest in real monsters and that whole mind/body schism once again. Because we draw so much of what we think of being unique about ourselves as an individual from our physical appearance—the way we sound, the way we stand, the way we look, our body language. If you think about the possibility that you were followed around by someone who looked exactly like you and sounded exactly like you and even thought very much like you, smelled like you—someone who other people confused constantly as you—then where does your individuality come from? You have to look elsewhere for it. (B. Gordon 2006, n.p.)

6. Beaty disagrees with Cronenberg's defense of this scene, that: "The idea in this sequence was to make Tom not be elegant and perfect in his disposal of the two bad guys, but awkward and nervous and worried and disturbed" (2008, 50). In fact, Tom does seem surprised, uncertain, and acts only as a reaction.

7. Beaty claims that in film noir, we would be given a flashback here, but none is forthcoming: "Instead of a fully fleshed out understanding of who Joey was, and how he became Tom, we glean mere fragments of the story that mesh with the little we know from Fogarty's testimony about

'crazy, fucking Joey.' We know that Joey killed for money, and he killed for enjoyment" (2008, 70).

8. Beaty offers a too-easy distinction between Tom and Joey, condemning Joey for his mere "vigilantism" (2008, 87). This is confirmed in his later claim that "by the end of the film, when we have been exposed to the full reality of who Joey is, it is easy to see that Tom Stall never existed except as a role that Joey successfully played for decades. Just as his family begrudgingly lets him back into the home, knowing what they know, the audience also realizes that they have always known they were watching Joey even when they hoped it was really Tom. . . . it is Joey who is the authentic self" (2008, 88).

Adam Ochonicky tends to agree, in alleging that even when the "Joey" persona appears in the film, at moments of violence, "Mortensen oscillates between the Tom and Joey personas, often with some degree of uncertainty as to which identity is dominant at a given moment" (2015, 134). Later he adds that in killing his brother, Tom/Joey "is developing the ability to inhabit either personality at will and for strategic purposes" (2014, 136).

9. Cronenberg insists that "the first scene is also of role play in sex, and so is the second one. We called that married sex and gangster sex. But the married sex is also a fantasy, where they decide to play roles to excite themselves, roles that they never played with each other. So, the whole question of identity in sexuality and violence in sexuality is there in those two scenes" (Grünberg 2006, 173). See also Freeland for support (2012, 29–30). Kent Jones claims: "We think we're going to see a rape—violent Joey Cusack coming back in full fury. Instead, they do what many couples do when things become too complicated to even formulate, let alone put into words: they have sex" (2007, 97).

10. Kent Jones is closer to the truth in his description of the first sex scene: "Two elements give this scene its strange undertone. First of all, there is something studied in Mortensen's reactions, as if he'd practiced them in his head. Every move, every gee-wiz exclamation, is letter perfect but betrayed by the slightest lack of spontaneity—a constant in the performance that becomes increasingly relevant as the film goes along, and this scene is where it becomes noticeable for the first time." He then adds, "What director has ever been better at finding the animal in the human, within the confines of ordinary gestures and behavior?" (2007, 97).

11. Amy Taubin declares that:

> The most powerful image in *A History of Violence* is of Edie, coming out of the bathroom, as she's probably done 5,000 times in the course of this marriage, with her robe carelessly open to reveal her naked body. But this time, when she sees the husband who has deceived and endangered her and her children, she reacts by tying the robe tight around her. The gesture is both instinctive and pointed, defensive and aggressive. This woman has reclaimed the body on which the marriage has been written, shutting her husband out, maybe forever, maybe not. The shot lasts only five seconds, and is the final stage of a fight that began the night before. (2005, 28)

12. As Dunlop and Delpech-Ramey observe: "Edie's forgiveness of Tom, and her silent complicity with him, despite her anger, is the most significant action of the film, far more dramatic than Tom's heroic rescue of the café or his daring trip back to Philly to confront Richie" (2010, 329).

13. As Roger Ebert argues:

> But what is Cronenberg saying about Tom, or Joey? Which life is the real one? The nature of Joey's early life was established by the world he was born into. His second life was created by conscious choice. Which is dominant, nature or nurture? Hyde, or Jekyll? Are we kidding ourselves when we think we can live peacefully? Is our peace purchased at the price of violence done elsewhere? In *A History of Violence*, it all comes down to this: If Tom Stall had truly been the cheerful small-town guy he pretended to be, he would have died in that diner. It was Joey who saved him. And here is the crucial point: Because of Joey, the son Jack makes discoveries about himself that he might not have ever needed (or wanted) to make (Ebert 2005).

14. For overly confident readings of the unresolved ending, see Mathijs (2008, 233) and Moseley (2012, 129). Steve Zimmerman says: "From the aching way they look at each other we get a sense that they've reached an understanding between them and that everything that was once their warm, loving family will again be as it was" (2010, 172–73).

15. Serge Grünberg claims that in the original 1997 graphic novel on which the film was based "there were all the clichés about the mafia, or the

mafia as a superfamily where family links are absolutely important, and the only family link that we discover between Joey and his brother is this phrase that he's repeating: 'You cost me a lot.' Which is superb, because you don't really imagine an Italian telling his brother, 'You cost me a lot.' It's true that it gives a dark feel about what family links generally are, what we know, what people feel" (2006, 175).

16. As Bart Beaty writes of the scene when Tom confronts Carl Fogarty in his frontyard: "The disguise is dropped, and an outsider is revealed in the midst of this all-American family" (2008, 4). Yet Beaty later more correctly observes, "In the end, there are no easy answers to either of these questions. Does Tom remain Joey, or has Joey grown to be Tom in the process of becoming a husband and father?" (2008, 11). Of the killing in the diner, Beaty argues: "Leland's quietly spoken 'Billy' raises Tom's eyes from the coffee mug and towards Charlotte. The part of him that is Joey knows precisely why Billy has been dispatched to the front door." And he then adds of Leland's smile that for Tom it is "a smile of recognition . . . the dark recesses of Tom's soul" (2008, 47). As Kent Jones observes: "*A History of Violence* presents us with a vision close to Buñuel's, in which sanity and normalcy are not pure states but compromises with madness and where everyone finds themselves trapped and dizzily looking for the escape hatch" (2007, 100).

17. According to Kent Jones, the Western genre structures the whole: "Cronenberg sticks very close to the standard narrative of the retired gunslinger, and he actually changes very little. . . . The strength of *A History of Violence* lies in its lucid understanding of its hero's core delusion: that he has successfully made himself over into a completely different human being. It's enough to make you laugh. Or cry. Or both" (2007, 98).

18. Daniel Mendelsohn is clearly correct in reading Ledger's performance in terms of Ennis's self-hatred for his desires: "On screen, Ennis's self-repression and self-loathing are given startling physical form: the awkward, almost hobbled quality of his gait, the constricted gestures, the way in which he barely opens his mouth when he talks all speak eloquently of a man who is tormented simply by being in his own body—by being himself" (2011, 35). But it is also true that Gary Cooper in *High Noon* or John Wayne in *The Searchers* (to take only two notable examples) might also

easily be described as physical actors in very similar terms, which may be construed as much Western as self-loathing homosexual.

19. As Elsie Walker adds, the film even distinguishes Jack and Ennis sonically, "aurally announc[ing] their differences" (2001, 8).

20. Ang Lee's high mountain vistas have been provocatively read in emotionally and temporally mixed tones by Anthony Lane:

> This is the most gorgeous part of the movie, and the least successful, partly because an idyll is less an event than a state of being. Lee wants to suggest the savoring of time, yet the camera tends to alight on ravishing formations of rock and cloud, grab them, and then move on, as if we were shuffling through a pile of photographs. (Does any director still have the patience to let our gaze rest without skittering upon the Western landscape?) On the other hand, you could argue that such transience sets the tone—at once wondrous and fleeting—for the rest of the movie, and that, if Ennis and Jack have fashioned a rough and rainy Eden for themselves, it is a paradise waiting to be lost. (2005, 117)

21. Gary Needham represents a certain overly politicized critical group that finds any questioning of the film's Western status automatically homophobic: "To deny *Brokeback Mountain*'s place within the Western genre is also to discount the ways in which the film reworks the Western formula through a specific set of political concerns that relates a troubled history of homosexuality and desire through national mythology and popular culture" (2010, 34). Yet questioning the film's generic status should not diminish its stature as a film; quite the contrary, the conflicts represented in the script's cross-fertilization actually enhance its critical (and commercial) success.

22. For fuller discussion of this theme, see pages 151–87. As Anthony Lane whimsically observes, "There is little in Lee's film that would have rattled the spurs of Montgomery Clift in *Red River*" (2005, 118).

23. Thomas Elsaesser has remarked, "In melodrama, violence, the strong action, the dynamic movement, the full articulation, and the fleshed-out emotions so characteristic of the American cinema become the very signs of the characters' alienation and thus serve to formulate a devastating critique of the ideology that supports it" ([1973] 2012, 455).

24. Elsaesser has observed certain standard poses and narrative rhythms, which seem characteristic of melodrama, that appear in *Brokeback Mountain*. The later scenes of Ennis alone in his double-wide trailer, or visiting Jack's bedroom in his childhood house, gazing at the shirt in the closet, is anticipated in Elsaesser's description of "the many films about the victimization and enforced passivity of women—women waiting at home, standing by the window, caught in a world of objects into which they are expected to invest their feelings" ([1973] 2012, 454). Earlier, the brutal scene of Ennis passionately embracing Jack outside Ennis's family house, overseen by a distraught Alma, is anticipated likewise: "Letting the emotions rise and then bringing them suddenly down with a thump is an extreme example of dramatic discontinuity, and a similar, vertiginous drop in the emotional temperature punctuates a good many melodramas—almost invariably played out against the vertical axis of a staircase" ([1973] 2012, 453).

Offering a similar assessment of literary melodrama, Peter Brooks speculates: "The critical resistance and embarrassment that melodrama may elicit could derive from its refusal of censorship and repression—the accommodations to the reality principle that the critical witness himself then supplies, from his discomfort before a drama in which people confront him with identifications judged too extravagant, too stark, too unmediated to be allowed utterance" (1976, 41–42). Interestingly, Brooks identifies the Western *with* melodrama: "If modern mass entertainment is so dominated by a limited number of fixed sub-genres—police story, western, hospital drama—it is because these offer the clearest possible repertories of melodramatic conflict. They provide an easy identification of villains and heroes (who can often be recognized simply by uniform), of menace and salvation. They give a set of situations in which virtue can be held prisoner, made supine and helpless, while evil goes on the rampage, and they offer highly exteriorized versions of its vindication and triumph" (1976, 204).

Mary Ann Doane, working through both Elsaesser and Brooks, claims the contrary:

> The maternal melodrama is maintained as a feminine genre by means of its opposition to certain genres specified as masculine (e.g., the Western, the detective film, the boxing film)—an opposition which in its turn rests

on another, that between emotionalism and violence. But theories of scopophilia, the imaginary relation of spectator to film, and the mirror phase all suggest that aggressivity is an inevitable component of the imaginary relation in the cinema. In the Western and detective film aggressivity or violence is internalized as narrative content. In maternal melodrama, the violence is displaced onto affect—producing tearjerkers. Its sentimentality is, in some respects, quite sadistic. (1987, 95)

And she then concludes: "The cultural denigration of the 'weepies' is complicit with an ideological notion of sexually differentiated forms of spectatorship. From this perspective, it is not at all surprising that the maternal melodrama tends to produce the uncomfortable feeling that someone has been had" (1987, 95).

25. Chris Berry has linked the film to Hollywood family melodrama and Chinese family-ethics films: "If we see *Brokeback Mountain* as a Hollywood-style family melodrama, then it can be understood as the struggle of Ennis to break free from conservative family values" (2007, 33). For others who have focused on the film's melodrama, see Joshua Clover and Christopher Nealon (2007, 62); Steven Cohan (2012, 237); Alan Dale; and Jim Kitses (2007, 26–27).

Ara Osterweil makes no mention of Elsaesser's essay, though she develops some of his ideas astutely and with specific reference to film melodrama:

Though they may superficially resemble screen cowboys, Ang Lee's protagonists can actually be usefully situated in a long lineage of melodramatic heroines—played by Lillian Gish in *Broken Blossoms* (1919), Barbara Stanwyck in *Stella Dallas* (1937), Jane Wyman in *All That Heaven Allows* (1955), or Julianne Moore in *Far from Heaven* (2002). Like the heroines in these screen melodramas, Ennis and Jack suffer for the transgression of choosing a socially unacceptable love object. And according to the conventions of the genre, Ennis and Jack must be punished in order for their essential innocence to be recognized. In the nineteenth-century stage set by the melodramatic imagination, the sacrifice of desire was rewarded, or at least compensated, by the belated revelation of virtue. (2007, 38).

It is also worth keeping in mind Linda Williams's more general claim about melodrama, pornography, and horror films: "We feel manipulated by these texts, an impression that the very colloquialisms 'tearjerker' and 'fearjerker' express" ([1991] 2012, 163).

26. As Dale goes on to argue, "If Ledger had been directed to play Ennis as a man responsible for his evasiveness and rage, for the brutality that comes from not thinking about your feelings and enforcing that clampdown on the people around you . . . the movie's vision would be far more penetrating than mere sympathy permits" (2011, 170). Dale counters critics who work "backward from ideological statements about homosexuality to a justification of the movie couched in aesthetic terms. But this kind of criticism comes close to eliminating aesthetics as a discipline" (2011, 173).

27. Elsaesser anticipates this description but more sympathetically, less judgmentally, outlining the "typical masochism of melodrama" in ways that seem perfectly to illuminate Lee's film:

> One of the characteristic features of melodramas in general is that they concentrate on the point of view of the victim: what makes the films mentioned above exceptional is the way they manage to present *all* the characters convincingly as victims. The critique—the questions of "evil," of responsibility—is firmly placed on a social and existential level, away from the arbitrary and finally obtuse logic of private motives and individualized psychology. This is why the melodrama, at its most accomplished, seems capable of reproducing more directly than other genres the patterns of domination and exploitation existing in a given society, especially the relation between psychology, morality, and class consciousness, by emphasizing so clearly an emotional dynamic whose social correlative is a network of external forces directed oppressingly inward and with which the characters themselves unwittingly collude to become their agents" ([1973] 2012, 457).

6. Dueling Genres

1. As Dennis Rothermal observes in more detail:

> The Coens invent these important purely cinematic touches: the wavering image of the wounded pit bull in the desert turning back to look at Moss, the raucous roar of the truck chasing Moss, the crinkling cashew wrapper on the counter, Chigurh drinking milk and staring at his reflection in

the TV set and Sheriff Bell repeating the same later, Moss pulling at the tag on his new shirt as he emerges from the riverbank weeds, the color of Sheriff Bell's uniform bleeding into the glint of light on the inside of the empty lock cylinder in the El Paso motel, Chigurh waiting inside in the darkness, Moss's embrace with the dead pit bull, the playing cards in the spokes of the boys' bicycles, the ironic supplicant gesture of Chigurh to the two boys. (2009, 196)

2. Ethan Coen has confessed: "There's always that decision when you're adapting a book, are we going to cheat using voice-over or are we going to put this into dialogue" (Baumbach 2007). Still, John Cant wryly makes us aware of how often they "cheat": "The Coens regularly make use of introductory voice-over. Examples include *Blood Simple*, *Raising Arizona*, *The Hudsucker Proxy*, *The Big Lebowski*, *The Man Who Wasn't There*: it is true to say that it is a characteristic feature of their style" (2012, 93).

3. In her essay on "title sequences in the Western genre," Deborah Allison has observed: "Until the late 1950s, films were most likely to present their titles over one or more still pictures" (2008, 109), invariably of landscapes. This suggests the Coen brothers are reaching back to a classical film history of the Western. As Allison adds, confirming the Coens' intent: "Whatever the case, the landscape almost invariably displays the characteristic John G. Cawelti has isolated: 'its openness, its aridity and general inhospitality to human life, its extremes of light and climate and, paradoxically, its grandeur and beauty'" (2008, 109–10).

4. Roger Deakins has accurately observed, "Probably, the bulk of the story takes place in motels, hotels, gas stations, and on the street, all of which were very evocatively described in the book" (2009. 221–22).

5. Among critics who deny any link to the Western, Pat Tyrer and Pat Nickell dismissively state that "References to traditional Westerns and to the history of this region arise periodically in the film, perhaps an homage to the dead, maybe a small inside joke for the fans of the Western, another dying breed" (2009, 89). More aptly, Sonya Topolnisky observes that "much of *No Country for Old Men's* visual language borrows from that of Western films, setting up expectations and assumptions for the audience only to challenge or contradict them" (2011, 111).

6. For a deft reading of this scene, see Ellis (2011, 103).

7. McCarthy's novel does make this clear (2005, 174). More generally, film noir often focuses on scenes in automobiles (much of *They Live by Night* and *Gun Crazy* takes place in cars), while the major crimes in both *The Postman Always Rings Twice* and Billy Wilder's *Double Indemnity* (1944) occur in automobiles, which function as amoral spaces.

8. Jay Ellis has observed that "The film helps us see how very many times we are in the same location but with different characters: Moss, then Chigurh, then Bell—Bell before Chigurh only in Carla Jean's case, and still that does her no good" (2011, 108). As he rightly adds, "None of these characters touch each other even when they manage to be in the same frame" (2011, 108).

9. Roger Deakins quizzically stated in response to a question of whether Chigurh is a "ghost" in this scene: "I think the book is as elusive as the film on this point" (Deakins 2009, 222). But of course the scene does not occur in the novel.

10. As Ellis points out, with evidence from the novel: "Moss is a man who chooses to take a risky shot at an antelope. Even with his special equipment and experience as a sniper in Vietnam, the shot is unethical" (2011, 113). Of course, his far more risky choice to bring water back to the injured drug dealer exposes him and his loved ones to all that ensues in the film.

11. "There really isn't any music in *No Country*" (Baumbach 2011), Joel Coen has said, though in fact some twenty seconds of diegetic music do occur, when a mariachi band serenades Moss. Elsewhere, Jay Ellis has noted "the extremely quiet but audible fade in of a few tones from a keyboard beginning when Chigurh flips the coin for the gas station man. This ambient music . . . grows imperceptibly in volume so that it is easily missed as an element of the mis-en-scene. But it is there, telling our unconscious that something different is occurring with the toss" (2011, 100). One other moment also slips in: the barely heard minor chords accompanying Chigurh's first appearance.

12. Geoffrey O'Brien inadvertently acknowledges the lack of motive among characters in the film, in noting with approval that Josh Brolin's "air of resigned detachment, before anything has even happened, serves quite well in the absence of any other motive for his character" (2007, 33).

13. Later, Flory adds in a claim that would seem to deny the novel's (and the film's) Western aspirations: "Crucially, the film comes to reject its earlier

evocation of nostalgia as a fitting attitude toward these 'new' problems of evil and even hints at alternatives" (2011, 126).

14. Eco invented the phrase, "l'école du regard," to explain the phenomenon of James Bond: "What is surprising in Fleming is the minute and leisurely concentration with which he pursues for page after page descriptions of articles, landscapes, and events apparently inessential to the course of the story and, conversely, the feverish brevity with which he covers in a few paragraphs the most unexpected and improbable actions" (1970, 165).

15. After seeing the openings of *Blood Simple* and *No Country* side by side, Ethan Coen responded, "It's not the first time that twenty years later we thought it would be a really good idea to start a movie with a character you don't know anything about and haven't seen talk tediously at length at things that have nothing to do with this story. Although Cormac [McCarthy]'s writing is better than ours" (Baumbach 2011).

16. In "Self-Reliance," Emerson claims that "Travelling is a fool's paradise," and then goes on to anticipate Moss's statement: "I pack my trunk, embrace my friends, embark on the sea, and at last wake up in Naples, and there beside me is the stern fact, the sad self, unrelenting, identical, that I fled from" (1990, 48).

17. Deakins seems to have been influenced by Barry Sonnenfeld's cinematography in the Coens's *Blood Simple* (1984), where the camera looks up and down through a ceiling fan on multiple occasions, or the aerial shot of the field where Ray buries Marty, with tracks of the car left perpendicular to the plowed furrows. Likewise, in *Fargo* (1996), Deakins offers an overhead shot of the parking lot where Carl Showalter (Steve Buscemi) murders Wade Gustafson (Harve Presnell) in a ransom exchange. This technique is hardly unique to the Coens, though it *is* characteristic of noir, beginning with Fritz Lang's *M* (1931), as Tom Gunning notably argues of high-angle topographical shots that signal not only "a new style of abstraction," but a style that "entraps" Beckert and visually "pursues him" from above (2000, 183, 186, 193).

18. Notably, Floyd Crosby, the cinematographer of *High Noon*, had studied Matthew Brady's Civil War photographs to achieve a similar high-contrast, unfiltered look. He also anticipated Deakins's noir style, focusing on body shots (Kane's legs walking, his hand over his pistol), with frequent

close-ups of Kane's face, of clocks, of Amy Kane; with low-angle shots of Kane in a bar, then on the street; or the arrival of Frank Miller, seen only from the back.

A different kind of Western echo occurs when Sheriff Bell exclaims to Deputy Wendell, "Who *are* these people?"—which seems (as mentioned above) a reference to the question that repeatedly punctuates George Roy Hill's *Butch Cassidy and the Sundance Kid* (1969), "Who *are* those guys?"

19. Dan Flory seems to me, then, mildly presumptuous in assuming that Ellis speaks for the film itself: "The rosy nostalgia in which Ed Tom has found comfort is rejected by his older, wiser peer, for to think in the way that Ed Tom does is, according to Ellis, to self-centeredly think that the whole world revolves around one's self. . . . The film here urges viewers to side with Ellis both affectively and intellectually" (2011, 127). Jay Ellis seems to me more accurate in describing Sheriff Bell's "reactionary call" of a dream: "But of course, this dream stretches and strains, as do all conservative visions, to get back to a past where the possibilities remain sufficiently uncorrupted by the chaos of change" (2011, 261).

20. Dan Flory argues instead: "The dream is a false hope, as Ed Tom realizes, which is why his statement 'And then I woke up,' his sense of shame, and his final look of defeat constitute essential cues for the audience. He does not live in a dream, where his steady, reliable father will be there to lean on and help him out" (2011, 128). Flory adds: "For the filmmakers and for McCarthy as well, the mood of nostalgia here becomes a trap. It prevents us from facing up to evil in the same way that it prevents Bell from facing up to the events involving Llewelyn Moss, Anton Chigurh, and the drug deal gone bad" (2011, 129).

7. Subverting Late Westerns

1. According to IMDB, the film was budgeted at an estimated $25 million, and by 2014 had grossed not quite $17 million.

2. In private correspondence, Fareed Ben-youssef has observed Scott's own predilection for sci-fi: the extraterrestrial of *Alien* (1979); the replicants of *Blade Runner* (1982); the android(s?) of *Prometheus* (2012). In the last, Fassbender plays the android David, while Charlize Theron described her own automatonlike role as "a suit who slowly sheds [her] skin through the

film." There seems a strong correlation between these films and Scott's uncanny characterizations in *The Counselor.*

3. Judging himself exempt from risk or consequence, he refuses to alter his ill-conceived plan, determined to defy the odds. Going well out of his way to purchase a lavish ring that surprises Laura, he puts himself in serious debt, raising the question of why. As well, he seems eager to copartner a nightclub with Reiner for similarly unexplained reasons, pressing the larger question of what drives him to take on such financial debts, at such exceptional risk.

4. Among other films that might be included in a survey of those offering a similar indictment, I have in mind Yoshitarô Nomura's *Castle of Sand* (1974), Ray Lawrence's *Lantana* (2001), David Lynch's *Mulholland Drive* (2001), David Mamet's *Heist* (2001), D. J. Caruso's *The Salton Sea* (2002), Park Chan-wook's *Oldboy* (2003), Jacques Audiard's *The Beat That My Heart Skipped* (2005), Atom Egoyan's *Where the Truth Lies* (2005), Sidney Lumet's *Before the Devil Knows You're Dead* (2007), Ridley Scott's *American Gangster* (2007), Martin Scorsese's *Shutter Island* (2010), and Nicolas Winding Refn's *Drive* (2011).

5. Or as McCarthy writes in *Blood Meridian*: "The truth about the world, he said, is that anything is possible. Had you not seen it all from birth and thereby bled it of its strangeness it would appear to you for what it is, a hat trick in a medicine show, a fevered dream, a trance bepopulate with chimeras having neither analogue nor precedent, an itinerant carnival, a migratory tentshow whose ultimate destination after many a pitch in many a mudded field is unspeakable and calamitous beyond reckoning" (1985, 256).

6. This is not altogether true of McCarthy's oeuvre, perhaps especially in the case of *The Road* (2006), which even as a postapocalyptic novel offers a humanist vision.

7. Russell Hillier has inventively given Malkina a psychology based on a reading of the conclusion of McCarthy's script and her presumed affair with Westray, whom he surmises is the father of her unborn child: "Malkina's endgame is to have the satisfaction of, first, avenging herself on Westray, the delinquent father of her child, and, second, securing a comfortable future for herself and for her child by appropriating Westray's assets" (2014, 154). As he adds, "McCarthy gives Malkina a personal justification for her

malice, both in Westray's rejection of her as a mate and in her protective and nurturing obligations as an expectant mother" (204, 156). The larger question, however, is whether the film and the script represent consistent narratives and whether they can be read interdependently.

8. Granted, following the opening credits there are a few long shots that establish a technique rarely used in the rest of the film (Malkina and Reiner watching cheetahs hunt jackrabbits; drug couriers driving their truck north, watching "illegals" crossing; and later, the Counselor driving, then walking into Reiner's place the first time; even later, of Wire-Man driving his truck on the road as if into the camera, before setting up his apparatus). But these are occasional exceptions to a dominant rule of close-up cinematography.

9. In "Diversions of Furniture," I explore the way irrelevant details in noir fiction actually center the reader's interest.

10. For a sampling of critics who savaged the film, see Peter Debruge, David Thomson, and Peter Travers. For those more genuinely enthusiastic, see Manohla Dargis and Scott Foundas.

11. Again, if this desultory vision helps explain the film's more general lack of appeal, it does extend a vision that Cormac McCarthy has expressed through many of his novels from *No Country for Old Men* (2005) back through *Blood Meridian* (1985) to *Suttree* (1979).

Epilogue

1. For the best discussion of these issues, see Ludwig Wittgenstein, *On Certainty*.

BIBLIOGRAPHY

Abbott, Carl. 2006. *Frontiers Past and Future: Science Fiction and the American West.* Lawrence: University Press of Kansas.

Allen, Martina. 2016. "The Heirs of Don Quixote: Representations of the World-Shaping Powers of Genre in Contemporary Fiction." In *The Poetics of Genre in the Contemporary Novel,* edited by Tim Lanzendörfer, 201–18. Lanham KY: Lexington Books.

Allen, William Rodney, ed. 2006. *The Coen Brothers: Interviews.* Jackson: University Press of Mississippi.

Allison, Deborah. 2008. "Title Sequences in the Western Genre: The Iconography of Action." *Quarterly Review of Film and Video* 25, no. 2 (February): 107–15.

Altman, Rick. 1984. "A Semantic/Syntactic Approach to Film Genre." *Cinema Journal* 23, no. 3 (Spring): 6–18.

———. 1987. *The American Film Musical.* Bloomington: Indiana University Press.

———. 1998. "Reusable Packaging: Generic Products and the Recycling Process." In *Refiguring American Film Genres,* edited by Nick Browne, 1–41. Berkeley: University of California Press.

———. 1999. *Film/Genre.* London: British Film Institute.

American Film Institute. "America's 10 Greatest Films in 10 Classic Genres." *AFI's 10 Top 10.* http://www.afi.com/10top10/.

Arreola, Daniel D. 2005. "'Forget the Alamo': The Border as Place in John Sayles' *Lone Star.*" *Journal of Cultural Geography* 23, no. 1 (Fall/Winter): 23–42.

Barker, Andrew. 2007. "James Mangold." *Variety,* December 5, 2007, A15.

Barr, Alan P. 2003. "The Borders of Time, Place, and People in John Sayles's *Lone Star.*" *Journal of American Studies* 37, no. 3 (December): 365–74.

Barthes, Roland. 1986. "The Reality Effect." In *The Rustle of Language,* translated by Richard Howard, 141–48. Berkeley: University of California Press.

Baumbach, Noah. 2011. Interview with Coen Brothers on June 13, 2011. YouTube. http://www.afi.com/10top10.

Bazin, André. (1948) 1997. "Adaptation, or the Cinema as Digest." In *Bazin at Work: Major Essays and Reviews from the Forties and Fifties*, edited by Bert Cadullo, 41–52. New York: Routledge.

Beaty, Bart. 2008. *David Cronenberg's "A History of Violence."* Toronto: University of Toronto Press.

Benjamin, Walter. 1969. "The Task of the Translator: An Introduction to the Translation of Baudelaire's *Tableaux Parisiens*." In *Illuminations*, edited by Hannah Arendt. Translated by Harry Zohn, 69–82. New York: Schocken Books.

Berkowitz, Roger, and Drucilla Cornell. 2005. "Parables of Revenge and Masculinity in Clint Eastwood's *Mystic River*." *Law, Culture and the Humanities* 1, no. 3 (October): 316–32.

Berliner, Todd. 2010. *Hollywood Incoherent: Narration in Seventies Cinema.* Austin: University of Texas Press.

Berry, Chris. 2007. "The Chinese Side of the Mountain." *Film Quarterly* 60, no. 3 (Spring): 32–37.

Bluestone, George. 1957. *Novels into Film.* Berkeley: University of California Press.

Borde, Raymond, and Etienne Chaumeton. (1955) 1996. "Towards a Definition of *Film Noir*." In *Film Noir Reader*, edited by Alain Silver and James Ursini, 17–25. New York: Limelight.

Borden, Diane M., and Eric P. Essman. 2000. "Manifest Landscape/Latent Ideology: Afterimages of Empire in the Western and 'Post-Western' Film." *California History* 79, no.1 (Spring): 30–41.

Breslin, Howard. (1954) 1989. "Bad Day at Honda." In *No, But I Saw the Movie: The Best Short Stories Ever Made into Film*, edited by David Wheeler, 16–30. New York: Penguin.

Brode, Douglas. 2012. "'Cowboys in Space': *Star Wars* and the Western Films." In *Myth, Media, and Culture in "Star Wars": An Anthology*, edited by Douglas Brode and Leah Deyneka, 1–11. Lanham MD: Scarecrow Press.

Brooks, Peter. 1976. *The Melodramatic Imagination: Balzac, Henry James, Melodrama, and the Mode of Excess.* New Haven: Yale University Press.

Browning, Mark. 2007. *David Cronenberg: Author or Film-Maker?* Bristol UK: Intellect Books.

Buscombe, Edward. (1970) 2012. "The Idea of Genre in the American Cinema." In *Film Genre Reader IV*, edited by Barry Keith Grant, 12–26. Austin: University of Texas Press.

Cahir, Linda Costanzo. 2006. *Literature into Film: Theory and Practical Approaches.* Jefferson NC: McFarland & Company.

Cameron, Ian, and Douglas Pye, eds. 1996. *The Book of Westerns.* New York: Continuum.

Campbell, Neil. 2011. "Post-Western Cinema." In *A Companion to the Literature and Culture of the American West*, edited by Nicolas S. Witschi, 409–24. Malden MA: Wiley-Blackwell.

———. 2013. *Post-Westerns: Cinema, Region, West.* Lincoln: University of Nebraska Press.

Cant, John. 2012. "The Silent Sheriff: *No Country for Old Men*—A Comparison of Novel and Film." In *Intertextual and Interdisciplinary Approaches to Cormac McCarthy: Borders and Crossings*, edited by Nicholas Monk, 90–99. New York: Routledge.

Carson, Diane, ed. 1999. *John Sayles: Interviews.* Jackson: University Press of Mississippi.

Carter, Matthew. 2014. *Myth of the Western: New Perspectives on Hollywood's Frontier Narrative.* Edinburgh: Edinburgh University Press.

Cawelti, John G. 1999. *The Six-Gun Mystique Sequel.* Bowling Green OH: Bowling Green State University Press.

Clarke, Roger. 2006. "Lonesome Cowboys." *Sight and Sound* 16, no. 1 (January): 28–32.

Clover, Carol J. 1992. *Men, Women, and Chain Saws: Gender in the Modern Horror Film.* Princeton: Princeton University Press.

Clover, Joshua, and Christopher Nealon. 2007. "Don't Ask, Don't Tell Me." *Film Quarterly* 60, no. 3 (Spring): 62–67.

Coen, Ethan and Joel, dir. 2007. *No Country for Old Men.* Bonus Feature of "The Making of *No Country for Old Men*." DVD.

Cohan, Steven. 2012. "'The Gay Cowboy Movie: Queer Masculinity on Brokeback Mountain." In *Gender Meets Genre in Postwar Cinemas*, edited by Christine Gledhill, 233–42. Urbana: University of Illinois Press.

Cronenberg, David. 2006. "Commentary." *A History of Violence.* New Line. DVD.

Cumbow, Robert C. 1987. *Once upon a Time: The Films of Sergio Leone*. Metuchen NJ: Scarecrow Press.

Dale, Alan. 2011. "In the Shadow of the Tire Iron." In *The Brokeback Book: From Story to Cultural Phenomenon*, edited by William R. Handley, 163–78. Lincoln: University of Nebraska Press.

Danks, Adrian. 2016. "This Room Is My Castle of Quiet: The Collaborations of Delmer Daves and Glenn Ford." In *ReFocus: The Films of Delmer Daves*, edited by Matthew Carter and Andrew Patrick Nelson, 102–17. Edinburgh: Edinburgh University Press.

Dargis, Manohla. 2013. "Wildlife Is Tame; Not the Humans: 'The Counselor,' a Cormac McCarthy Tale of Mostly Evil." *New York Times*, October 25, 2013. http://www.nytimes.com/2013/10/25/ movies/the-counselor-a-cormac-mccarthy-tale-of-mostly-evil.html.

Daves, Delmer, dir. 1957. *3:10 to Yuma*. Columbia Pictures. DVD.

Davis, Todd F., and Kenneth Womack. 1998. "Forget the Alamo: Reading the Ethics of Style in John Sayles's *Lone Star*." *Style* 32, no. 3 (Fall): 471–85.

Deakins, Roger. 2009. "Interview." In *No Country for Old Men: From Novel to Film*, edited by Lynnea Chapman King, Rick Wallach, and Jim Welsh, 219–25. Lanham MD: Scarecrow Press.

Debruge, Peter. 2013. Review of *The Counselor*, directed by Ridley Scott. *Variety*, October 24, 2013. http://variety. com/2013/film/reviews/film-review-the-counselor-1200758390/.

Deleyto, Celestino. (2011) 2012. "Film Genres at the Crossroads: What Genres and Films Do to Each Other." In *Film Genre Reader IV*, edited by Barry Keith Grant, 218–36. Austin: University of Texas Press.

Dimendberg, Edward. 2004. *Film Noir and the Spaces of Modernity*. Cambridge: Harvard University Press.

Dixon, Wheeler Winston. 2009. *Film Noir and the Cinema of Paranoia*. Edinburgh: Edinburgh University Press.

Doane, Mary Ann. 1987. *The Desire to Desire: The Woman's Film of the 1940s*. Bloomington: Indiana University Press.

Ducker, Guy. 2013. "Snakes, Funerals, and Clint Eastwood." *Salon*, August 12, 2013. https://cuttingroomtales.wordpress.com/2013/08/12/snakes-funerals - and-clint-eastwood/.

Dunlop, Aron, and Joshua Delpech-Ramey. 2010. "Grotesque Normals: Cronenberg's Recent Men and Women." *Discourse* 32, no. 33 (Fall): 321–37.

Ebert, Roger. 2005. Review of *A History of Violence*, September 22, 2005. http://
www.rogerebert.com/reviews/a-history-of-violence-2005.

———. 2007. Review of *The Assassination of Jesse James by the Coward Robert
Ford*, October 4, 2007. http://www.rogerebert.com/reviews/the-assassination
-of-jesse-james-by-the-coward-robert-ford-2007.

Eco, Umberto. 1970. "Narrative Structures in Fleming." In *The Role of the Reader:
Explorations in the Semiotics of Texts*, 144–72. Bloomington: Indiana University Press.

Eliot, T. S. 1919. "Tradition and the Individual Talent." http://www.bartleby.com
/200/sw4.html.

Elliott, Kamilla. 2003. *Rethinking the Novel/Film Debate*. Cambridge UK: Cambridge University Press.

Ellis, Jay. 2006. *No Place for Home: Spatial Constraint and Character Flight in
the Novels of Cormac McCarthy*. New York: Routledge.

———. 2011. "'Do you see?': Levels of Ellipsis in *No Country for Old Men*." In
*Cormac McCarthy: "All the Pretty Horses," "No Country for Old Men," "The
Road,"* edited by Sara L. Spurgeon, 94–116. New York: Continuum.

Elsaesser, Thomas. (1973) 2012. "Tales of Sound and Fury: Observations on the
Family Melodrama." In *Film Genre Reader IV*, edited by Barry Keith Grant,
433–62. Austin: University of Texas Press.

Emerson, Ralph Waldo. 1990. *Essays: The First and Second Series*. New York:
Library of America.

Esther, John. 2007. "Avoiding Labels and Lullabies: An Interview with James
Mangold." *Cineaste* 33: 28–30.

Falconer, Pete. 2009. "*3:10* Again: A Remade Western and the Problem of
Authenticity." In *Adaptation in Contemporary Culture: Textual Infidelities*,
edited by Rachel Carroll, 61–71. London: Continuum.

Flory, Dan. 2011. "Evil, Mood, and Reflection in the Coen Brothers' *No Country
for Old Men*." In *Cormac McCarthy: "All the Pretty Horses," "No Country for Old
Men," "The Road,"* edited by Sara L. Spurgeon, 117–34. New York: Continuum.

Foundas, Scott. 2013. "*The Counselor*." *Variety*, October 28, 2013. http://variety
.com/2013/film/ columns/ the-counselor-rearview-ridley-scott-1200770790/.

Freeland, Cynthia. 2012. "Tragedy and Terrible Beauty in *A History of Violence*
and *Eastern Promises*. In *The Philosophy of David Cronenberg*, edited by Simon
Riches, 24–35. Lexington: University of Kentucky Press.

French, Philip. 1977. *Westerns: Aspects of a Movie Genre*. New York: Oxford University Press.

Gallagher, Tag. 1986. "Shoot-Out at the Genre Corral: Problems in the 'Evolution' of the Western." In *Film Genre Reader*, edited by Barry Keith Grant, 202–16. Austin: University of Texas Press.

Gaunson, Stephen. 2013. "Murder Ballad: *The Assassination of Jesse James by the Coward Robert Ford*." In *Contemporary Westerns: Film and Television Since 1990*, edited by Andrew Patrick Nelson, 63–75. Plymouth, England: Scarecrow Press.

Godard, Jean-Luc, dir. 1963. *Contempt*. Embassy Pictures. DVD.

González, Jesús Ángel. 2015. "New Frontiers for Post-Western Cinema: *Frozen River, Sin Nombre, Winter's Bone*." *Western American Literature* 50, no. 1 (Spring): 51–76.

Goodman, Amy. 2011. "A Moment in the Sun": An Extended Interview with Independent Filmmaker, Author John Sayles." *Democracy Now: A Daily Independent Global News Hour*. June 17, 2011. http://www.democracynow.org/2011/6/17/a_moment_in_the_sun_an.

Gordon, Bette. 1989. "David Cronenberg." *BOMB Magazine* 26 (Winter 1989). http://bombmagazine.org/article/1160/david-cronenberg.

Gordon, Rebecca A. 2006. "Psychic Borders and Legacies Left Hanging in *Lone Star* and *Men with Guns*." In *Sayles Talk: New Perspectives on Independent Film-maker John Sayles*, edited by Diane Carson and Heidi Kenaga, 215–37. Detroit: Wayne State University Press.

Grünberg, David. 2006. *David Cronenberg: Interviews with Serge Grünberg*. London: Plexus.

Gunning, Tom. 2000. *The Films of Fritz Lang: Allegories of Vision and Modernity*. London: British Film Institute.

Handley, George B. 2004. "Oedipus in the Americas: *Lone Star* and the Reinvention of American Studies." *Forum for Modern Language Studies* 40, no. 2 (April): 160–81.

Harries, Dan. 2002. "Film Parody and the Resuscitation of Genre." In *Genre and Contemporary Hollywood*, edited by Steve Neale, 281–93, London: British Film Institute.

Hillier, Russell M. 2014. "'Nor Hell a Fury': Malkina's Motivation in Cormac McCarthy's *The Counselor*." *The Explicator* 72, no. 2 (May): 151–57.

Horne, Thomas A. 2013. "James Mangold's *3:10 to Yuma* and the Mission in Iraq." *Journal of Film and Video* 65, no. 3 (Fall): 40–48.

Hurst, Rochelle. 2008. "Adaptation as an Undecidable: Fidelity and Binarity from Bluestone to Derrida." In *In/Fidelity: Essays on Film Adaptation*, edited by David L. Kranz and Nancy C. Mellerski, 172–96. Cambridge UK: Cambridge Scholars Publishing.

Jameson, Fredric. 1981. *The Political Unconscious: Narrative as a Socially Symbolic Act*. Ithaca: Cornell University Press.

Jones, Kent. 2007. *Physical Evidence: Selected Film Criticism*. Middletown CT: Wesleyan University Press.

———. 2013. "Curious Distances." Criterion Collection of *3:10 to Yuma*. https://www.criterion.com/current/posts/2766-3-10-to-yuma-curious-distances, n.p.

Jones, Tommy Lee, dir. 2005. *The Three Burials of Melqiades Estrada*. Sony Classics. DVD.

Kaminsky, Amy. 2001. "Identity at the Border: Narrative Strategies in Maria Novaro's *El jardín del Edén* and John Sayles's *Lone Star*." *Studies in Twentieth-Century Literature* 25, no. 1 (Winter): 91–117.

Kaufman, Millard. 2008. "A Vehicle for Tracy: The Road to Black Rock." *The Hopkins Review* 1, no. 1 (Winter): 70–88.

Kitses, Jim. 2007. "All that Brokeback Allows." *Film Quarterly* 60, no. 3 (Spring): 22–27.

Klawans, Stuart. 2005. "Lessons of Darkness." *The Nation*, October 24, 2005, 48–52.

Kollin, Susan, ed. 2007. *Postwestern Cultures*. Lincoln: University of Nebraska Press.

Kowalewski, Michael. 1993. *Deadly Musings: Violence and Verbal Form in American Fiction*. Princeton: Princeton University Press.

Kranz, David L. 2008. "The Golden Continuum of Probability." In *In/Fidelity: Essays on Film Adaptation*, edited by David L. Kranz and Nancy C. Mellerski, 202–4. Cambridge UK: Cambridge Scholars Publishing.

Lane, Anthony. 2005. "New Frontiers." *New Yorker*, December 12, 2005, 117–19.

Leach, Stephen. 2011. "Evaluating the Representation of Violence in David Cronenberg's *A History of Violence*. *Film Matters* 2, no. 1 (Spring): 13–20.

Leitch, Thomas. 2003. "Twelve Fallacies in Contemporary Adaptation Theory." *Criticism* 45, no. 2 (Spring): 149–71.

———. 2007. *Film Adaptation and Its Discontents: From "Gone with the Wind" to "The Passion of Christ"*. Baltimore: Johns Hopkins University Press.

———. 2012. "Adaptation and Intertextuality, or, What Isn't an Adaptation, and What Does It Matter?" In *A Companion to Literature, Film, and Adaptation*, edited by Deborah Cartmell, 87–104. Somerset UK: Blackwell.

Leonard, Elmore. 2004. "3:10 to Yuma." In *The Complete Western Stories of Elmore Leonard*, 179–93. New York: William Morrow.

Levy, Shawn. 2007. "Interview: James Mangold on *3:10 to Yuma*." *The Oregonian*, September 2, 2007. http://blog.oregonlive.com/madaboutmovies/2007/09/interview_james_mangold_on_310.html.

Lovell, Glenn. 2008. *Escape Artist: The Life and Films of John Sturges*. Madison: University of Wisconsin Press.

Lowenstein, Adam. 2009. "Promises of Violence: David Cronenberg on Globalized Geopolitics." *Boundary 2* 36, no. 2 (Summer): 199–208.

MacCabe, Colin. 2011. "Introduction: Bazinian Adaptation: *The Butcher Boy* as Example." In *True to the Spirit: Film Adaptation and the Question of Fidelity*, edited by Colin MacCabe, Kathleen Murray, and Rick Warner, 3–25. New York: Oxford University Press.

MacCurdy, Carol A. 2009. "Masculinity in *3:10 to Yuma*." *Quarterly Review of Film and Video* 26, no. 4 (July): 280–92.

Magowan, Kim. 2003. "'Blood Only Means What You Let It.' Incest and Miscegenation in *Lone Star*." *Film Quarterly* 57, no. 1 (Fall): 20–31. http://www.jstor.org/stable/10.1525/fq.2003.57.1.20?origin=jstor-pdf.

Mangold, James. 2007. Interview in ComingSoon.Net. September 6, 2007. http://www.comingsoon.net/movies/features/36601-director-james-mangold-on-310-to-yuma.

———, dir. 2007. *3:10 to Yuma*. Lionsgate Films. DVD.

Mathijs, Ernest. 2008. *The Cinema of David Cronenberg: From Baron of Blood to Cultural Hero*. New York: Wallflower Press.

McCarthy, Cormac. 1985. *Blood Meridian: or, The Evening Redness in the West*. New York: Vintage Books.

———. 2005. *No Country for Old Men*. New York: Knopf.

———. 2013. *The Counselor: A Screenplay*. New York: Vintage Books.

McGuire, Don, and Millard Kaufman. 2015. "'Bad Day at Black Rock': Screenplay, Shooting Draft." http://www.weeklyscript.com/Bad+Day%20at%20black%20rock.html.

McMurtry, Larry, and Diana Ossana. 2013. *Brokeback Mountain: A Screenplay.* Adapted from an Annie Proulx Story. February 1, 2013. 99 pp. http://www .screenplayexplorer.com/wp-content/scripts/brokeback_mountain.pdf.

Mellen, Joan. 2008. "Spiraling Downward: America in *Days of Heaven, In the Valley of Elah,* and *No Country for Old Men.*" *Film Quarterly* 61, no. 3 (Spring): 24–31.

Mendelsohn, Daniel. 2011. "An Affair to Remember." In *The Brokeback Book: From Story to Cultural Phenomenon,* edited by William R. Handley, 31–38. Lincoln: University of Nebraska Press.

Merritt, Russell. 1983. "Melodrama: Post-Mortem for a Phantom Genre." *Wide Angle* 5, no. 3 (September): 24–31.

Meuel, David. 2015. *The Noir Western: Darkness on the Range, 1943–1962.* Jefferson NC: McFarland.

Mitchell, Lee Clark. 1996. *Westerns: Making the Man in Fiction and Film.* Chicago: University of Chicago Press.

———. 2009. "Fairy Tales and Thrillers: The Contradictions of Formula Narratives." *Literary Imagination* 11, no. 3 (January): 278–90.

———. 2015. "Diversions of Furniture and Signature Styles: Hammett, Chandler, Macdonald." *Arizona Quarterly* 71, no. 3 (Autumn): 1–26.

Moseley, Daniel. 2012. "Self-Creation, Identity, and Authenticity: A Study of *A History of Violence* and *Eastern Promises.*" In *The Philosophy of David Cronenberg,* edited by Simon Riches, 125–39. Lexington: University of Kentucky Press.

Murray, Simone. 2012. *The Adaptation Industry: The Cultural Economy of Contemporary Literary Adaptation.* London: Routledge.

Neale, Steve. 1990. "Questions of Genre." *Screen* 31, no. 1 (Spring): 45–66.

———. 1999. *Genre and Hollywood.* New York: Routledge.

———. 2002. "Westerns and Gangster Films Since the 1970s." In *Genre and Contemporary Hollywood,* edited by Steve Neale, 27–47. London: British Film Institute.

Needham, Gary. 2010. *Brokeback Mountain.* Edinburgh: Edinburgh University Press.

Nelson, Andrew Patrick, ed. 2013. *Contemporary Westerns: Film and Television Since 1990.* Plymouth UK: Scarecrow Press.

———. 2015. *Still in the Saddle: The Hollywood Western, 1969–1980.* Norman: University of Oklahoma Press.

Newman, Kim. 2010. "Bad Luck in Threes: Coin Tosses and Death Triangles in *No Country for Old Men*. *Screen Education* 59 (January): 139–43.

Nixon, Rob. n.d. "Behind the Camera on *Bad Day at Black Rock*." TCM Film Article. Accessed June 17, 2015. http://www.tcm.com/this-month/article /288809|296104/Behind-the-Camera-Bad-Day-at-Black-Rock.html.

O'Brien, Geoffrey. 1992. "Killing Time." Review of *West of Everything* by Jane Tompkins. *New York Review of Books*, March 5, 1992, 38–42.

———. 2007. "Gone Tomorrow": The Echoing Spaces of Joel and Ethan Coen's *No Country for Old Men*." *Film Comment* 43, no. 6 (November/ December): 28–31.

Ochonicky, Adam. 2015. "The Millennial Midwest: Nostalgic Violence in the Twenty-First Century." *Quarterly Review of Film and Video* 32, no. 2 (December): 124–40.

Osterweil, Ara. 2007. "Ang Lee's Lonesome Cowboys." *Film Quarterly* 60, no. 3 (Spring): 38–42.

Patterson, John. 2007. "We've Killed a Lot of Animals." *Guardian*, December 21, 2007. https://www.theguardian.com/film/2007/dec/21/coenbrothers.

Paz, Octavio. 1962. *The Labyrinth of Solitude*. New York: Grove Press.

Petch, Simon. 2007/2008. "Return to Yuma." *Film Criticism* 32, no. 2 (Winter): 48–69.

Pheasant-Kelly, Fran. 2016. "Delmer Daves' *3:10 to Yuma*: Aesthetics, Reception, and Cultural Significance." In *ReFocus: The Films of Delmer Daves*, edited by Matthew Carter and Andrew Patrick Nelson, 149–65. Edinburgh: Edinburgh University Press.

Powell, Liz. 2011. "The Good, the Bad, and the American: Interrogating the Morality of the Western in *A History of Violence*." *Cinema Journal* 51, no.1 (Fall): 164–68.

Pye, Douglas. 2010. "At the Border: The Limits of Knowledge in *The Three Burials of Melquiades Estrada*." *Movie: A Journal of Film Criticism* 1 (August): 1–9.

Rothermel, Dennis. 2009. "Denial and Trepidation Awaiting What's Coming in the Coen Brothers' First Film Adaptation." In *"No Country for Old Men": From Novel to Film*, edited by Lynnea Chapman King, Rick Wallach, and Jim Welsh, 173–98. Lanham MD: Scarecrow Press.

Ryan, Jack. 2010. *John Sayles: Filmmaker: A Critical Study and Filmography*. 2nd ed. Jefferson NC: McFarland.

Sayles, John. dir. 1996. *Lone Star*. Sony Classics. DVD.

———. 1998. *"Men with Guns" and "Lone Star."* London: Faber and Faber.

Schary, Dore. 1979. *Heyday: An Autobiography*. Boston: Little, Brown and Company.

Schrader, Paul. (1972) 1996. "Notes on Film Noir." *Film Noir Reader*, edited by Alain Silver and James Ursini, 52–63. New York: Livelight.

Scott, Ridley, dir. 2013. *The Counselor*. 20th Century Fox. DVD.

Shepler, Michael. 2008. "Sagebrush Noir: The Western as 'Social Problem' Film." *Political Affairs*, October 27, 2008 http://www.politicalaffairs.net/sagebrush-noir-the-western-as-social-problem-film/.

Shumway, David. 2012. *John Sayles*. Urbana: University of Illinois Press.

Silver, Alain. 1996. "Introduction." In *Film Noir Reader*, edited by Alain Silver and James Ursini, 3–15. New York: Limelight.

Simmon, Scott. 2003. *The Invention of the Western Film: A Cultural History of the Genre's First Half-Century*. New York: Cambridge University Press.

Singer, Ben. 1990. "Female Power in the Serial-Queen Melodrama: The Etiology of an Anomaly." *Camera Obscura* 8, no. 1 (January): 90–129.

Slotkin, Richard. 1992. *Gunfighter Nation: The Myth of the Frontier in Twentieth-Century America*. New York: Atheneum.

Smith, Gavin, ed. 1998. *Sayles on Sayles*. London: Faber and Faber.

Smith, Imogen Sara. 2011. *In Lonely Places: Film Noir beyond the City*. Jefferson NC: McFarland.

Somerson, Wendy. 2004. "White Men on the Edge: Rewriting the Borderlands in *Lone Star*." *Men and Masculinities* 6, no. 3 (January): 215–39.

Spurgeon, Sara L., ed. 2011. *Cormac McCarthy: "All the Pretty Horses," "No Country for Old Men," "The Road."* New York: Continuum.

Stewart, Jon. 2008. "Jon Stewart's Oscar Monologue." In *Kentucky Democrat* (February 25, 2008). http://kydem.blogspot.com/2008/02/jon-stewarts-oscar-monologue.html.

Streamas, John. 2003. "'Patriotic Drunk': To Be Yellow, Brave, and Disappeared in *Bad Day at Black Rock*." *American Studies* 44, no. 1/2 (Spring/Summer): 99–114.

Sturges, John, dir. 1955. *Bad Day at Black Rock*. Metro-Goldwyn-Mayer. DVD.

Sutter, Greg. 2004. "A Conversation with Elmore Leonard." In *The Complete Western Stories of Elmore Leonard*, xi–xiv. New York: William Morrow.

Tatum, Stephen. 2011. "'Mercantile Ethics': *No Country for Old Men* and the Narcocorrido." In *Cormac McCarthy: "All the Pretty Horses," "No Country for Old Men," "The Road,"* edited by Sara L. Spurgeon, 77–93. New York: Continuum.

Taubin, Amy. 2005. "Model Citizens." *Film Comment* 41, no. 5 (September/October): 24–28.

———. 2012. *Taxi Driver.* 2nd ed. London: Palgrave Macmillan.

Thomson, David. 2013. "Cormac McCarthy's Disastrous Hollywood Debut." *New Republic,* October 23, 2013. http://www.newrepublic.com/article/115317/counselor-review-mccarthys-dialogue-ruins-ridley-scotts-film.

Topolnisky, Sonya. 2011. "For Every Tatter in Its Moral Dress: Costume and Character in *No Country for Old Men*." In *Cormac McCarthy: "All the Pretty Horses," "No Country for Old Men," "The Road,"* edited by Sara L. Spurgeon, 110–23. New York: Continuum.

Torres, Steven L. 2009. "Generic Subversion in *The Three Burials of Melquiades Estrada*." *The Journal of Latino-Latin American Studies* 3, no. 4 (Fall): 158–70.

Travers, Peter. 2013. Review of *The Counselor,* directed by Ridley Scott. *Rolling Stone,* October 24, 2013. http://www.rollingstone.com/movies/reviews/the-counselor-20131024.

Tyrer, Pat, and Pat Nickell. 2009. "'Of What Is Past, or Passing, or to Come': Characters as Relics in *No Country for Old Men*." In *No Country for Old Men: From Novel to Film,* edited by Lynnea Chapman King, Rick Wallach, and Jim Welsh, 86–94. Lanham MD: Scarecrow Press.

Walker, Elsie. 2015. *Understanding Sound Tracks through Film Theory.* New York: Oxford University Press.

Walker, Janet. 2001. "Captive Images in the Traumatic Western: *The Searchers, Pursued, Once upon a Time in the West,* and *Lone Star*." In *Westerns: Films through History,* edited by Janet Walker, 219–53. New York: Routledge.

Walker, Michael. 1996. "The Westerns of Delmer Daves." In *The Book of Westerns,* edited by Ian Cameron and Douglas Pye, 123–60. New York: Continuum.

Warshow, Robert. (1954) 1962. "Movie Chronicle: The Westerner." In *The Immediate Experience: Movies, Comics, Theatre, and Other Aspects of Popular Culture.* Garden City NY: Doubleday.

Wenders, Wim. 2001. "Re: *Bad Day at Black Rock*." In *On Film: Essays and Conversations,* 48–50. London: Faber and Faber.

Williams, Linda. 1989. *Hard Core: Power, Pleasure, and the "Frenzy of the Visible."* Berkeley: University of California Press.

———. (1991) 2012. "Film Bodies: Gender, Genre, and Excess." In *Film Genre Reader IV*, edited by Barry Keith Grant, 159–77. Austin: University of Texas Press.

———. 1998. "Melodrama Revised." In *Refiguring American Film Genres*, edited by Nick Browne. 42–88. Berkeley: University of California Press.

Wister, Owen. 1902. *The Virginian: A Horseman of the Plains.* New York: Macmillan.

Wittgenstein, Ludwig. 1969. *On Certainty.* Edited by G. E. M. Anscombe and G. H. von Wright. Translated by Denis Paul and G. E. M. Anscombe. New York: Harper & Row.

———. 1998. *The Collected Works of Ludwig Wittgenstein. Philosophical Investigations.* Edited by G. E. M. Anscombe, G. H. von Wright, Rush Rhees, and Heikki Nyman. Translated by G. E. M. Anscombe. Charlottesville VA: InteLex.

Zimmerman, Steve. 2010. *Food in the Movies.* 2nd ed. Jefferson NC: McFarland & Co.

INDEX

automobiles, 194, 255n9; in film noir, 252n22, 285n7; sonic disruptions of, 47, 53; as static spectatorial sites, 188–90

Bad Day at Black Rock (Sturges), 35–36, 41–63, 98, 240; and absence, 47, 48, 50, 51, 52, 54, 61, 62, 255nn10–11, 256n13; artificiality of staging in, 49–50, 61, 255n10; and civic obligation, 52–53; and film noir, 31, 41, 42, 44, 53, 61, 62; ghostly town of, 42–43, 47–49, 50–51, 53, 55, 60, 62–63, 76, 255n9, 257n18; and hero as phantom embodiment, 42, 46, 47, 58, 59–60, 61, 256n13; lack of economy in, 36, 49–50, 51, 55; lack of resolution in, 46, 62–63, 257n18; and outsiders, 52, 54, 56, 57, 58–59, 257n18; plot repetition in, 34, 58, 60; self-consciousness of, 41, 49, 60, 62; and turn from landscape, 32, 41, 43, 48, 49, 53, 55, 56. *See also* cinematic openings; Kaufman, Millard; Mellor, William C.; Previn, André; sound track; Sturges, John

Bale, Christian, 85, *86*, 87, 88, 91

Bardem, Javier, 226

Barr, Alan P., 269n18

Barthes, Roland, 196

Bazin, André, 66, 257n2

Beaty, Bart, 159, 274nn1–2, 276nn6–8, 279n16

Beltrami, Marco, 138, 273n7

Benjamin, Walter, 258n2

Ben-youssef, Fareed, 287n2

Berkowitz, Roger, 252n21

Berliner, Todd, 36, 68, 84, 93, 258n4, 259n6, 262n17

Berry, Chris, 282n25

Bluestone, George, 258n3

Boetticher, Budd, 15, 17, 47

—Works: *Buchanan Rides Alone*, 248n10; *Ride Lonesome*, 141; *The Tall T*, 22

Borde, Raymond, 252n24

Borden, Diane, 14

Brady, Matthew, 286n18

Brandt, Michael and melodramatic revision, 87–91; and violence, 92

Breslin, Howard, 47, 254n5

Brode, Douglas, 251n21

Brokeback Mountain (Lee), 33, 149, 150–51, 166–76; and cinematography, 167, 241, 280n20; and claustrophobia, 170–72, 175; family dynamics of, 173–74, 177; and homosexuality, 24, 168–69, 170, 174–75, *175*, 280n21, 282n25, 283n26; and landscape, 166–67, 280n20; as melodrama, 38, 170–75, 176, 177, 280nn23–25, 283n27; and social strictures, 175–76, 283n25, 283n27; and violence, 169, *171*. *See also* Lee, Ang; McMurtry, Larry; Ossana, Diana; Prieto, Rodrigo; Proulx, Annie; Santaolalla, Gustavo; sound track

Fuller, Samuel, 15, 184
Fuqua, Antoine: *The Magnificent Seven*, 242

Gallagher, Tag, 17
Garnett, Tay: *The Postman Always Rings Twice*, 252n22, 285n7
Gaunson, Stephen, 251n20
gender: and absence of women, 50, 52; boundaries, 107, 266n8; and melodrama, 247n9, 281n24, 282n25; and race, 266n8; roles, 151–52, 153, 226; and women in Westerns, 24–25, 213–17, 215. *See also* masculinity
genre, 3–6, 14, 228, 237–40, 243–44, 245n3; expectations, 10, 12–13, 27, 65, 67, 237–38, 239–40, 242; "family resemblance" of, 3, 245nn2–3; hybridization of, 7, 10, 12–13, 27, 65, 237–39; myth of purity of, 9–10, 13, 15, 67, 238, 248n10; outliers, 7, 9–10, 238; "post," 4–5, 239; retrospective coherence of, 5, 10–11, 14, 238; and syntax and semantics, 9, 10, 12, 15, 27, 247n8, 249n12; theories of, 9–15, 17, 247n8. *See also* film noir; horror; late Westerns; melodrama; Westerns
Gingrich, Brian, 269n19
Glass, Philip, 230
Godard, Jean-Luc, 2
—Works: *Contempt*, 256n14
González, Jesús Ángel, 246n7, 250n16
Gordon, Rebecca, 269n20

Gray, Zane: *Riders of the Purple Sage*, 5
Grünberg, Serge, 278n15
Gunning, Tom, 286n17

Hammett, Dashiell, 229
Hancock, John Lee: *The Alamo*, 97
Handley, George, 267n12
Harris, Ed: *Appaloosa*, 27
Hathaway, Henry: *True Grit*, 8, 107
Hawks, Howard, xii, 241
—Works: *The Big Sky*, 8; *Red River*, 17, 22, 24, 107, 138, 152, 167
Heflin, Van, 76, 78, 87, 91, 264n20
Hemingway, Ernest, 82
Hill, George Roy: *Butch Cassidy and the Sundance Kid*, 8, 23, 136, 287n18
Hillcoat, John: *The Proposition*, 27
Hillier, Russell, 288n7
A History of Violence (Cronenberg), 33, 38, 241, 278n15; family dynamics of, 153, 155–56, 159–62, 163–64, 278n11, 278n15; hero's capacity for change in, 162, 279n17; masculinity in, 153, 156; open ending of, 162, 166; overlapping identities in, 34, 156–61, 157, 164–65, 275nn4–5, 276nn7–8, 277n10, 279n16; second viewing of, 162–63; sexuality in, 159–60, 277nn9–10; and time, 155, 275n4; and violence, 153–54, 156–58, 165. *See also* cinematic openings; Cronenberg, David; Shore, Howard; sound track; Suschitzky, Stephen

late Westerns (*continued*)
  identity, 19–26, 34–35, 39, 169–70;
  influence of film noir on, 30–31, 33,
  242; thematic shifts in, 18–26; as
  meta-Westerns, 35, 37, 83–84, 98,
  124, 263n19; self-consciousness of,
  35, 38–40. *See also* cinematography;
  film noir; genre; landscape; melodrama; viewers; violence; Westerns;
  *and under individual films, directors,
  and cinematographers*
Lawrence, Ray: *Lantana*, 288n4
Lawton, Charles, Jr., 32, 79–82, 199,
  240, 241, 261nn12–13; and crane
  shots, 80, 80–81, 199, 263n8; noir
  perspectives of, 79, 81–82, 81,
  259n7, 261n12
Ledger, Heath, 166, 171, 279n18, 283n26
Lee, Ang, 184; and casting, 166,
  279n18; and screenplay, 166, 169,
  173; and Western semantics, 166–
  68, 176
—Works: *Brokeback Mountain*, 24,
  33, 35, 38, 149, 150–51, 166–76,
  181, 211, 241
Leitch, Thomas, 66, 257nn1–2
Leonard, Elmore: equivocal history in,
  70–71; and film industry, 68, 259n5,
  260n11; psychology of minimalism
  in, 68, 70–73, 78, 82, 83, 94; sound
  and silence in, 72, 73; and Western
  conventions, 72, 259n5
—Works: "3:10 to Yuma," 65, 67–69,
  70–73, 78, 82, 83, 94, 127, 259n5,
  260n11

Leone, Sergio, 17, 20, 95, 181, 256n14
—Works: *A Fistful of Dollars*, 2,
  248n10, 264n1
Levering, Kristian: *Salvation*, 243
Lewis, Joseph H.: *Gun Crazy*,
  252n22, 274n9, 285n7
Lone Star (Sayles), 37, 97–122; and
  cinematography, 33, 100, 101–
  3, 102, 111–20, 240–41, 265n6,
  268n15, 269n18, 269n20; and
  contested history, 100–101, 103–4,
  117, 118, 268n16; fragmentation
  of, 103, 108, 112–16, 267n12;
  gendered boundaries in, 107,
  266n8; generational borders in,
  100, 104–7; idealism of, 106,
  108–9; and incest, 110–11, 120–21,
  152, 266n10, 270n23; institutional
  corruption of, 102, 102, 108; and
  landscape, 99–100, 264n2; and
  film noir, 98, 103, 106; racial
  borders in, 104, 109–10, 116,
  266nn8–9; temporal borders of,
  21, 99, 101–3, 116–20, 121–22,
  268n15. *See also* cinematic openings; Dryburgh, Stuart; Sayles,
  John; sound track
Lovell, Glenn, 255n10
Lowenstein, Adam, 160
Lucas, George: *Star Wars*, 251n21
Ludlum, Robert: *The Bourne Identity*
Lumet, Sidney: *Before the Devil Knows
  You're Dead*
Lynch, David: *Mulholland Drive*,
  288n4

Pheasant-Kelly, Fran, 259n7, 261nn12–13, 263n18

Pitt, Brad, 226

postwestern, 6, 14, 15–18, 238–39, 245n5, 249n14; alternative terms for, 15, 238, 246n7; as diminishing genre, 7; as semantic shift, 16. *See also* genre; late Westerns; Westerns

Powell, Liz, 157

Previn, André, 41, 42, 45–48, 53, 59, 253nn3–4

Prieto, Rodrigo, 167, 241

Proulx, Annie, 166, 167, 168

Pye, Douglas, 128, 133, 274n10

Quietism, 217, 232–33

race, and gender, 266n8; and interracial relationships, 104, 110, 266nn8–9; and racism, 42, 51–52, 54, 58, 109–10, 116, 255n11. *See also* African Americans; Asian Americans; Mexican border, immigrants; Native Americans

Raimi, Sam: *The Quick and the Dead*, 24

Ray, Nicholas: *The Lusty Men*, 8, 32; *Rebel without a Cause*, 76, 259n6; *They Live by Night*, 198, 202, 252n22, 274n9, 285n7

reflection theory, 69–70, 259n6

Refn, Winding: *Drive*, 288n4

Reich, Steve, 230

Richardson, Tony: *The Border*, 264n1

Ritt, Martin: *Hombre*, 259n5

Rodriguez, Robert: *El Mariachi*, 26, 97; *Once upon a Time in Mexico*, 22, 97

Roeck, Lawrence: *Diablo*, 243

Romero, Eddie: *Black Mama, White Mama*, 267n13

Roth, Philip: *American Pastoral*, 266n10

Rothermal, Dennis, 283n1

Ryan, Jack, 117, 264n2, 268n15

Santaolalla, Gustavo, 166–67, 280n19

Sayles, John, 187, 220; on borders, 100, 265n3, 267n14, 268n15; and influence of Ford, 98, 104, 111–12, 117, 266n7; and meta-Western, 98, 104, 111, 124; and screenplay divergences, 108, 113–14; undermining of Western conventions by, 98–99, 104, 106–7, 111–12, 120, 264n2

—Works: *Lone Star*, 21, 33, 37, 97–122, 152, 240–41

Schary, Dore, 45, 46

Schlesinger, John: *Midnight Cowboy*, 8

Schrader, Paul, 252n23

Scorsese, Martin: *Shutter Island*, 288n4; *Taxi Driver*, 252n21

Scott, Randolph: *Buchanan Rides Alone*, 248n10

Scott, Ridley, 220; and antigeneric premise, 210–13, 218, 220–21, 224–25, 229, 231, 232–33; and casting, 225–26; and sci-fi, 287n2; and screenplay modifications, 211, 218, 221, 227–28, 231–32, 234, 288n7

linity, 127, 143; narrative structure of, 37–38, 123, 125, 126–27, 128–30, 135, 142, 272n5; replicated scenes of, 130–31, 132, 146; and resurrection of the Western, 38, 124, 126, 138. *See also* Arriaga, Guillermo; Beltrami, Marco; cinematic openings; Jones, Tommy Lee; Menges, Chris; sound track

Tiomkin, Dimitri, 45, 138

Topolnisky, Sonya, 284n5

Tóth, André de, 15, 47

Tourneur, Jacques: *Out of the Past*, 191, 195, 198, 274n9; *Stars in My Crown*, 32

Tracy, Spencer, 48, 58, 253n1

trains: in *Bad Day at Black Rock*, 41, 43, 44, 45–46, 62, 253n2, 253n4, 257n17; and landscape, 41, 43, 45, 253n2; and sound, 46, 73, 253n3

Turner, Frederick Jackson, 52, 58, 61, 136

Tyrer, Pat, 284n5

Verbinski, Gore: *The Lone Ranger*, 242

viewers, 11, 36, 199, 216–17, 224, 233–35; and adaptations, 257n1; and desire for violence, 37, 94, 210, 211–12, 233–34; expectations of, 4, 10, 12–13, 27, 38–39, 68, 84, 180–81, 183, 186, 237–38, 239–40, 242, 243, 284n5; and noir estrangement, 33, 199, 201–2; and previews, 45. *See also under individual films and directors*

violence, 17–18, 74–75, 110, 169, 188–89; cinematic, 22–23, 47, 153–54; and genre conventions, 106, 123, 150, 154, 156, 165, 204, 251n19; institutional, 108; and late Westerns, 20, 22–23, 37, 90–91, 92–93, 95, 181, 182; retaliatory, 106; "value of," 18, 20, 31, 107, 181, 209, 210; viewer desire for, 37, 94, 210, 211–12, 233–34. *See also under individual films, directors, and cinematographers*

Walker, Elsie, 280n19

Walker, Janet, 106, 270n23

Walker, Michael, 75, 260n9

Walsh, Raoul: *Pursued*, 31, 34; *White Heat*, 28

Warren, Charles: *Flight to Tangier*, 193–94

Warshow, Robert, 251n19; and "value of violence," 18, 20, 31, 107, 181, 209, 210

Wayne, John, xii, 126, 271n3, 279n18

Welles, Halsted, 73–79, 82, 93, 180; and civic obligation, 76, 78; and family dynamics, 67, 74, 78–79; and psychological complexity, 75, 76–78

Welles, Orsen: *The Lady from Shanghai*, 191; *Touch of Evil*, 274n9

Wenders, Wim, 246n5; on *3:10 to Yuma*, 82–83; on *Bad Day at Black Rock*, 48–49, 254n8

—Works: *Don't Come Knocking*, 28–30, 29, 152

IN THE POSTWESTERN HORIZONS SERIES

Dirty Wars: Landscape, Power,
and Waste in Western
American Literature
John Beck

Post-Westerns: Cinema, Region, West
Neil Campbell

The Rhizomatic West:
Representing the American West
in a Transnational, Global,
Media Age
Neil Campbell

Positive Pollutions and Cultural
Toxins: Waste and Contamination
in Contemporary U.S. Ethnic
Literatures
John Blair Gamber

Dirty Words in Deadwood:
Literatures and the Postwestern
Edited by Melody Graulich
and Nicolas Witschi

True West: Authenticity
and the American West
Edited by William R. Handley
and Nathaniel Lewis

Postwestern Cultures:
Literature, Theory, Space
Edited by Susan Kollin

Westerns: A Women's History
Victoria Lamont

Manifest and Other Destinies:
Territorial Fictions of the
Nineteenth-Century United States
Stephanie LeMenager

Unsettling the Literary West:
Authenticity and Authorship
Nathaniel Lewis

Morta Las Vegas: CSI and
the Problem of the West
Nathaniel Lewis
and Stephen Tatum

María Amparo Ruiz de Burton:
Critical and Pedagogical Perspectives
Edited by Amelia María de la Luz
Montes and Anne Elizabeth
Goldman

Late Westerns:
The Persistence of a Genre
Lee Clark Mitchell

To order or obtain more information on these or other University of
Nebraska Press titles, visit nebraskapress.unl.edu.